'*No Way But Gentlenesse* pulls no punches on the issues of class and entitlement – or lack of – that also made *Kes* so ground-breaking . . . As he describes so evocatively in the book, he too was earmarked in early life and by an inflexible education system to a lesser lot' Conor Jameson, *BritishBirds.co.uk*

'The writing is vivid and direct, with many telling anecdotes and perceptive reflections . . . Richard Hines's book holds the reader throughout' *Times Literary Supplement*

'Rarely, if ever, have I had such a feeling of intimacy with an author as he tells me about his life and draws me in completely' Mary Whipple, author of *Seeing The World Through Books*

## A NOTE ON THE AUTHOR

RICHARD HINES has worked as a building labourer, in an office, and he was Deputy Head in a school but has spent most of his career as a documentary filmmaker, starting his own production company and working for the BBC and Channel 4, before becoming a lecturer at Sheffield Hallam University. He lives in Sheffield and frequently walks on the nearby moors.

# No Way But Gentlenesse

*A memoir of how Kes, my kestrel,
changed my life*

Richard Hines

BLOOMSBURY

LONDON • OXFORD • NEW YORK • NEW DELHI • SYDNEY

Bloomsbury Paperbacks
An imprint of Bloomsbury Publishing Plc

50 Bedford Square          1385 Broadway
London                     New York
WC1B 3DP                    NY 10018
UK                         USA

www.bloomsbury.com

BLOOMSBURY and the Diana logo are trademarks of Bloomsbury Publishing Plc

First published in Great Britain 2016
This paperback edition first published in 2017

© Richard Hines, 2016

Extracts from the works of Jack Mavrogordato are reproduced by kind permission of
Western Sporting. Extracts from *The Goshawk* and *The Godstone and the Blackymor*
by T. H. White, published respectively by New York Review of Books and
Jonathan Cape, are reproduced by kind permission of David Higham Associates
Limited. Extracts from *The Peregrine* © 1967 by J. A. Baker, are reproduced by kind
permission of HarperCollins Ltd.

Every reasonable effort has been made to trace copyright holders of material reproduced
in this book, but if any have been inadvertently overlooked the publishers would be glad to
hear from them.

British Library Cataloguing-in-Publication Data
A catalogue record for this book is available from the British Library.

ISBN: HB: 978-1-4088-6801-0
PB: 978-1-4088-6802-7
ePub: 978-1-4088-6803-4

2 4 6 8 10 9 7 5 3 1

Typeset by Newgen Knowledge Works (P) Ltd., Chennai, India
Printed and bound in Great Britain by CPI Group (UK) Ltd, Croydon CR0 4YY

MIX
Paper from
responsible sources
FSC
www.fsc.org          FSC® C020471

To find out more about our authors and books visit www.bloomsbury.com.
Here you will find extracts, author interviews, details of forthcoming events and the
option to sign up for our newsletters.

*For Jackie, John and Katie*

There is no way but gentlenesse to redeeme a Hawke

– Edmund Bert, *An Approved Treatise of Hawkes and Hawking*, 1619

# PROLOGUE

In February 2012 I walked to the ruins of Tankersley Old Hall, a sixteenth-century mansion set in farmland close to my home in South Yorkshire. It was a cold overcast afternoon with drizzle in the air, and as I stood there my eyes went up to the high, crumbling ledge in the wall before me. The stones which had once surrounded the nest had fallen away, but in 1965 that was where my first kestrel had spent the first month of her life.

I'd kept the kestrel, which I'd called Kes, in a Second World War air raid shelter in my older brother Barry's garden. One evening, Barry told me he had come up with an idea for his second novel, a story about a lad named Billy Casper who trains a kestrel called Kes. The book, *A Kestrel for a Knave*, became a Penguin Twentieth-Century Classic and was made into the film *Kes*, directed by Ken Loach. In one scene Billy calls his kestrel to the glove in the very field in our mining village where, forty-seven years ago, I trained and flew my own kestrel, Kes.

Two other kestrels that I trained also came from that high ledge, hatching from their reddish-brown blotched eggs. I could remember how, once, my excitement had turned to despair when I reached into the nest hole. Empty, I had thought, cursing the fact I was too late, that all the young kestrels must have fledged. Yet when I reached in further, burying my arm shoulder-deep in the stonework, a gasping young hawk had lashed at my hand with its talons.

Today, almost half a century later, a kestrel called: 'kikiki . . . kikiki . . .' I could see his blue head and tail, as with fast, shallow wingbeats the male kestrel flew out of the ruins of Tankersley Old Hall and landed on a telegraph pole. Moments later, he launched into flight again and then hovered over a verge of tall grasses beside the cart track opposite the ruined Hall. His long wings flickering, his tail fanned, and his head looking down, he hovered in the air, dropped a few feet, hovered again, then, closing his wings, plunged into the tall vegetation with his yellow legs outstretched. A minute or two later he flew up and over a hedge in the direction of the pit village where I'd been brought up, half a mile away across the fields and meadows.

Turning back to gaze at the nest ledge I wondered how my life might have turned out if kestrels hadn't nested there and I hadn't trained Kes. Back then, in the mid-1960s, I could never have guessed my experiences would spark an obsession for hawks that would transform my life.

# PART ONE

# ONE

... you must by kindness make [the hawk] gentle and familiar with you ...

– Nicholas Cox, *The Gentleman's Recreation*, 1674

I was born in 1945, and brought up in Hoyland Common, five miles south of the town of Barnsley in South Yorkshire. Rockingham Colliery was the reason for the existence of the village. Had things turned out differently in 1875 the site of the village might still be farmland today. In March of that year, as the pit shaft of Rockingham Colliery was being sunk, gas ignited by the blasting set a seam of coal on fire and sent flames leaping into the sky. If relays of men hadn't rhythmically pumped water into the shaft and quenched the flames, the colliery would have been destroyed and the village of Hoyland Common wouldn't have existed.

From our small rented terraced stone cottage with its low ceilings and deep windowsills I could see Rockingham Colliery's winding gear, half a mile away across the fields. Silhouetted against the sky, the winding gear consisted of two large black wheels that turned as the cables holding the 'cage', a lift, sent clean-faced miners or empty pit tubs – the small trucks which carried coal – plunging to the depths. Later they hauled the cage back up again, the miners' faces now black with coal dust and the pit tubs full of coal. For a place so embedded with coal dust the irony is that no part of the pit village, with its streets of stone and brick Victorian terraced houses, was more than a few hundred yards away from the fields of crops, grazing cows or flower meadows which surrounded it. The floor of the 'Little Wood', which was a stone's throw away from the colliery slag heap, was covered with bluebells in spring. Sometimes as I lay in bed I could hear lapwings calling 'peewit . . . peewit' in the night, and on spring mornings I would wake to the song of skylarks.

Our terraced cottage had no bathroom and I can remember having my baths in a tin bath in front of a blazing coal fire when I was little. My mother, who had shoulder-length dark, wavy hair and strikingly blue eyes, seemed to be moved by my vulnerability as I sat with my eyes shut tight, while waiting for her to rinse the soap from my hair. She would dip my fingers into the large pan of clean warm water, before saying, 'Don't ever let anyone pour water on your head, without you first checking it isn't too hot', and only rinsed my hair after I'd confirmed the water was the right temperature. Bath time was the only time my mother was openly affectionate, although I know she must have occasionally felt affection towards me when I was asleep, because some mornings I'd wake and find lipstick on my cheek. Showing affection seemed to embarrass my mother, but my dad, with his brushed-back dark wavy hair, dark eyebrows and gentle blue eyes, was the opposite and openly showed his emotions. The first two or three days of my life, before Mother returned home, had been spent in a maternity home in a nearby village. The rules didn't allow Dad to visit his newly born son. Instead, Mother held me up to a window, and as Dad stood outside in the grounds, his eyes filled with tears. When I was at infant and junior school I loved it when Dad returned home from the night shift at the colliery. After he'd greeted me with a smile and

'All right, son?' he'd cook my breakfast while I sat in my pyjamas reading the *Dandy* or *Beano*. Our rented cottage not only lacked a bathroom, there was no lavatory either. So we had to walk about thirty yards to use a shared lavatory in someone else's backyard. That was our life until 1955, when one momentous day, along with Barry, who was six years my senior, I helped our parents carry all our furniture out of the terraced cottage, then further up Tinker Lane. Our new semi-detached and stone-fronted house had been built in the 1880s. My parents bought it for three hundred and fifty pounds and added a bathroom and indoor lavatory.

I can recall an awful occasion from around this time, when Dad had been working the morning shift and I'd returned home from school to find a neighbour sitting in our house waiting for me. She told me Dad had had an accident at the colliery and Mother was at the hospital with him. Mother eventually returned home white-faced from visiting the hospital, and later I overheard her telling the neighbour that my dad had been shovelling coal on his hands and knees when a lump of 'muck' – a large piece of coal or rock – had fallen on him, pinning my dad's chest to the floor and breaking his back. Luckily the doctors' diagnosis was wrong. It turned out that Dad's back wasn't broken after all, and he was transferred from hospital to a miners' rehabilitation home in Firbeck, a village on the Yorkshire/Nottinghamshire border. Those weeks without Dad were awful and I recall running up to greet him on the day he came in through the door, smiling and carrying a suitcase and a wooden lamp-stand he'd made in the miners' rehabilitation home. Soon he was back working on the coalface deep underground. The pit would continue to take its toll of lives.

I loved my kind, gentle dad. One day I'd taken his best trilby out of the wardrobe, pulled it low over my brow, then, sitting on a rusty sheet of corrugated iron, I'd repeatedly slid down the colliery slag heap, coal dust billowing up behind me. Later cloud after cloud of coal dust filled the backyard as my mother beat my dad's hat against a wall to clean it, ranting in anger at me as she did so. It was no good. The hat was ruined and she threw it in the dustbin. Later when Dad returned home from work and she told him what had happened, he shook his head solemnly but couldn't conceal the smile flickering across his lips.

The six-year difference in age meant that Barry had his own friends, and I had mine, but I can remember him vividly when he was seventeen and I was eleven. I was proud of Barry because he was a Teddy boy of sorts, albeit a polite, sixth-form grammar school version. Real Teddy boys were usually ex-secondary modern school youths who worked in manual jobs and had a reputation for gang violence. Barry wore a fingertip-length jacket and narrow-legged trousers, and I thought he looked great dressed up in his suits, with his striking pale blue eyes and brushed-back fair hair. At a local dance I flushed with pride when he jived to a rock 'n' roll number with his girlfriend.

Barry and I shared a bedroom and some nights we would talk and laugh until late. If Dad was on the day shift at the colliery and had to get up early, the noise we made would keep him awake. When he first came into the bedroom he would ask us to be quiet. If we ignored him, as we often did, he would march back into the bedroom and warn us that if we didn't shut up we wouldn't be laughing in the morning when he woke us up at half past four and made us get up with him. Of course he never carried out his threat, and the next morning, when he got up in the dark to go to work, he would tiptoe downstairs so as not to disturb us.

One of my best friends at junior school was called Budgie. A small stocky lad with sandy hair, he lived around the corner in Queen Street in a row of prefabs, which had been built after the end of the Second World War to replace a row of grim terraced houses. The kind couple who lived next door to Budgie were one of the first families in the village to have a television, and they invited kids in to watch children's programmes. I first got to know Budgie, when, along with a line of five or six other kids, we queued outside waiting to see *The Adventures of Kit Carson*, a western about a frontier scout. On one day of the week, I think it was Friday, the traders opened their stalls in the village market place to sell their wares – freshly baked bread, cakes and bilberry pies; fish; curtains, pots and pans. The toy stall had two shutters which were secured by a padlock when the market was closed. One evening I pulled hard on the bottom shutter, while Budgie reached into the gap between the bottom and top shutter and took out a few toy cars, which we played with in his grandad's allotment shed. A few days later, on my way to call for Budgie, I turned into Queen Street and stopped dead, my heart pounding. Looking tiny between them, Budgie was walking down the street between two policemen. I was terrified, thinking they were on their way to arrest me. To my great relief they walked past, Budgie looking straight ahead as if he didn't know me. Later he had to attend court in Barnsley, where he was fined five shillings and had to apologise to the magistrate. Throughout his ordeal he never let on that he'd had an accomplice in the market toy stall robbery. I was moved and grateful and we became even closer friends.

Something else which bound Budgie and me was our love of nature. In the summer of 1956, the year we left junior school at the age of eleven, we spent our time wandering the meadows, crop fields and woods which surrounded Hoyland Common. Whenever I met up with Budgie, he would shout, beating me to it, 'Bags the first animal or bird we find', ensuring the first creature we came across would be his to take home, once he had caught it. His quick thinking paid off.

On one occasion when we came across an escaped budgerigar, he chased it up and down the colliery slag heap until it landed, too tired to fly any longer. Budgie picked it up and carefully carried it home – that's why I called him Budgie. Another time he took home and successfully reared a young song thrush we had found in the fields. One day I managed to get in my claim for the first animal or bird we found, and I thought I was going to be lucky. We were at a pond which fascinated us because it contained newts, when we saw a grass snake, head held high, its greenish body zigzagging through the water. But by the time we had raced around to the other bank to try and catch it, the snake had vanished into the grass.

We weren't only interested in things we could take home and rear. On one occasion in a field, when the white may blossom on the hawthorn had gone to seed but the hedgerows were still coloured by creamy white elder flowers, delicate white bramble flowers and pink dog roses, we walked through tall grass covered in cuckoo spit, which looks like bubbly saliva. Crouching down and running our first finger and thumb carefully up a grass stem, we both marvelled at the tiny green frog hopper nymphs with their tiny black eyes that had produced the frothy grass sap on our fingers.

Towser, my other best friend, had black curly hair. We'd been in the same class throughout junior school but we became closer friends one day when we discovered a shared interest in guns. My parents had bought me a toy silver six-shooter pistol, the type cowboys used in shoot-outs in films. I told Towser about my gun, and he told me his dad had taken a gun from a dead German soldier in the Second World War, and invited me around to his house to see it. Towser lived four streets away from me in a stone terraced house, and one evening after school I sat on the edge of his bed in his attic room while he sneaked into his parents' bedroom, took the gun from a drawer and brought it up for me to look at. My heart raced as he handed me the German Luger. It was so exciting holding it, its brown ribbed handle heavy and snug in my hand as I admired its black barrel with its gunsight at the end.

One Saturday morning, along with Budgie and a couple of other lads from the village, I stood on the pavement outside Towser's house. Unable to contain our excitement, as Towser came out of the front door we all rushed forward and simultaneously asked: 'Has tha got it?'

Grinning, he opened his jacket and showed us the Luger, then reached into his pocket and held up a single bullet between his finger and thumb. We all trailed through the fields to the slurry pond behind the slag heap, then watched fascinated as Towser fired the bullet into the black slurry. The terrific bang forced us to cover our ears and set dogs off barking in a row of cottages half a mile away.

There were two colliery slag heaps. The 'Big Tip' had a truck running up a single rail to its top which dumped slag there night and day. The 'Little Tip' was no longer used and behind it was a barren area made up of grey black slag and compacted coal dust which we called the Lost Valley. One afternoon in the Lost Valley we came across an old pit tub, a small narrow-gauge railway truck made of blackened planks of wood. Upturned, it now looked like a tiny flat-roofed shed with an old sack for a door and a pair of axles with small railway wheels lying across the flat roof.

The old sack covering the sawn-out doorway wouldn't budge when I pulled at it. One of the other lads tried. Still the sack wouldn't move. Then we heard laughter from inside as two kids who lived a couple of streets away from me loosened their grip on the sack door, pulled it to one side and invited us into their den. As I crawled into the upturned pit tub I was amazed. The two lads had lined it inside with floral wallpaper and even fitted a carpet.

Thirty years earlier my dad had worked as a boy pit pony driver at the colliery, and it fascinated me that the very pit tub the two boys had commandeered for their den might have been pulled in a procession of pit tubs through underground tunnels by a pony led by my dad. Dad had told me about those days, and how, as well as leading the pony, he often sat on the first pit tub behind the pony holding its reins. In places where the mine's tunnel was particularly narrow and the roof really low, and Dad couldn't get out of range of the pony's back legs, one crafty pony always stopped for a long rest. It knew Dad daren't give it a whack to get it moving because if he did it would shoot out a back leg and kick him.

When he started work at the age of fourteen, he had been scared of the pit ponies. They could be surly and unpredictable animals, and some of the rebellious ones kicked and bit. Over time he grew to know and like them, but he never fully conquered his fear of being alone, sitting on the pit tub behind his pony holding its reins as they travelled the dark tunnels, the only source of light his miner's lamp, throwing spooky shadows on the tunnel walls.

One pit pony, Dad had told me, had bolted from its underground stables and galloped down a tunnel where the roof descended lower than expected. As it careered along in the dark it had the top of its head cut off by a metal arch holding up the roof. My dad had a similar accident when working as a boy with the pit ponies deep underground. The location of his wound suggests he'd been distracted, maybe looking at a looming shadow, or ducking under a piece of old sacking hanging down from the low roof which, unknown to him, concealed a roof beam. Whatever the reason, as he sat holding the pony's reins he wasn't looking ahead, and, thud, the roof beam hit him at the side of the head, sending him crashing off the pit tub. The fall extinguished his miner's lamp, and Dad, at the age of fourteen and alone, had become aware of warm blood pouring out of a gash on the side of his face as he crawled around in the pitch blackness frightened and crying. Coal dust had entered the wound and the scar, as deep blue as a tattoo, marked him for the rest of his life. When little, I would trace the scar from the front of his ear down to his lower jaw with my finger, marvelling at its blueness.

One day my brother Barry told me of a family member who hadn't been so lucky. It had happened when I was still a baby, and Barry was seven years old. It was 1946 and Barry was playing in some prefabricated bungalows that were being built after the Second World War, when scores of miners came walking up the road hours before the shift was due to end. As women came to their doors to see why the men were returning home from work early, some of the miners called to them, telling them the news: 'Doug Westerman's been killed.' Being only seven, and only knowing him as Grandad, Barry hadn't realised that it was Mother's dad, our grandad, whose name was being called along the village streets. Until, that is, he returned home and saw Mother crying, and our dad standing awkwardly beside her. After Barry told me that, I feared that one day Dad might not return home from the colliery alive.

# TWO

The origin of the word 'kestrel' is somewhat uncertain. By some
it is derived from 'coystril,' a knave or peasant, from being the
hawk formerly used [trained] by persons of inferior rank . . .

– J. E. Harting, *The Ornithology of Shakespeare*, 1864

One early Monday morning in September 1956, I lay in
my bed in the dark listening to Dad cleaning out the
ashes and laying the coal fire for my mother to light when
she got up. Moments later, I heard him close the door and
leave the house to join other miners heading for the colliery.
Later still came the mournful wail of a siren, the 'pit buzzer'
as we called it, signalling to everyone in the village the start
of the 6 a.m. shift at the mine. Trying to calm the anxiety that
had awoken me so early, I attempted to go back to sleep.

Later that morning, around eight o'clock, I called for
Budgie and then at Towser's house, but both of my friends
from junior school had already set off. Turning left at the
top of Towser's street I walked along Sheffield Road, the
old turnpike road, then turned left at Allott's Corner, which
was named after the grocer's shop there, and along Hoyland
Road. In those few hundred yards I'd walked past some of
the nineteenth-century stone buildings in the village that
had been built to sustain the growing population of miners
and their families: the Hare and Hounds pub where the

Rockingham Colliery Brass Band practised in an upstairs room, a bank, an infant and a junior school, which in my parents' and grandparents' day had been a boys' and a girls' school, a post office, two doctors' surgeries, a chemist and lots of shops. Through a gap between a cobbler's and a greengrocer's, where a track led to a farm, I could see meadows and fields of golden stubble, and beyond them the dump truck at Rockingham Colliery making its way up the slag heap to tip its black dusty load.

I was on my way to begin my first day at Kirk Balk Boys' Secondary Modern School on the edge of the village. The system in those days was for all eleven-year-olds to sit an exam, the eleven plus, the results of which dictated whether you were one of the few who went on to grammar school or among the vast majority of kids who were sent to secondary modern school. I don't remember taking that exam myself, but I do remember after the exam one lad had run around the playground shouting it was easy, his arms raised like aeroplane wings. He hadn't done as well as he thought. He failed the exam and didn't get into grammar school, but his dad owned the local bakery and he was sent to a private school in Sheffield.

The playground was full of new boys standing in lines, and when I saw Budgie and Towser I joined their line. Standing in front of us that morning was my new headmaster, Ben, as the older boys called him. He was small and plump with a bald head and round gold-rimmed glasses. As he organised us into our new classes he frequently checked the time on a gold pocket watch which he took out of his waistcoat pocket. Ben called out Budgie's name and he joined the line of boys who had been put in 1C. When the headmaster called out my name I could feel my heart thumping and the blood rising to my face, but when he said what form I'd been put in, my embarrassment was overridden by disappointment. I hesitated, wondering whether I dare tell Ben in front of all those lads lined up in the playground that he'd made a mistake and that I should be in 1A, the top-ability stream.

'Get a move on, boy,' Ben roared, and I quickly joined the line of lads who'd been told they were in 1B. Soon afterwards I was joined by Towser.

Later, as we lined up outside the classroom a big man wearing a tweed jacket marched down the corridor. This was Idle Jack, our new form teacher. He slapped the first boy in the line across the face. Then, after he'd walked along and slapped each one of us across the face, he warned us that's what we got for doing nothing wrong, then asked us to imagine the beating we'd get if we *did* do something wrong.

By the time I got home Idle Jack's red finger marks had worn off my face and I didn't tell my mother about the slap, but I did tell her of my disappointment at discovering I'd been put in 1B, rather than 1A. Next day the classroom door opened and in walked Ben.

'Where's Hines?' the headmaster asked.

Blushing, I raised my hand.

'Your mummy says you're a clever little boy,' he said in a whining voice while moving his head from side to side.

For a moment I didn't know what he was talking about, then I realised that after I'd complained to Mother about being put into 1B, she'd come up to school to try and persuade the headmaster to move me up into the A stream.

'Come with me,' Ben ordered.

Humiliated and burning with shame, I rose to my feet. Some of the lads in our class wore their older brothers' tattered handed-down clothes and boots with steel studs in the soles. As I followed Ben out of the classroom under their sneering gaze I was uncomfortably aware of my tie, my neatly pressed short trousers, knee-length stockings and new Clark's shoes. If only my mother had let me come to school in my jeans and sneakers.

I followed Ben to his office and he told me to wait outside with an older boy called Herb, who I knew by reputation. He was a wild, rough lad with jet-black hair, the kind of lad you dreaded coming across when out walking in the countryside. Once I'd seen him throwing stones at a man cycling to work. So my heart raced when he turned to me and asked: 'Was that thi mother who's just been to see Ben?'

'Yeah,' I said, blushing.

Mother was a good-looking woman who was interested in fashion. She travelled on the bus to Sheffield to buy her clothes, and when she dressed up and put on make-up, as I knew she would have before coming up to school, she looked so glamorous she embarrassed me. As Herb stood facing me in his scruffy, tattered clothes I was expecting him to insult my mother. Instead he smiled and said: 'She's nice, her.'

Mother could weigh up a situation in an instant. When she'd seen Herb standing outside the headmaster's office, she would have guessed he wasn't the type of lad to have been sent on an errand by a teacher, and, realising he was waiting to be caned, she would have smiled and spoken to him kindly.

Moments later Ben called me into his office, and I noticed three or four canes on the top shelf of the bookcase as he irritably searched the shelves. Ben found a book, handed it to me and told me to read from it. I stood there fumbling to find the first page.

'Any page will do,' he said.

I let the book fall open and looked at the page in front of me. The print was tiny, the lines close together. I started to read, but when I discovered that the passage I was reading contained words I'd never come across I faltered. Ben muttered and on the edge of my vision I could see him shaking his head. After I'd read three or four sentences he took the book away from me.

'1B? You're lucky you're not in 1C, boy,' he said. 'Now get back to your class.'

On that first morning when Idle Jack had slapped all the class across the face, I'd feared that, as our form teacher, he would teach us every subject, like the class teachers did in junior school. So I was relieved to discover Idle Jack only marked the register each morning and afternoon, and taught us art, and that we had different teachers for different subjects. Ronnie, our friendly first-year history teacher, wore a blue tracksuit. In our first lesson he smiled and asked us to take our seats when we entered the classroom. He began telling us about the Spartans in ancient Greece, about their habit of throwing unhealthy babies off a mountain to their deaths, and about how Spartan boys aged eleven – the age we were – would already have had four years' military training. If we had been Spartans, he told us, we would only have been allowed to have a gravestone with our name on it if we had been killed in battle. I was engrossed. Then, about ten minutes into the hour-long lesson, one of the lads homed in on the football coaching badge on Ronnie's tracksuit and asked him if he'd seen our local team Barnsley's match at the weekend. That was the end of the Spartans, and Ronnie talked about football until the bell rang to signal the end of the lesson. As we left the classroom delighted boys congratulated the lad who'd got the history teacher talking about football. I liked football but I didn't want to hear the teacher talk about it in a history lesson. I had only left junior school a few weeks earlier. I hadn't thought much about school before, but that wasted lesson brought home to me the fact that I'd been dumped in a school where my education didn't matter.

One evening, soon after my parents had heard I'd failed my eleven plus exam, and that I wouldn't be going to grammar school, I'd overheard a snippet of an argument they were having. Dad said if I'd passed the exam it would have reflected well on Mother, and would have been a feather in her cap, just as Barry gaining a place at grammar school had been, and that was the main reason she was upset that I'd failed. Mother responded that she had been proud of Barry. Then she furiously demanded to know if Dad really believed she hadn't just wanted what was best for me. In the end Dad had apologised. The previous year, while still at junior school, I'd seen Mother standing at the garden gate hardly able to contain her pride. When Barry had finally come down the lane dressed in his dark red grammar school blazer, and she'd told him the results of his GCE O level exams, he'd vaulted over the gate and run into the house to check the good news for himself. Back then, I'd wondered what all the fuss was about. Now, each evening, when I walked home from school and past lads in red blazers who'd got off the bus from grammar school, I longed to be like them, part of their world.

One evening when I arrived home from school I opened the gate and walked down the path beside our house. Perched on top of the shed in our backyard was my magpie, Maggie, a beautiful bird with her black head and white breast, her blue-green wing feathers and her long tail shining in the late afternoon sun. She had been special to me ever since I'd carried her home that May evening nearly five months ago, my hands, arms and face covered in scratches from the thorns of a hawthorn tree that I'd had to climb, so I could reach into the large bundle of sticks that was her nest and take her.

'Not be long, Maggie,' I called to her as I opened the door and went into the house.

There was no one home as I changed into jeans and sneakers before boiling a couple of eggs and mashing them up on a saucer to feed to Maggie. If there was a joint of meat in the

17

pantry I'd usually cut off a few pieces and mix them in with the boiled egg. Sometimes I'd also break off bits of vegetables and add them to the saucer but this evening I could only find a few radishes. I'd never fed her radish before but I thought I'd see if she liked it and chopped one into Maggie's boiled egg.

As I carried Maggie's saucer of food out of the back door my mother walked down the path carrying a shopping bag in each hand. She looked furious. Nodding towards Maggie, who was still perched on the shed roof, she said that after I'd gone to school in the morning 'that blasted magpie' had landed on the flowers and berries decorating an old lady's hat, and that the old lady's screams had brought out the neighbours who then had to sit her down on a wall where her nerves were calmed with a sip of water.

When I laughed I sensed that my mother was so angry that for once in her life she might have hit me, and that only the shopping bags she held restrained her. Only yesterday, she reminded me, a neighbour had complained after Maggie flew inches above her dog's head, chasing it up the street, her dog 'yelping as if it had been shot'. Then she went on to recall how, a week earlier, a furious woman had banged on the door complaining how 'that damned magpie' had terrified her two boys by looking through the window as they ate their breakfast. She was 'sick of it', Mother told me, and said I had to get rid of her. As I walked behind the shed carrying Maggie's saucer of food, she called: 'And I mean it.'

Placing the saucer of food on the ground behind the shed, I sat on the compacted earth beside Maggie. She seemed to be enjoying the radish, holding the small chopped pieces in the tip of her beak, then tilting her head back to swallow them. This wasn't the first time Mother had insisted that I get rid of Maggie. Once was after a neighbour had complained that my magpie had flown in through the open window of her bedroom and at that moment was perched on top of the dressing-table mirror.

I'd always been drawn to wild creatures. There was a newt pond with overhanging trees beside the colliery railway line, and holding a fishing net I'd dip it into the clear water of the pond and scoop out great crested newts, then carry them home in a jam jar of water and tip them into a fish tank on an old chest of drawers in the shed. Four or five inches long, jagged crests along their backs and orange and black spots on their bellies, the great crested newts swam around like little lizards, fascinating me for a few days before I returned them to the pond. Yet the newts I'd caught, the frogs I'd reared from tadpoles or the hedgehogs I'd kept didn't have the same appeal as Maggie. I looked at her lovely long blue-green tail as she pecked at her food and remembered how short and stumpy it had been when I'd carried her home.

Leaning back against the shed, I watched Maggie as she pecked and swallowed the last pieces of mashed-up egg from her saucer. To my horror she suddenly seemed to be struggling for breath, then began to vomit the chopped-up chunks of radish. She looked so ill, so vulnerable, as she retched and retched. How could I have been so unthinking as to feed her such hard food? I'd reared her from a stubby-tailed fledgling, kept her fit and alive until she'd become a healthy, beautiful juvenile, and now I was convinced she was dying in front of my eyes. I began to cry but moments later Maggie recovered miraculously and was up to her old mischief, pulling the laces on my sneakers with her beak, pecking at the turn-ups of my jeans. Nevertheless, I couldn't stop crying.

Later that warm September evening I sat on the back doorstep, knowing Maggie would fly down from wherever she was perched. As she took one of my shoelaces in her beak and pulled it, I clamped my hand across her back then stuffed her into an old shopping bag and zipped it up.

Carrying the bag, I walked through the village, through Bell Ground Wood, past Tankersley Old Hall and through fields enclosed by hedges and drystone walls; farmland which in the past had been the Old Hall's deer park. When I reached the field with the hawthorn tree and the now deserted bundle of twigs that had been Maggie's nest, I unzipped the shopping bag and Maggie flew out. I walked away, repeatedly glancing over my shoulder to watch her fly and land on stone walls as she followed me along the field paths. Occasionally walking backwards, I watched as she flew between trees as I made my way up the track that led to Tankersley Old Hall. If Maggie kept this up, and followed me back home, I would be able to tell Mother I had done my best to release her but that she wouldn't go. However, when we got to Tankersley Old Hall farm, which stood in the grounds of the Old Hall, Maggie landed on the roof of a stable and reached down to peck insects from between the stones of the wall. When I called her she flew away across the farmyard, over a stone barn and out of sight, her blue-green wings and long tail shining in the evening sun.

It was unlikely I'd see Maggie again and my heart ached. I'd thought of her as my pet, but the way she had ignored me and flown off made me realise I was nothing to her. At first I was upset but as I walked along the lane I began to feel differently. I was only eleven, and probably couldn't explain it at the time, but there was something about my magpie never having truly lost her wildness that had a strange appeal. Mixed in with my sadness was a feeling of pride; I'd been honoured to have reared and kept a wild bird like Maggie.

A couple of evenings later, still missing Maggie, I decided to wander around Tankersley Old Hall farm, hoping to see her. I didn't, but as I made my way home I stopped in my tracks to gaze up at a male kestrel hovering a few yards away beyond a drystone wall. Caught in the evening sun, the underside of its outstretched flickering wings and fanned tail shone a brilliant white. I'd never been so close to a kestrel. I could clearly see its blue head, large brown eyes, curved beak and the black talons at the end of its yellow clasped feet. I'd never found a kestrel's nest, and I didn't know if it was possible to rear one, but as I stood gazing up at that beautiful hovering kestrel, so aloof, so wild, I knew that I'd love to bring one into my life.

# THREE

*... it is no kindnesse, but violence and churlish usage, which must never be offered to a Hawke ...*

– Edmund Bert, *An Approved Treatise of*
*Hawkes and Hawking*, 1619

Smithy glanced around the classroom and called my name.

'Hines?'

'Yes, sir.'

He stared at me for a few moments then ticked off my name in the register. He called out another boy's name, gazed at him for a while and then marked him present. After coming second in the end-of-term exam in 1B, I'd been moved up into the A stream. Now aged fourteen, I was in my fourth year at secondary modern school and it was my first morning in 4A, where Smithy, my new form teacher, was trying to match the names in the register with the faces of the boys in his new class.

Smithy, who was in his forties, had a small moustache and wore a tweed jacket with leather elbow patches. When he'd finished marking the register he got up and stood in front of the class. I thought he was going to welcome us and perhaps give us an encouraging speech on how we needed to work hard in our final year at school, but instead he told us secondary modern school lads like us, who would leave at the end of the year aged fifteen, had an easy time at school. Much easier than his two daughters, he explained, who, because they were at grammar school, had to do homework and stay on at school to take GCE O and A level exams because they wanted to go to university and have professional careers.

Later that term Smithy chalked SOCIAL CLASS in capital letters on the blackboard. Underneath he wrote WORKING CLASS, before asking some of us what jobs our dads did as examples of the type of work done by the working class. Then, after he'd written MIDDLE CLASS on the blackboard Smithy asked for examples of middle-class professions.

'Bank manager,' said one kid.

'Good,' said Smithy.

'Vicar,' said another lad.

'Yes,' said Smithy.

Further examples were called out – doctor, lawyer, accountant – but Smithy wasn't satisfied. He demanded more examples, then more still. Finally, it dawned on us he was waiting for someone to call out teacher and acknowledge he belonged to a higher social class than us. Without a word or a glance at each other we somehow decided that we wouldn't give Smithy what he sought, as the examples of middle-class professions became more mischievous.

'Scissor grinder,' one lad shouted.

Fred, our English teacher, who had a kind face and wore an unbuttoned jacket and corduroy trousers, looked more bohemian than the other teachers. One day he read poetry to us. One of the poems was *Horatius at the Bridge* by Lord Macaulay. In the poem, in a desperate attempt to save Rome, Horatius stood on a narrow bridge that crossed the river Tiber and fought off the Etruscans as the bridge was being chopped from beneath him. I was so taken by the poem that at the end of the lesson I stayed behind pretending to be looking for something I'd misplaced. Then, when everyone had left the classroom, I took a copy of the poetry anthology from the cupboard in which they were stored, sat down at a desk, and began reading the poem again.

Earlier I'd shielded my eyes with my hand when Fred reached the part of the poem where Horatius, bleeding and in great pain, weighed down by his armour, struggled to swim back to Rome. Now, alone in the classroom, when I read 'And oft they thought him sinking, But still again he rose,' the tears rolled down my face as I urged Horatius to keep going and make it to the riverbank.

Budgie had found new school friends. Towser, who had also been moved up into the A stream, was now my best mate and like me he enjoyed poetry. We both liked Irene Rutherford McLeod's poem 'Lone Dog', particularly the line: 'I love to sit and bay the moon, to keep fat souls from sleep.'

We also enjoyed fiction, and were amused by a description from J. D. Salinger's novel *The Catcher in the Rye* in which the protagonist, Holden Caulfield, said his teacher had picked up his exam paper and was holding it as if it was a turd. After we'd both finished reading the book anyone who picked up anything – a book, a pen, a piece of chalk – seemed to us to be handling it as if it was a turd. Towser spoke in a Barnsley dialect, as we all did, and although he lived in a stone terraced house, unlike the rest of us he came from a middle-class family that ran shops in the village. His parents had sent him for elocution lessons when he was younger, and he could speak Standard English without a trace of accent and had won prizes for reading aloud to audiences. So when Fred needed a passage from a novel or a poem reading out he would hand the book to Towser who would captivate the class with his delivery.

One morning as we walked together along the school corridor he told me that the previous evening, while out in the countryside with some other kids, they'd come across an injured 'standing hawk', a local name for a kestrel. My heart began to race. Ever since I had looked up at that hovering kestrel, at the underside of its outspread flickering wings and fanned tail shining white in the evening sun, that was the bird I'd yearned to keep. I still hadn't discovered a kestrel's nest. Heart thumping, I desperately hoped that whoever was looking after the injured kestrel would now pass it on to me.

'Who's got the kestrel?' I asked.

'Nobody,' Towser said.

'How's tha mean?'

'We killed it – with sticks.'

I rammed Towser against the wall and held him there with my arm across his neck.

'It'd flown into the telegraph wires,' he shouted into my face. 'It was dying. We were putting it out of its misery.'

One day in a science lesson a lad called Denny sat on a stool at the bench in front of Towser and me. He'd had a haircut. The back and sides were shaved but the floppy hair on top of his head seemed to have been untouched. From the bench where we were doing work in our science books it looked as if Denny was wearing a cap.

'Denny,' I called in a loud whisper.

He turned round.

'It's bad manners to wear thi cap in class.'

'Shut thi gob, Hinesy.'

He turned back to his work.

'Denny,' I called again, 'take thi cap off in class.'

I hadn't realised Denny was so sensitive about his hair. To my surprise he jumped up and marched over to the science teacher who, at that point, was sending an electric shock through half a dozen lads who were holding hands, making them writhe in pain. He turned off the electricity when Denny approached, and as Denny spoke to him and occasionally pointed to his hair the science teacher looked across the science benches at me, then he said something to Denny. Grinning, Denny walked out of the classroom. When he returned he sat back on his stool at the bench in front of me, turned, and told me: 'Tha's to go and see Ben.'

And so I did.

Ben the headmaster reached up to a high bookshelf in his office and brought down four canes, one straight and three with curved ends like walking sticks. He chose the straight cane. Ben taught us history now we were in our fourth year, and his knowledge and his love of the subject engaged my interest. One day he'd even embarrassed me by praising my work in front of the class. He seemed to like me and sent me on errands out of school. Now, looking exasperated, he asked: 'What are you playing at, Hines?'

'I only meant it as a bit of fun, sir.'

With a couple of flicks of the cane Ben indicated I should raise my hand. I'd once seen a lad who had been caned by Ben rush out of school and do three laps around the playground holding his thumb in agony. Other lads offered the advice that, to lessen the pain, you needed to make sure the skin on your hand was loose. Thumb tucked behind my first finger, skin nice and loose on my palm, I stood with my hand raised, steeling myself for the first blow. It didn't come. I looked at Ben. He had the cane raised but he was shaking his head as if he couldn't make up his mind whether to thrash me or let me off. Then he stopped shaking his head and looked at me angrily.

'You've got intelligence, boy,' he said, 'but it's not human intelligence.'

Swish. Swish.

'Other hand.'

Swish. Swish.

Blowing on my hands, rubbing them together, blowing on them again, I tried to lessen the pain of the four strokes of the cane as I made my way back to class. Suddenly, Herb, the wild rough lad who had told me my mother was nice, came sprinting down the corridor. Herb must have fled the classroom to escape a beating, because, running behind him, red-faced, breathing heavily and calling, 'Come back here, you imbecile', was Idle Jack, the art teacher.

One morning I came within a second of fleeing Idle Jack's classroom myself. I can't remember what I'd done to cause him to call me out to the front of the class. Using the first finger and thumb on each hand he took hold of the hair above my ears and then he slowly lifted me up. The skin on either side of my head was pulled so tight that I was frightened it would tear. Idle Jack was a lot bigger than me and, when he'd lifted me to my full height and I was standing on tiptoes, my eyes level with his mouth, I could feel his breath on my face. I was suddenly overcome with rage. My fingers squeezed into a fist, and for a moment I was going to smack Idle Jack on the nose.

But I didn't. Idle Jack, still holding the hair at the side of my head between his fingers and thumbs, let me down on to the soles of my shoes and finished off my punishment by ordering me to bend over, then using his full power hit me at least six times across the backside with one of those large blackboard T-squares.

'Now get back to your place, you cretin, you imbecile,' he roared.

In one English lesson I looked up the dictionary definitions of Idle Jack's two favourite insults – *cretin*: 'a physically deformed and mentally retarded person'; *imbecile*: 'a person of abnormally weak intellect'. Idle Jack wasn't the only one to insult us; other teachers would call us halfwits, morons, numbskulls, retarded. Even well-behaved lads couldn't escape put-downs, as a teacher, while smirking or winking at other staff, would say, 'I'm looking for an *intelligent* boy to do a job for me', emphasising intelligent. Were the grammar school kids constantly told they were stupid? If they were maybe they'd have the confidence to know they weren't, but for me, a lad who'd racked his brain over his eleven plus exam to no avail, the insults struck home.

Idle Jack left while I was in my last year at school and I thought I'd seen the last of him. Then one evening when I switched on the television there he was talking about his new venture on the regional news. I thought he might have become an artist because his figurative pencil drawings were brilliant but instead he'd set up a business making fibreglass car bodies. When asked why he'd left teaching Idle Jack didn't hold back, telling the interviewer that the pupils he'd taught in our secondary modern school were cretins and imbeciles.

I was almost fifteen and soon I'd have to leave and find a job. In this my final year I had become so fed up with school I was often late. Some days I'd just sleep in despite my mother's repeated calls, but in spring and summer I'd walk through the fields and take a long route to school.

I was still fascinated by nature. One morning I had to put six fully feathered young blue tits back into their nest, when, to my amazement, I'd found them clinging to my fingers when I'd pulled my hand out of a hole in a tree. On another occasion I watched as a young moorhen chick pecked its way out of its egg in a nest at the edge of a pond. On another morning, only a few minutes' walk from school, I saw a mistle thrush dive-bombing another late schoolboy, forcing him back down a tree after he'd tried to climb up to its nest. But these sightings were nothing compared to the morning I went a long way round to school, and spent at least half an hour, sitting in Tankersley churchyard, gazing skywards after a 'kikiki . . . kikiki . . . kikiki . . .' had drawn my attention to three kestrels, the dark bars on the underside of their tails and wings clearly visible as they flew and soared together above the church.

One day in metalwork I was making a sugar bowl that Wee Georgie, the metalwork teacher, was going to send off to be silver-plated. I can't remember what I needed but, whatever it was, Wee Georgie sent me to the stockroom to get it. On a shelf I spotted a patterned length of metal and pulled it out. It was wafer-thin, about a quarter of an inch wide and looked like a strip of silver lace. Later, when Wee Georgie was overseeing a lad who was holding a piece of white-hot metal in tongs and plunging it into steaming water, I sneaked back into the stockroom with a hacksaw.

At my bench I filed and bent the piece of patterned metal I'd sawn off into a silver band. I slipped it on my ring finger and it fitted perfectly. A touch of solder, discreetly applied when I soldered the handles on to my sugar basin, and I'd made a lovely ring.

'Give it to me.'

It was Wee Georgie, his face white with anger. I hid my hand with the ring on it behind my back.

'What, sir?'

'Give it to me.'

Realising that some kid had shopped me, I took off the ring I'd so lovingly fashioned and handed it to Wee Georgie. He dropped it into his grey overall pocket, grabbed my wrist, raised my hand and held it there.

Swish. Swish. Swish.

I hadn't realised he was carrying a cane and the first stroke crashed down on to my thumb. He grabbed my other wrist, raised my hand and once again held it high.

Swish. Swish. Swish.

The last three strokes were delivered with so much anger that it felt as if they were going to fetch off my finger ends.

Over the four years at school I'd guess I'd been given the slipper and the cane by teachers three or four times a month, but the thrashing from Wee Georgie for sawing off a small piece of fancy silver-coloured metal worth a few pennies affected me more than any of the other beatings. Before Wee Georgie confronted me I remember feeling pleased with myself as I crafted that silver band of metal into a ring. I couldn't understand his anger. Maybe the strip of fancy metal was for the exclusive use of the adults he taught in a metal-work night-school class. Perhaps he'd had unruly classes all day and was at the end of his tether with disruptive boys. It wasn't just the physical pain, or my bruised thumb and fingers: I felt as if I had been emotionally assaulted.

Later, still seething with resentment, I wandered around the metalwork room seeking to do damage that really would have justified such anger and such a beating. I spotted a small portable hand vice and, guessing that would cost Wee Georgie a lot more to replace than the few pence worth of metal I'd helped myself to, I drilled out the screws. The hand vice fell apart, and the damaged threads where the screws had been meant it couldn't be put back together again.

A few days later, I was walking down the corridor at break time when I saw a kid standing outside the staff-room. Realising Wee Georgie, along with all the other teachers, would be in there enjoying a cup of tea, a surge of mischievousness and defiance overcame me. I flung open the door, grabbed the lad by the scruff of the neck and the back of his trousers and threw him in. Conversation stopped mid-sentence, laughter died and a couple of dozen teachers stared in astonished silence, as, hunched into a crouched run, the lad tried to keep his balance as he stumbled across the staffroom. I couldn't see Wee Georgie, but Fiddler, our music teacher, who was lying back in a chair with his feet on a table, jumped up, spilling tea down his jacket, and Fred, the English teacher, choked on a biscuit. The lad's momentum was brought to a halt when one of the teachers grabbed him as he stumbled into a group standing by a table.

'A kid threw me in, sir.'

A gang of angry male teachers, all of them seemingly wearing tweed jackets, now marched the lad towards the open staffroom door where I was standing facing them.

'Did he throw you in?' asked one of the teachers.

'Yes, sir,' said the lad.

A cane seemed to appear from nowhere and I was told: 'Get your hand up, Hines.'

I was then given six strokes of the cane as I stood in the corridor.

Towards the end of the summer term of 1960 Ben stood on the school hall stage, thrashing the lectern with a cane. It was Speech Day, and the proceedings had reached the point where a school prefect was supposed to give a speech and Ben was demanding that someone tell him where the prefect had gone. I don't know if Ben realised he had done a runner. Or if he'd remembered the owner of the local drapery shop, who donated and handed out the prizes, was sitting on a chair on the stage behind him, but he stopped thrashing the lectern with the cane and said, 'We'll move on'.

The fourth-year lads whose fifteenth birthdays had fallen before Easter had left school at the beginning of the Easter holidays to work down the mines or in the steelworks. So, rather than being 4A, 4B, 4C, 4D, in the summer term we'd been split into L4 and U4, an abbreviation of Lower and Upper 4th year. In previous years I'd always won one or two prizes on Speech Day, but this year, because several of the kids who were good at specific subjects had left, there wasn't so much competition and I won three or four prizes.

Returning from the stage after receiving my first prize, *The Observer's Book of Birds' Eggs*, I sat on the school hall floor and turned to the picture of the kestrel's mottled reddish-brown egg. My anger rose when I read that although kestrels feed only on voles, mice and shrews, like most birds of prey they'd often been ruthlessly destroyed and ended up on gamekeepers' gibbets. My brother, Barry, had inherited a collection of birds' eggs from an uncle who had collected them as a boy. The eggs were kept in a box, the catch of which I'd sometimes unfasten carefully before easing open the lid to look at the kestrel's egg cushioned in sawdust in its own square compartment. I had no interest in taking eggs. Instead, as I sat on the school hall floor, in my imagination I scaled a cliff to a nest and took a young kestrel to rear.

There was an inscription at the front of the book. Ben must have run out of ink midway and refilled his pen with a different colour, for using both blue ink and black he'd written:

Form U4
1st Place
Awarded to
Richard Hines
July 1960

Although I was top of the class I wasn't cleverer than the other kids. Maybe they hadn't cottoned on – or more likely knowing they'd end up doing manual work whatever the results of the exams, they didn't care – but when each subject teacher started going over work we'd done previously I realised he was preparing us for questions he'd set in the exam. Unlike a lot of the lads I stopped messing about and listened.

The drapery shop owner was now handing out prizes for coming top in a specific subject. Each time I was called up on stage to receive yet another book prize, Fiddler, the music teacher, clapped so gingerly he looked as if he feared he'd get an electric shock if he brought his palms together too enthusiastically. By contrast, Fred, the English teacher, clapped heartily and even gave me the thumbs-up a couple of times.

# FOUR

... hawking ... is ... uncertaine and subject to mischances ...

– King James VI of Scotland, later King James I of
England, *Basilikon Doran*, 1599

One evening after school I went to our local cinema, the Kino, with Towser, and as we walked home he suddenly quoted, 'I love to sit and bay the moon, to keep fat souls from sleep', before crouching down on his haunches and howling at the full moon. I was still grinning when I entered the house and saw Mother sat in an armchair, her face white with anxiety.

'What's up?'

'Your dad hasn't come home from work yet.'

My stomach churned as I glanced at the clock. It was nearly eleven. The colliery had three shifts: mornings, afternoons and nights. Each week Dad worked on a different shift; today he'd been on the 2 p.m. to 10 p.m. afternoon shift. He would usually be home by ten thirty. Knowing why Mother was so worried I sat down to wait with her. She was still haunted by that awful day when my grandad Westerman, who wore a pink dog rose in the buttonhole of his lapel in spring, hadn't returned home from the colliery.

Suddenly Mother jumped up and hurried to the door. I thought she'd heard Dad coming down the path but she was only going outside to stand at the gate to see if she could see him walking down the lane. Had Dad been home tonight when I'd returned from the cinema he'd have greeted me with his usual smile and an affectionate 'All right, son?' as he ate his supper. I thought about when I'd last seen him this morning through the open shed door as I set off to school. Kneeling on the floor, he'd cut a dark red patch from an old grammar school blazer of my brother's, and then had glued it over the rip on a pair of work trousers spread on the shed floor. Grinning at the large deep red patch on the dark-coloured trousers, I'd told him they looked daft. 'They'll do for the pit,' he'd replied, adding, 'after two minutes it'll not matter what colour they are – they'll be black with coal dust.'

'There's no sign of him,' Mother said as she came back into the house. Ten minutes later, and then again ten minutes after that, she went out to stand at the gate and gaze up the lane. It was nearly half past eleven when we heard the gate latch click and someone walking down the path. We both looked at the door. Would it open, or would we hear the knock of someone bringing bad news? The wait was unbearable. Then the door opened and Dad walked in grim-faced, his blue-checked 'pit scarf' knotted around his neck.

'Thank God,' Mother said, her relief turning to anger as she asked, 'Where've you been?'

'Digging out Jimmy Pole.'

Dad told us Jimmy Pole, a Polish man who'd come to work in the pits after the Second World War, had been partially buried by a roof fall.

'Is he all right?' Mother asked.

'We thought he was,' Dad said, 'but when we got him out we saw his foot was hanging off.'

I'd had my fifteenth birthday in May 1960, a few weeks earlier. Now it was nearing the end of the summer term and I would soon leave school, along with all the other fourth-year lads. To help us with our search for work the school had arranged for a Youth Employment Officer to visit. On the day of the interviews I sat on one of a row of chairs, which had been placed outside the headmaster's office where the interviews were being held. When I heard my name called and entered the office I was struck by the unusual sight of the Employment Officer sitting behind Ben's desk, and, as I sat down, behind his head I could see Ben's canes on the top shelf of the bookcase.

'You must have given it some thought – the kind of job you want to do.'

I sat looking at him.

I'd never wanted to be a miner like my dad and both my grandads. Wee Georgie, our metalwork teacher, had once taken us around the steelworks in Sheffield, about ten miles away. I'm not sure why but I hated it: the high cavernous factory, the smoke, the blazing red furnaces, sweating men pouring white-hot molten metal. Worse than that was a workshop where, time after time, women and lads picked up a hacksaw blade, tapped it on a bench, then, after deftly flicking it over and holding the other end, tapped it on the bench again. If satisfied with the sound it made they threw it into a box with hundreds of already tested blades. I'd rather have worked down the pit than do that.

'There must be something you're interested in,' the Youth Employment Officer said.

There was: wildlife, literary fiction, history. Six years older than me, my brother was already training to be a PE teacher, and, fascinated, I'd read every psychology book on his college reading list from cover to cover, but I couldn't see how any of this stuff would help me find a job. I remained silent.

'What about hobbies? Do you like constructing Meccano sets, for example?'

I racked my brain trying to give him something to work with. Barry was good at sport and had won lots of prizes in local athletics meetings. It was this that had encouraged him to train to be a PE teacher. I remembered how the last time he'd been home from college he'd filled a fancy dish he'd won with soil and planted some cacti.

'Cactuses,' I said.

'Cacti,' the Youth Employment Officer corrected.

'Yeah.'

'Planting them?' he asked. 'Making little cacti gardens?'

I nodded, and he wrote 'gardening' under my name in his notebook.

I'd no interest in cacti or gardening but I couldn't think of anything else to do. I don't recall if the Youth Employment Officer arranged it, or if I'd seen the job advertised in the local newspaper but I had an interview with the owner of a local landscape gardening business.

The offices were in a large shed. A secretary showed me into the boss's office. He was a big bloke in his early forties working at a desk. He didn't look up and left me standing there awkwardly. When eventually he looked up I thought he might ask me to sit down. He didn't. I stood there as he asked me questions.

'Start next Monday – 7.30 a.m.,' he said finally, before turning back to the paperwork on his desk.

'Excuse me,' I said.

He looked up, glaring at me.

'Yes?'

I told him I had another interview to attend for a similar gardening labourer's job with the parks department of the local council. I said if I was offered that job and decided to take it I'd come and tell him immediately, rather than just not turn up to work for him next Monday. Anger drained his face white and in a quiet, threatening voice he asked: 'Who do you think you are?'

'Pardon?'

'Coming here wasting my time?'

'I thought . . .'

'GET OUT,' he roared.

Frightened, I tiptoed out of the office, quietly closing the door behind me.

My parents had warned me of the indignities suffered by working-class people. From the age of fourteen until she was twenty-one, when she married Dad, my mother had worked as a servant. Although a feisty lass who often ranted in the privacy of her attic bedroom at the way she'd been spoken to, she needed the job badly, and whatever degradations she suffered at the hands of her employers she said she always 'bit her tongue' and told me that's what I'd have to learn to do.

When I was younger a coal lorry had pulled up in the lane outside our house. When the driver knocked on our door, Dad had left his dinner half eaten and climbed into the lorry with the driver before he drove off. My mother anxiously told me that earlier at work Dad had argued with a deputy manager, and had been summoned to see the colliery manager. When he returned home I asked him what the pit manager had said. He said he'd told him 'not to get aggressive with the officials'. I laughed but Dad didn't, for they'd threatened him with the sack. Dad said he hoped I wouldn't end up like him, an unskilled labourer, but told me if I did, even if they are wrong, you don't argue with the bosses, because they can take away your livelihood and make it difficult for you to get a job anywhere else. He gave me the same advice as my mother: 'Bite your tongue.'

What my parents had told me about the realities of working-class people's lives probably never crossed my mind. If it did, I ignored it that day in the interview at the landscaper's office. I was suddenly overcome by a rage and turned around abruptly, marched back to the office door I'd so meekly closed seconds before, and flung it open with such force that it banged on the inside of the office wall. Startled, the man looked up from his work as I strode back to his desk. I told him – probably while jabbing my finger at him – that I'd tried to be fair to him and would have kept my word, and that owning a company didn't give him the right to treat people the way he'd treated me.

He picked up the telephone receiver, held his finger above the nine on the dial, and spoke in that official way that people seem to adopt in such circumstances as he threatened to call the police and have me escorted off the premises.

# FIVE

CAST, a 'cast' of hawks, i.e. two . . .

— J. E. Harting, *Bibliotheca Accipitraria*, 1891

At the very end of term at secondary modern school, when I was fifteen, the headmaster, Ben, had marched into the classroom and asked if any boy wanted to take an entrance exam for a new two-year course at Barnsley Technology College, which would give them the opportunity to study for GCE O levels. I took the entrance exam but I was so convinced that I'd failed, I'd already started the job as a labourer in the council parks department after leaving school. It came as a pleasant surprise when I received a letter telling me I'd been accepted on the full-time course. This meant I could leave my job and begin attending Barnsley Tech in September 1960, along with Towser, who had also passed the entrance exam. We both passed a few GCE O levels and in 1962, aged seventeen, we transferred to Ecclesfield Grammar School to study GCE A levels and travelled the three miles to get there on the bus.

I can remember how, after failing my eleven plus exam, I'd longed to wear that deep red grammar school blazer. Yet by the time I'd passed my O levels, and transferred to Ecclesfield Grammar School, I'd cultivated my own style of dressing: open-necked shirts, usually dark blue or dark red. If it was cold

I wore arty-looking sweaters, polo- and round-necked, sometimes ribbed, usually black or dark blue. Wearing the grammar school uniform now made me feel daft, like some big awkward kid. Nevertheless I tolerated it, although I drew the line at the school tie. The teachers who taught me A level History and Geography didn't seem to notice, or care. Similarly the deputy head who taught me A level English Literature didn't seem offended by my open-necked collar. Unfortunately my other literature teacher, Brooky, wasn't having it. Wherever he spotted me, walking up the school drive, along a corridor, entering a classroom, he'd call: 'Necktie, Hines.'

One summer afternoon it was so hot that some girls in the classroom were fanning their faces with the essays that Brooky had just handed back to us. Brooky, wearing a black gown and mortarboard, stood in front of us, and when he started talking about the poems of John Donne I thought he was going to let it go for once but he noticed me.

'Necktie, Hines,' he roared.

'It's too hot to wear a tie, sir.'

'Nonsense,' he said. 'I'm wearing a shirt, tie, jacket and gown. It's about discipline, boy. Something you obviously know nothing about.'

Irritated, I asked: 'Doesn't it make you sweaty, sir – wearing all that stuff?'

As the other boys and girls struggled to suppress laughter, Brooky quickly returned to talking about John Donne.

A couple of days later Towser approached me in the corridor looking extremely amused.

'What tha grinning at?' I asked.

'I've just been talking to Brooky about my essay.'

'So?'

'He said "Your friend Hines is a philistine".'

I was upset. Not because Brooky had insulted me, but because I feared what he'd said was true.

41

Although I had managed to get myself into the sixth form of grammar school to study A levels, that awful sense of failure and low self-worth brought about by my time at secondary modern school still haunted me. That wasn't the only legacy of my experience. Had I entered grammar school at eleven and met classmates from different areas and social classes, either consciously or unconsciously I would have modified my local dialect so they could understand me more easily. But in our pit village and at secondary modern school, where all the lads spoke in the regional dialect, had I attempted to speak in Standard English I would have been thought of as trying to get above myself, and been scornfully asked: 'Who's tha think thy are?'

And, of course, speaking dialect all the time meant when we had to revert from dialect to a more standard way of speaking we had a strong regional accent. At Barnsley Tech we were almost all local working-class secondary modern school kids, and I hadn't thought about how I spoke. I like the Barnsley dialect; it's often warm and humorous. Even so, when I'd moved to grammar school to spend my days among A level students and gowned ex-Oxbridge teachers, I became aware I was the only pupil with a strong accent, and when Brooky told Towser I was a philistine, uncultured, it played on the insecurity I'd felt since arriving at grammar school; that I was crude and unrefined. I'd become self-conscious, socially awkward.

By contrast Towser felt at ease at grammar school, switching in an instant from the Yorkshire dialect we used when speaking together to the beautiful accentless voice that he used in class discussions or with teachers. For Towser, grammar school had opened up the kind of life he wanted to live.

One morning in assembly in the school hall a girl wearing a white blouse and green skirt stood beside a grand piano waiting to sing. The sweet sad music played by the teacher sitting at the piano moved me, but when the girl took a deep breath and opened her mouth and sang, her voice sounded so beautiful I thought my heart would break.

'I was nearly roaring when that lass was singing,' I told Towser as we walked out of assembly. Roaring meant crying.

'Was tha?' asked Towser. 'I've heard her before, it's Elizabeth Gale. I know her from when we did elocution lessons together as kids.'

Towser rekindled his friendship with Elizabeth – she later became an international opera singer – and became mates with a kid called Fred who composed classical music. He also took up drama and landed himself the lead male role in several school productions.

One evening when I called around to see Towser his mother told me he was upstairs. I could hear Howlin' Wolf's deep voice and the sound of his whining electric guitar becoming louder as I climbed the second set of stairs to Towser's attic bedroom. White smoke drifting up from his cigarette emphasised the blackness of his curly hair as he sat in a chair reading. Becoming aware of my presence in the doorway, Towser put down his book, stood up and turned down the record player.

'I'm going to make a coffee. Does tha want one?'

'Please.'

I spotted a book I'd lent him a few nights earlier which I'd really enjoyed, *This Sporting Life*, David Storey's novel about a working-class professional rugby league player.

'Has tha read it yet?' I asked, pointing to the book.

Towser nodded.

'What did tha think?'

'It was all right,' he said unenthusiastically, pulling a pained face before asking: 'Does tha want a piece of cake?'

'What kind?'

'Ginger,' he said, knowing I hated it.

'Piss off,' I said, as Towser walked laughing down the attic stairs.

I picked up the book he had been reading. It was *The Caucasian Chalk Circle*, a play by Bertolt Brecht. In our first year in the sixth form at grammar school, Towser and I had started going to the theatre in Sheffield and Rotherham. We'd seen the Brecht play, which, set in Soviet Russia, is about a dispute between two communes over who should manage the land abandoned by the Nazis at the end of the Second World War. Towser liked it because it used a folk tale and music to tell the story in a non-naturalistic style. I enjoyed it, too, but I found myself drawn to what I thought were more authentic plays, like Arnold Wesker's *Roots*, which was about a farm labourer's daughter gaining self-confidence. Towser had become fed up with the stuff I loved most, the new wave of novels and films such as *This Sporting Life*, *Saturday Night and Sunday Morning* and *The Loneliness of the Long Distance Runner*, which realistically portrayed northern working-class life. Our tastes had diverged.

I put the copy of *The Caucasian Chalk Circle* back on Towser's desk and walked across his bedroom to the bookshelf where I'd spotted a grammar school magazine in which we'd each had a poem published. Mine was about the hovering male kestrel I'd seen as an eleven-year-old near Tankersley Old Hall, the underside of its outstretched wings and fanned tail shining white in the evening sun. I was reading Towser's poem when he entered the bedroom carrying two mugs of coffee.

'What're tha grinning at?' asked Towser.

After getting off the school bus I occasionally walked home with a lad who was about to go to Oxford University in the autumn, and I'd just remembered something that he had said. Showing Towser the cover of the school magazine, I said: 'What that kid – him that got in at Oxford – said about our poems. Mine was bad but thine was worse.'

'Piss off,' said Towser, handing me my coffee.

# SIX

O, for a falconer's voice,
To lure this tassle-gentle [male peregrine] back again!

– William Shakespeare, *Romeo and Juliet*, 1597

My favourite book while studying A level English Literature at grammar school was D. H. Lawrence's *Sons and Lovers*. It was the first book I'd read about a mining family, and I shared with Lawrence the experience of being a miner's son living in a pit village surrounded by fields, farms and woods. This shared history brought his novel vividly to life, although Dad's experiences of family life in a mining village were much closer to Lawrence's than mine. So I persuaded him to read the novel. He said the scene in the first chapter, where Walter Morel returns home late and drunk to the fury of his wife, reminded him of an afternoon when his own dad, my grandad, returned home hours late from the pub and discovered my grandma had thrown his dinner on the coal fire. My dad said he, his brother and six sisters were expecting my grandad to start shouting. Instead he had picked up an apple from the fruit dish, and before taking a bite had said, 'I could eat a horse, and I've got to be content with an apple'. Yet although Dad said the novel perfectly captured what life had been like in his childhood, after he'd read the first chapter he abandoned *Sons and Lovers* and returned to reading westerns written by Zane Grey, his favourite author. He didn't want to read about the goings-on in a mining village, he told me; he preferred to get away from his own life experiences.

In our village in the late nineteenth and early twentieth centuries, the shaking, hallucinations and delusions caused by withdrawal from alcohol were called the 'blue devils'. When my mother was a girl she once saw a neighbour with the blue devils lying on his back kicking the bottom out of the sideboard. Although he didn't behave quite as dramatically, my great-grandad Hines often suffered from the blue devils. He drove a shunting engine, moving waggons of coal around the local pit yard. In his spare time Great-grandad would cut old clothes up into 'clippings', and then, using a wooden clothes' peg shaved to a point, he fixed these different coloured clippings into a piece of hessian, to make patterned 'pegged' rugs, which he sold. The front room of his small terraced brick cottage was his workshop, where he also carried out woodwork repairs and made furniture to sell. This extra income he used to buy beer and whisky. After his heavy drinking sessions, in the early hours of the morning he'd sit in front of the fire rocking backwards and forwards, moaning. Sometimes his suffering became so bad that his wife, Sophia, would step out into the moonlight, cross the narrow street, open a gate and hurry up a garden path where she would beat on Dr Allott's door, begging him to come and help her husband.

Perhaps it was this family history of heavy drinking which had put my dad off alcohol, for unlike most miners he didn't go to the pub. And unlike most miners at that time, he thought that the women who stayed at home, looking after kids day and night, forever washing and ironing clothes, cleaning and cooking, had a more difficult life than miners like him. I can remember when I was younger I was petrified one of my mates would call at the house, see my dad helping with the housework or cooking, and call him a sissy.

It was not long after he'd abandoned reading *Sons and Lovers* that Dad noticed a lump on his neck while shaving. The diagnosis was Hodgkin's disease, cancer in the lymph glands, although the doctor didn't tell my parents the prognosis at the time. Unknown to me, my mother looked it up in our home medicine book with its severe black cover. No known cure, she read. Removing the dustbin lid in the backyard she threw in the book, tipped in a cloud of ashes from the ash pan from under the fire grate to hide it, and 'didn't tell a soul' that dad was dying – including him.

After his hospital visits for radium treatment on his throat, Dad was unable to swallow. He grew thin, so much so that I could have used a finger and thumb to span those biceps that used to shovel sixteen tons of coal a day at the coalface. Over half a century after my great-grandma Sophia had knocked on old Dr Allott's door and begged him to help my alcoholic great-grandad, on two or three occasions in the summer of 1963 I ran through the empty village streets in the moonlight and knocked on young Dr Allott's door. Although wearing pyjamas, he always greeted me in the same friendly manner as when he passed me in the street in the daytime, before saying he'd get dressed and would be at my dad's bedside in a few minutes' time.

One evening, when I was helping Dad into bed, he pointed at his swollen feet and ankles.

'It's just your slippers,' I told him, 'they're too tight.'

'You're trying, aren't you lad?' he said.

Then as I left the bedroom he asked: 'You know that book you gave me to read that I didn't finish?'

'*Sons and Lovers*?'

'Yes. Can you find it for me, please?'

From that point onwards, each time I popped in to see him he was reading *Sons and Lovers*. One evening as I sat on the edge of the bed he told me that although the arguments between Paul Morel's haughty mother and drunken miner dad brought his own family experiences as a child to life, there was a crucial difference. Although his dad was a heavy drinker, unlike the drunken miner in *Sons and Lovers* he was never physically violent, and was always gentle and tolerant with his kids.

Sitting in bed with *Sons and Lovers* lying open on the bed covers before him, he also told me about something which had happened when he was little. His dad sent him to the shop to buy two ounces of sweets – I think he was going to take them to work. On the way home from the shop my dad helped himself to a couple of his dad's sweets, but when he arrived home his dad told him he'd bought the wrong ones and sent him back to the shop to change them. The shopkeeper weighed them, and, seeing there was less than two ounces of sweets in the bag, he refused to exchange them.

'What did your dad say when you got home?' I asked.

'He told me I was a snip,' Dad said, his gaunt face tinged yellow by jaundice, smiling at the memory. 'Snip' meant 'mischievous rogue'.

Occasionally people asked my mother if she smoked. 'Only on Tuesdays,' she replied – Tuesday evening was when she went to a dance in a nearby village with her female friends. At one point Dad had been in hospital but had been discharged and seemed a little better. He was even sitting up in a chair, downstairs, and so my mother had decided to go to the dance with her friends and leave me looking after him. That evening he was telling me that if he did manage to get better he didn't think he would be strong enough to do his old job on the coalface, and so would ask for a 'button job' operating the conveyor belt that the coal was carried out on. There was a knock on the door. I opened it and Towser was standing there, smoking a pipe.

'Coming for a pint?'

I glanced at Dad sitting beside the coal fire, his feet on a stool.

'I'll be all right,' he said.

In the Prince of Wales pub a voice said, 'Get them down your necks', as two plates with hot dogs and onions were plonked on the table beside Towser and me. Looking up, we saw a youth with shoulder-length bleached blond hair and tattooed forearms. It was Budgie, who I'd robbed the toy stall with, and who had become my nature-loving best friend in junior school. He'd also been a friend of Towser's at that time, but we'd hardly seen him since he'd been put into a different class at secondary modern school, and he had found new friends.

'What're you lads doing now?' Budgie asked.

Towser told him we were studying A levels at grammar school.

'Bloody hell . . . well done both on ye,' said Budgie, his surprise turning to an unselfish delight for us.

'Where tha working? The pit?' I asked Budgie, after thanking him for the hot dogs.

'Foundry – got sacked from the pit.'

'What for?'

'Threatening to chuck a boss down the pit shaft.'

Towser picked up our empty beer glasses and stood up laughing.

'Sit down. I'll get thi a pint.'

'No, tha right – I'm with them,' Budgie said, pointing at a group of youths sitting at a table across the room.

Budgie and Towser walked away, Budgie to join his mates and Towser to the bar. When Towser returned, carrying two pints of beer, he sat down and said: 'I've got to get out of the village. Move away. I'm going to apply to drama college.'

I don't know if it was Towser's change of mood, but I seemed to suddenly come to my senses and realise how stupid and selfish I'd been leaving Dad by himself.

'I've got to go.'

'I've just got thi a fresh pint,' Towser said.

'Thee sup it,' I said, 'or give it to Budgie or one of his mates.'

By now I was captain of the grammar school rugby union team and extremely fit, and when I opened the door and entered the house I wasn't even slightly out of breath. Only the beads of sweat on my forehead gave away that I'd run the half a mile or so from the pub almost at a sprint. Dad, his thin, anxious face still slightly yellow from jaundice, was sitting strangely upright in a chair with a woman neighbour sitting nearby.

'What's wrong?' I asked.

'I'm frightened,' he said.

'He managed to crawl to the fireplace on his hands and knees and bang on the fireback with the poker till I came,' said the neighbour.

'Have you sent for the doctor? Called an ambulance?'

'He won't let me – till your mother gets home,' she replied.

So I immediately ran to the Working Men's Club where I found Ken, a family friend who owned a car, who fetched my mother home from her Tuesday evening dance.

Maybe it was my mother's own guilt but as we waited for the ambulance she berated me for my thoughtlessness. She went on and on. Finally I lost my temper.

'I know,' I shouted, 'I should be shot.'

Still sitting curiously upright in his chair, Dad quietly said: 'Shut up, Richard. You weren't to know lad.'

Riding in Ken's car under a late August full moon, my mother and I followed the ambulance to the Royal Infirmary in Sheffield. There the ward sister wouldn't let us stay with Dad and we returned home.

Next day we travelled on two buses to visit Dad in hospital. It was 1963 and walking into the cancer ward felt like walking into a hospital from the Victorian age. There were at least forty men in that ward, old men with white hair, men around my dad's age – he was fifty-three then – and younger men. There was even a fourteen-year-old boy dying of leukaemia. All the patients lay in beds facing each other across a large ward with a high ceiling. As each became more ill they were moved closer to the door to save the doctors and nurses having to walk far. In his previous stays in this hospital Dad had watched the drama of other men's failing health played out in bed moves as they'd been edged closer to the door. Finally they would end up in the bed right beside the door, where before long the curtains would be swished around the bed, and in the quiet half-light of night Dad would see the man's body carried out of the ward, freeing up the bed for the next doomed occupant. Terrified, he'd asked my mother to ask the nurses not to move him into the bed next to the door. She did ask but when we next visited, two days after he'd been admitted, that's where Dad was lying, hallucinating, saying things we couldn't make sense of.

A few weeks before he was admitted, Ken had driven Dad, accompanied by my mother, into the Derbyshire Peak District to look at a particular view he'd asked to see, where, as a young man standing astride his bike as skylarks sang high in the sky, he'd gazed across the moors to distant peaks. Maybe a road had been slightly altered, or walls had fallen down or been rebuilt, or maybe after nearly forty years he'd misremembered, but after hours of driving the moorland lanes they had to return Dad home exhausted. Through the window of the cancer ward I could see industrial wasteland, and beyond that an ugly red-brick council estate that stretched for miles. I desperately hoped this wouldn't be the last view my dad would ever see.

We were never allowed to stay on outside the strict visiting hours, but that evening my mother decided that she needed to see my dad regardless of hospital rules. I remember just one detail from that journey. The green tunnel created by overhanging branches from a wood was lit by the headlights, before we once again drove out into moonlight. Eventually we reached Sheffield. After disappearing into the hospital for a few minutes my mother returned to the car, and, under a full moon, she told Ken and me through wound-down car windows that Dad had died half an hour earlier.

Early the next morning I walked through the village to the undertaker's, which was only a few minutes away. He lived in a detached house and as I knocked on the back door, across the yard I could see the carpenters' shop where the coffins were made. An upstairs window opened, and when the undertaker stuck out his head, his hair was ruffled and he was wearing a white vest under an open striped pyjama jacket. Despite my grief, I couldn't stop grinning, and he must have thought I was heartless as I called up and told him my dad had died. I was grinning even more when, seemingly only seconds later, he stood at the open door before me with a grave look on his face, his hair immaculately combed, and dressed in a white shirt, black tie, black jacket with tails, black trousers with razor-sharp creases and shiny black shoes. All that was missing was his black top hat.

'It's not fair . . . It's not fair,' my mother called out in heartbroken despair when, a few days later, she saw Dad lying in an open coffin standing on trestles in our front room. With his arm around her waist and gently taking her wrist in his hand, the undertaker led my sobbing mother to the coffin and placed her hand on Dad's forehead. The curtains were closed, as was the custom, and the shades of blue, green and red on the loosely woven curtains made the September light filtering through seem as if it had passed through stained glass. The coloured light, and the cool marble feel of Dad's forehead when I placed my hand on it, reminded me of touching those white statues which lie on tombs in medieval churches.

One moment Dad's kind, gentle face was there. Then it was gone, never to be seen again as the undertaker screwed down the coffin lid.

A brass plaque on the coffin lid read: RICHARD LAWENCE HINES.

Whoever had inscribed that plaque had missed out the R in Lawrence. I know Dad wouldn't have minded. He'd have seen it as a mistake that anyone could have made.

Although I'd been robbed of a future with my dad, nothing had been left unsaid, nothing had been left unresolved. And my grief in the years following his loss took the form of a longing, a continuation of the sad sweet yearning evoked in me by the autumn song of the robin that had sung in the graveyard on that sunny September day when, the grass glistening with dew, my dad's coffin had been slowly lowered into the earth.

# SEVEN

Falconry is not a hobby or an amusement; it is a rage . . .

     – T. H. White, *The Godstone and the Blackymor*, 1956

One evening I found myself filling in an application for an administrative job in the housing department at the Town Hall. I landed the job, and soon after Dad's death in 1963, aged eighteen, I was working for the local council in Hoyland, a small town – more a large village, really – on the eastern border of our village. The office, which was about fifty yards behind the Town Hall, and across a car park, was housed in a century-old converted stone cottage with wide windowsills and low ceilings.

One day the bell rang to alert me that someone was waiting for attention. When I left my desk and walked to the counter there stood Mrs Mardy. One of the two or three women teachers who'd taught at my all-boys' secondary modern school, she was unsmiling, had dark hair and was in her forties. I'd never been taught by her or been rude to her, but she'd seemed to have it in for me. Once when she'd tried to slap me across the face (I don't recall why) I'd grabbed her hand, put my other arm around her waist and infuriated her by waltzing her along the school corridor. She'd punished me for that by giving me an essay to write. When she handed it back she said, 'That's very good'. For once I thought she was going to be nice to me, until she asked, 'Who wrote it for you?'

'I didn't expect to see you here,' Mrs Mardy said, remembering me from school as I faced her across the counter.

'Why not?'

'I thought you'd need qualifications for this job,' she replied, a scornful grin on her face.

Irritated, I was about to tell her that I'd studied for GCE O levels, but, guessing she'd ask who took the exams for me, I decided to remain silent as I sullenly went about sorting out the business that had brought her into the office – maybe she'd come in to put her parents' names on the waiting list for a council bungalow.

Outside, there was a small garden which had belonged to the old cottage before it had been converted into an office. The garden had been left to run wild, but flowers planted by the generations of people who'd previously lived in the cottage still bloomed and marked the seasons. One morning when I walked out of the office, dark pink Michaelmas daisies were in flower in the once-tended garden borders. Picking up a folder of 'work cards', on which were written requests for building repairs, I'd told a colleague I was going to visit council house tenants to check out these repair requests, but instead I walked across to the Town Hall and up the steps beneath its clock tower. To my relief the grand entrance hall was empty, eerily quiet, with no voices or the tapping of typewriters coming from any of the offices. Easing the door shut behind me, I entered the sombre, high-ceilinged council chamber where the councillors met. There, sitting on one of the tiered leather benches, I opened my folder of work cards and took out a book: *The Goshawk* by T. H. White. I removed the bookmark and began to read.

It was the story of how in 1937, the author T. H. White had abandoned his teaching job in a public school to live in a gamekeeper's cottage in woods in Buckinghamshire. There, using knowledge he'd gleaned from reading medieval falconry books, he'd trained a young goshawk that had been taken from a nest deep in the forests of Germany, and flown over in an aeroplane. The book had gripped me the moment I'd opened it the previous evening. In the first paragraph of the first page, White's goshawk had just arrived in a basket covered with sacking and 'was bumping against it from underneath: bump, bump, bump, incessantly, with more than a hint of lunacy'. Captivated by the goshawk's wildness I read on. In its early stages of training, time after time, with 'talons like scimitars' it would clutch White's leather glove as it perched there, then, with 'mad' yellow eyes staring, the young goshawk would leap off in a headlong 'dive of rage' in 'a wild bid for freedom', only to hang upside down by the leather thongs around its legs. Until, with 'gentleness and patience', T. H. White would once again lift it back on to the glove. Even when the goshawk had been trained well enough to fly a hundred yards to his raised glove, White still couldn't help feeling a little afraid of Gos's wildness, as 'the horrible aerial toad, the silent feathered owl, the humped back aviating Richard the third, made toward [him] close to the ground'. Enthralled, last night I'd read into the early hours, then brought the book into work in the morning to continue reading, desperate to discover if Gos, who had escaped and disappeared into the woods, would be found alive. I don't know how long I read, but by the time I sneaked back out of the council chamber I discovered White never did find his beloved goshawk, which, he speculated, would have most likely ended up 'a bundle of green bones and ruined feathers . . . swinging in the winter wind', after the leather thongs around its legs had become entangled in a tree.

Later that day I visited a woman who lived in a rented caravan, whose name was nearing the top of the council house waiting list. The caravan site, which had a dozen or so caravans, was in a field behind a farm, on high ground. As I searched for the caravan, below I could see fields and woods, and in the distance our village of Hoyland Common. To qualify for a council house, people who lived in rented private properties needed to have kept their home clean and tidy and have paid their rent regularly. After I'd noted that the woman's cosy caravan was immaculate, and flicked through her rent book and seen the payments were up to date, I was able to give her an idea of how long it would be before she and her husband could move into their council house. She chatted as I sipped the tea she had made, but I wasn't listening. Gazing out of the caravan window at the surrounding fields and woods, my mind drifted back into that world of 'mists, wet boots . . . solitude' where T. H. White lived as a 'deluded and imaginative recluse' in a gamekeeper's cottage and kept his goshawk in a barn with a brick floor and criss-crossed laths across its windows.

Sunlight poured in through the high windows above the rows and rows of bookcases. Nearby a newspaper rustled as a man sitting at a large wooden table turned a page. It was a Saturday, my first day off work since I'd read *The Goshawk*. Still enthralled by White's book, I'd caught the bus into Barnsley to search the bookshelves at the library there for books about hawks. Suddenly my heart raced. On a high shelf I'd seen the spine of a hardback book which read FALCONRY. Reaching up, I took down the book and flicked through the pages to a photograph of three falcons on a long perch, and another of a falcon perched on weighing scales. There were also drawings, with one showing how to tie the falconer's knot, and another of falcon hoods with feather plumes.

I put the book on the desk in front of the librarian.

'I'd like to take this out, please.'

'You can't borrow that one, love,' she said.

'Can't I join the library?'

'You can join, love, and take other books out. But that's a reference book – you can only read it in the library.'

So I left the library and headed straight for a bookshop a couple of streets away, where a bell tinkled as I burst through the door. Usually I'd have wandered around looking at the books on the shelves but today I was too fired up and waited impatiently by the counter until a male assistant appeared from a backroom.

'Have you got *A Manual of Falconry* by M. H. Woodford, please?'

They didn't have the book in stock, but he said he could order it and it would arrive in a couple of weeks. I ordered the book. I'd hoped it would be in stock and I was bitterly disappointed that I'd have to wait so long to read it. Then, as the bookshop assistant copied the book's details from the piece of paper on which the librarian had written them, I had an idea. I didn't need to wait two weeks or more. This was the early 1960s, before photocopiers, but I could copy out the reference book in the library by hand and read my own notes, while I looked forward to the arrival of the book itself with its illustrations and photographs.

I hurried back to the library with a pen and large notepad, bought from a nearby stationery shop. Sitting at a library table I began copying sections of M. H. Woodford's book by hand: the equipment needed for falconry; how to train falcons such as the peregrine. I copied out passages taken from medieval falconry books, as well as a glossary of ancient falconry terms. I felt like a scholar who had come across an ancient manuscript, as words from a long-lost age came to life:

BATE, BATING . . . fluttering or flying off the fist.

FULL-SUMMED . . . when a hawk has got all her new feathers after moulting.

Everyday words took on a vivid history:

PERCH . . . is that whereon you set down your hawk when you put her off your fist.

– J. Ray, *Summary of Falconry*, 1678.

I was amused to learn 'booze' originates from the falconry word for drink: 'BOWSE . . . to drink; variously spelt "bouse", "boose", "bouze", and "booze".' Above all, I loved the line from a book written by Edmund Bert in 1619: 'There is no way but gentlenesse to redeeme a Hawke.' I found this quote fascinating and strangely moving, just as I had when I'd read in *The Goshawk* of T. H. White's knowledge, that only 'gentleness' could win over his crazy wild hawk, Gos.

Items of falconry equipment, called 'hawk furniture', are of 'supreme importance' to the falconer, M. H. Woodford says, and it 'behoves him to take great care they are of the best materials obtainable'. Returning from the library, still fired up, I went straight upstairs and into my parents' bedroom and rummaged around until I found what I was looking for. Feeling the soft thin leather of my mother's best gloves I worked out how I could cut them up to make a pair of 'jesses', the leather straps which fit around a hawk's legs. The cobblers in the village had closed for the weekend, but on Monday lunchtime I called in and walked over to a display of dog leads. Picking up the different sized leads, I carefully examined the metal figure-of-eight-shaped swivel which holds the fastener that clips on to the dog's collar. If I ever managed to get a hawk I could cut one of these swivels from the dog lead, and it would make a swivel to which I could fasten the jesses. Next I moved on to a stand displaying leather bootlaces and picked out the longest lace. With a knot tied at one end so it didn't slip through the swivel, I could use a leather bootlace like this one for a hawk's leash.

In copying out sections of *A Manual of Falconry* and reading *The Goshawk*, I had discovered that both hawks and falcons were referred to by falconers as 'hawks' and distinguished by the different shape of their wings. So peregrines, for instance, were known as 'longwings', for these falcons of the open moors and cliffs have evolved long pointed wings to minimise air resistance, when with deep pumping wingbeats they come hurtling out of the sky in pursuit of their quarry. Goshawks and sparrowhawks, by contrast, were 'shortwings'. Their broad, rounder wings have evolved for acceleration, allowing them to reach full speed within a second, or suddenly to change direction or height with a flick of their wings as they swerve around tree trunks, flashing through a wood or over a hedge like a grey shadow as they pursue their prey.

On my walks I often went along Hoyland Road to the crossroads at the centre of the village, crossed the turnpike, then headed west along Tankersley Lane, where, after a couple of hundred yards or so, I entered the parish of Tankersley. To me the woods and fields there had previously been just that, woods and fields, but now I found myself walking through 'shortwing' country. Historically, those who flew 'shortwings' were divided into 'austringers', who flew goshawks, and 'sperviters', who flew sparrowhawks. Out walking one morning I accidentally flushed a covey of partridge from under my boots. Rather than watch them whirr away on their sweptback wings, as I had in the past, I now imagined a goshawk powering off the glove of an austringer of old, flying a few feet above the meadow in a desperate sprint to catch one of the partridges before it made it to the hedge bottom and escaped.

Passing a cornfield of golden wheat stubble, I continued my walk and called into Tankersley church with its square Norman tower. As sunlight flooded through the stained-glass windows and threw patches of colour on to the stone-flagged floor, I stood gazing into a glass display case at the cannonballs that had been fired in the 1643 Battle of Tankersley during the English Civil War. What excited me was where they had been found, for the sign said Tankersley *Moor*. Around here used to be moorland: 'longwing' country. Tankersley church is located in fields, half a mile or more from Tankersley village, and, as I walked out of the church and past the rectory, I visualised the moorland which would have stretched out in front of me three centuries earlier. Again I imagined a falconer, this one casting off his peregrine to circle up to a thousand feet into the sky, before it plummeted to earth in pursuit of a covey of grouse flying across the purple heather.

Not far from the church I paused at a stone dovecote and read a plaque which said the dovecote had been built in 1735. Above this was an entrance where the pigeons flew in and out, and, in an attempt to try to make sure that all the pigeons provided eggs or ended up on the owner's dinner table, it had been surrounded by iron spikes designed to impale marauding wild hawks. Although disgusted at that thought, as I gazed up at the iron spikes I was fascinated by the fact that the moors and cultivated land around Tankersley church would have once been the haunt of peregrines, goshawks and sparrowhawks. Yet, had I lived in those times, I wouldn't have been allowed to fly a peregrine on the moor. I knew from reading Woodford and White, that, in 1486, when the Abbess Juliana Berners wrote about Tudor etiquette in her *Boke of St Albans*, she allocated particular hawks to different classes of people. She assigned the female and male peregrine – the 'falcon gentle' and 'tiercel gentle' – to a prince: 'Ther is a Fawken gentill. And a Tercell gentill. And theys be for a prynce.'

And, according to the Abbess, I wouldn't have been able to fly a goshawk: 'Ther is a Goshawke. and that hauke is for a yemen.' Or a sparrowhawk: 'Ther is a Spare hawke. and he is an hawke for a prest.'

The kestrel is a falcon, a 'longwing' like the peregrine, but because it hunts voles and insects and the occasional small bird it was derided by falconers in the Middle Ages. So much so, that the Abbess Juliana thought it unworthy of inclusion in the *Boke of St Albans*. It does get a mention in a medieval Harleian manuscript where it is assigned to the knave.

I'd never even seen a peregrine, or a goshawk, or a sparrowhawk, and in 1963, almost five hundred years after the *Boke of St Albans* had been published, I still hadn't a hope of flying one. I'd read enough to know that after shotguns had improved in the eighteenth and nineteenth centuries and shooting game birds had become popular, hawks had lost the esteem they had enjoyed in earlier centuries. And that gamekeepers, who were paid by their employers to rear game birds and to protect them from predators, had poisoned, trapped and shot goshawks into extinction in Britain by the 1880s. Although they hadn't been similarly wiped out, sparrowhawks had often ended up swinging in the wind on a gamekeeper's gibbet. Now in the 1960s news stories were reporting that sparrowhawks and peregrines were also on the verge of being poisoned into extinction by the overuse of dangerous agricultural pesticides.

The only hawks I'd ever seen were the kestrels hovering over the meadows and verges beside the country lanes around Hoyland Common and Tankersley. Had I been able to choose one of the hawks listed in the medieval texts I would have chosen a goshawk. T. H. White had written to a German falconer and arranged for his goshawk to be transported to Britain in an aeroplane. I didn't know any falconers, German or British, so if I was going to fly a hawk it would have to be a kestrel.

# EIGHT

When all the feathers are hard at the base the hawk is said to be 'hard penned' and is ready to be taken up for training.

– M. H. Woodford, *A Manual of Falconry*, 1960

In the spring of 1964 I was still working in the housing department at the Town Hall. Towser was in the final year of his A levels and had been provisionally accepted at drama college. Unlike Towser, who'd discovered his talent for acting at grammar school, I still had no idea what I wanted to do in life. Things weren't all bad, though. I'd met Lynn at a local dance. She was good-natured, had brown eyes, black hair, a lovely smile and worked as a secretary. On one of our first dates she invited me to sneak into the house of friends of her parents, whom she was babysitting for, to keep her company. Watching from a bus shelter I saw her parents' friends, the local chemist and his wife, come out of their house wearing formal evening dress and climb into Lynn's parents' car. As soon as the car rounded a bend I hurried up the pavement and rang the doorbell. We'd only been sitting on the sofa a few minutes when we heard the front door being unlocked.

'Hello,' her dad called from the hall.

Lynn jumped to her feet and her beautiful brown eyes desperately looked around the room, almost as if she expected to discover a previously hidden door she might bundle me through. She then started jabbing her finger at the sofa.

'What?' I silently mouthed.

'Behind it,' she mouthed back. 'Get behind it.'

I leapt from my sitting position and dived behind the sofa. To make sure my legs didn't stick out I pulled myself into a crouching position as Lynn's dad entered the room.

'Are you all right?' he asked.

The sofa moved as Lynn sat down.

'Yes. Why?'

The sofa sank as her dad sat down beside her.

'You look as if you've seen a ghost.'

I seemed to be crouched behind the sofa for a long time before he left.

Lynn's fear that her dad would find out she had a boyfriend lasted for months, and when we walked through the village together she would suddenly let go of my hand and anxiously check out any car resembling her dad's. So I was amazed when one day I was invited to a meal with family and friends. I was nervous walking up the drive to their new bungalow, and after I'd rung the doorbell I was disappointed to see Lynn's dad's shape through the glass door rather than hers, but when he opened the door he smiled as he invited me in. Lynn's lovely mother made me feel welcome, and her investment banker brother and the family friends were all friendly. So much so that when we were all seated around the table eating, and one of the older male guests started talking about his schooldays, I joined in the conversation.

Everyone listened as I told them that at junior school, when I was eight or nine years old and all the boys wore short trousers, our headmaster was renowned for slapping misbehaving boys hard on the backs of their legs. Continuing my tale I told them how one day a lad who'd been sent to the headmaster's office for misbehaving was told to come back the following morning for his punishment, and how next day after hearing the headmaster had died in the night, the lad danced a jig in the playground to celebrate his unexpected escape from having his legs slapped. I laughed at my own story, but before anyone else could respond Lynn's dad looked at me angrily and said: 'I don't think that's funny.'

Everyone ate on in embarrassed silence.

I thought I'd lost my chance to make a good impression on Lynn's dad but later, after Lynn had told him of an incident in which I'd gone to the aid of an old man and carried his flaming chip pan out of his council bungalow, he seemed to warm to me, and to my surprise invited me to accompany them on their family holiday in Cornwall.

It was June. Pink wild dog roses were blooming in the overgrown cottage garden when I walked out of the housing department office. Earlier that day a council workman had told me he'd just finished working at a house where a teenager called John kept a kestrel. I could hardly believe it. The council were trying to cut their repair bill, and part of my job was to check if the repairs requested by tenants were really necessary. By chance my grandma Westerman, whose husband, my grandad, had been killed at the pit all those years ago, lived on the same council estate as the teenager and had requested a new set of kitchen taps. After hurriedly putting her work card in my folder, along with several other work cards requesting repairs I needed to check, I was now heading to John's house hoping to see his kestrel. As I walked along the street of 1930s council houses where he lived, I passed dogs barking so crazily at the end of their chains I feared one might break loose. As I approached John's house his grandma came out of the kitchen door and threw something in the dustbin. She told me John wasn't in. I asked if I could see his kestrel and she led me into the living room.

Pointing to a cardboard box on the floor beside the television, John's grandma said: 'She's in there.'

I couldn't tell if the young kestrel crouched inside was a he or a she. In their first-year plumage male and female kestrels are identical but 'she' sounded appropriate. Taken by her beauty, her large brown eyes, her buff-coloured breast streaked with black, and forgetting what I'd read about the wildness of yet-to-be-trained hawks, I reached into the box to touch her. Suddenly animated and gasping with fear, the young kestrel struck out at my hand with her talons.

John was a nice friendly lad, with jet-black collar-length hair, and was always smiling. We knew each other from secondary modern school, but later, when I saw him walking down the street and told him his grandma had shown me his kestrel, he wouldn't tell me where he'd got his hawk from, or whether there were other young ones still in the nest. When I asked if he thought I could get a kestrel this year he said I'd no chance, and when I asked him if he could get me a kestrel next year he refused to commit himself. Even so I told him I lived down Tinker Lane if he needed to find me.

I was about to have a week off work, and delighted with myself that I was packing to go on holiday with Lynn and her family. When I was younger our family holidays were taken during the local colliery's annual week-long summer break, when most people from the village went to the seaside, and often stopped to chat together on the seafront. We travelled by coach to either Blackpool or Scarborough. I can remember how at Blackpool Tower zoo a monkey reached through the bars and grabbed my brother Barry's hair; and also a single-propeller aeroplane flying a banner over Scarborough beach, the numbers under its wings suddenly becoming big and clear through the new plastic binoculars Dad had just bought me. I also remember drab 1950s backstreet guest houses with overbearing landladies, their strict rules forbidding guests to return until evening, and days spent wandering around aimlessly in drizzle and rain. This year, however, I would be staying in a seafront hotel. It was all exciting and new. I'd never been on holiday in a car, I'd never been to Cornwall, and for the first time I was going on holiday with a girlfriend.

Later that evening there was a knock on the back door. I assumed it was Lynn and opened the door smiling, keen to tell her I was all packed up and ready to go; but standing on the doorstep was John, holding something in his cupped hands. It took me a moment to realise it was a young kestrel. My mind was in turmoil. I'd been looking forward to going to Cornwall with Lynn for months. I'd dreamt of keeping a hawk for years. And now . . .

'Does tha want it?' John asked, surprised by my hesitancy.

'Err . . . yeah . . .' I said as I carefully took the young kestrel from him.

Later, after I'd put the hawk into a cardboard box, I trailed a piece of beef across her yellow feet. She grabbed the meat and held it in one foot, and as I slowly backed away she lowered her head, tore off a piece of meat and swallowed it. At last I had a hawk. I should have been delighted but I felt troubled. Soon I'd have to tell Lynn she would have to go on holiday without me. Then, as I watched my kestrel tear and swallow more meat with her curved beak, I recalled from reading my falconry books that a young hawk's feathers wouldn't be fully grown for at least two weeks after she'd been taken from the nest. I realised it wouldn't be detrimental to her health if the cardboard box acted as a nest until I returned from my week's holiday. Barry liked birds – he'd kept an injured crow as a lad when I was at infant school – and I decided to ask him if he would feed my young kestrel while I was on holiday.

Barry's teenage Teddy-boy style of dressing hadn't lasted long. Aged seventeen or eighteen, he'd been selected to attend the trials for the English Grammar Schools' football team, which were held at Cambridge University. Barry made it into the England team, but while staying and dining in one of the older Cambridge colleges he'd not only met posh southern grammar school boys, but public school boys as well, and it had made him self-conscious. Or as he'd put it when he returned home, 'I felt like an oik, dressed in my fingertip-length jacket and tight trousers.' To my dismay, soon afterwards he stopped wearing his hair brushed back, and instead had it neatly parted, and he began to wear respectable-looking jackets and trousers.

After he'd left Loughborough College, and taught physical education in a London school for two years, Barry had returned home to teach the same subject in a secondary modern school in Barnsley. As a teenager Barry had called me 'Our Nipper', and had ignored me when we met while he was out with his friends. Now the six-year age gap between us no longer mattered. We were good friends, and each Monday and Thursday evening we met up and drank a few pints of Barnsley Bitter together in the Star. Now married, Barry lived on the edge of the village in a detached 1930s house with bay windows, and a long garden which backed on to fields. His house was about half a mile away from the family home, where I still lived with my mother. To get there, I could either go up Hoyland Road, past the church mission hall and a couple of farmhouses and old stone cottages, or through the fields. This evening it was sunny, so I walked through the fields, opened a gate into Barry's back garden and walked up to the house. His wife Margaret said he was working and sent me upstairs.

As well as being a teacher, Barry was also a writer, the last thing I would have imagined him becoming. For as far as I knew, despite his grammar school education Barry had never read a novel in his life. Then, one wet day, when eighteen or nineteen years old and stuck in his lodgings at college, bored out of his mind, he'd asked his room-mate if he had anything to read. I think the book he was handed was George Orwell's *Animal Farm*. Whatever the book, it sparked Barry's interest and set him off reading every novel he could find, and finally led to his decision to become a writer. He'd already written radio plays for the BBC, and when I reached the top of the stairs I could see him through the open door of a small spare bedroom, biro in hand, sitting at his desk writing on a sheet of lined paper as he worked on his first novel. When he looked up and saw me in the doorway his striking blue eyes looked as if they were trying to focus, as he came out of the world of fiction that he was writing about and adjusted to the reality of me standing there. Barry was happy to help me out with my kestrel until I told him the harsh reality: beef was all right in an emergency, but the young kestrel would need to be fed wild prey, which was much more nutritious and would ensure healthy growth. Barry didn't fancy stalking the hedgerows with an air rifle, and so later that evening I arranged for Towser's younger brother Chris to shoot birds for Barry to feed to my young kestrel.

On the journey to Cornwall in the front seats of the car Lynn's mother and dad sang:

Ramona, I hear the mission bells above
Ramona, they're ringing out our song of love . . .

Sitting in the back of the car Lynn and I smiled at the sweet love song, written by Mabel Wayne and L. Wolfe Gilbert, for the 1928 film *Ramona*, but this was 1964, the Beach Boys were on the airwaves, and we were excited to be on our way to St Ives.

When we arrived at the seafront hotel I was stunned by the views, the golden beach, the turquoise sea, the harbour across the bay. As I sunbathed on the beach with Lynn I watched gulls soaring in the clear blue sky, dreaming of the time when my young kestrel would be flying across the field to my raised glove. Before we left I'd taken a last look at her crouched in her box. With her large brown eyes looking at me, flecks of down still on her head, she had looked so beautiful that I wished I'd cancelled my holiday. But as we lay on the beach together, and spent our evenings hand in hand, smiling and chatting, as we walked around the fishing village streets with their quaint shops, their white cottages and hanging baskets full of flowers, I was convinced I'd done the right thing. My young kestrel wouldn't be ready to start training for at least a fortnight, Barry was looking after her and I'd be back home in a few days after the best holiday of my life.

It was a beautiful sunny evening when I arrived back home in the village. Desperate to see my kestrel, I hurried up to Barry's house through meadows golden with buttercups. I opened the gate which led from the field into Barry's garden, approached the corrugated-iron air raid shelter and carefully opened the door so as not to alarm the young kestrel. It wasn't there. I hurried up the garden path and looked in the garage. The kestrel wasn't there either. I knocked on Barry's door and entered the kitchen, thinking that he must have brought the kestrel into the house in its box.

'Hello,' I called.

Barry walked in from the hall. He looked awful. Against his white face his pale blue eyes looked bluer than ever. I thought he was ill.

'It's dead.'

He told me he'd followed my instructions and cut up the sparrows Chris had shot and fed the hawk three times a day. He said it seemed all right but a couple of mornings ago when he'd gone into the air raid shelter he'd found it dead in its box. I guessed a sharp bit of bone must have perforated its crop – part of the gullet where food is stored before being digested – or it had swallowed some large feathers and died of inflammation of the crop. I tried to console Barry yet inside I was raging. I could hardly believe what I'd done. Unexpectedly I'd been given what I'd dreamed of, longed for, a hawk, but rather than take care of it myself I'd handed it over to someone else while I went on a week's holiday. Now my chance to train a kestrel had gone. On my way back home I stopped and gazed at the patch of recently disturbed earth in the field where Barry had buried the young kestrel.

Two or three months after our return from holiday, Lynn borrowed her parents' car. The plan had been to go for a drive together, but even before we'd got out of the village she suddenly pulled into the side of the road, turned off the car engine and stared through the windscreen.

'What's wrong?'

She continued to look straight ahead.

'You want to dump me, don't you?'

'I think we should stop seeing each other,' she said, turning to me.

She said I'd been her first boyfriend. Had we met when we were both a little older, she added, things would have probably worked out. She was kind and didn't want to hurt me, but she couldn't soften what she said next: 'I've been seeing Alan.'

'Towser?'

She stared out of the windscreen again.

'You've teamed up with Towser?'

Strange, isn't it? How when we've been dumped, instead of accepting the other person has got fed up with us, we feel betrayed and rage against them for having the audacity to prefer someone else to us. I flung open the car door and climbed out.

'Richard, I'm sorry,' Lynn said with genuine feeling.

I swung the door shut and marched off into the village.

Towser and I had been friends at junior school, at secondary modern school, at Barnsley Tech, and then at Ecclesfield Grammar School. When I'd jacked in grammar school we'd remained best mates, going to the pub and theatre together and lending each other books. On occasions Towser and his girlfriend had joined Lynn and me for a night out. On that day, as I strode along Hoyland Road raging against Towser I saw him walking towards me with my brother. Of the two, Towser looked more like a writer, with his earnest way of talking and his interested, thoughtful way of listening. Barry, with his slim build and the sleeves of his V-neck sweater pushed up to his elbows, looked more like an athlete. As I approached them I could hear them discussing Dylan Thomas's play *Under Milk Wood*. Towser and I loved that play, we both liked the character Organ Morgan and we were both amused by a description of the starless night in the play – 'bible-black'. My intention that day was only to tell Towser what I thought of him. Admittedly I suspected I might give weight to my thoughts by pinning him against a wall, but when I saw his 'bible-black' curly hair and handsome face I was surprised to feel my arm swing through the air and my fist smack into his nose.

Poor Barry, who seconds earlier had been discussing Dylan Thomas, was so surprised and shocked it seemed to affect his vocal cords. Speaking in a posh formal voice which sounded nothing like his usual speaking voice, Barry said: 'You disgust me.'

Towser didn't look disgusted or even the least bit surprised. Except for the blood pouring out of his nose he looked quite normal. Taking a white hankie from his pocket he held it on his nose, pinched his nostrils together with his finger and thumb, and in a nasal tone said: 'I think we need to talk about this.'

Which we did. I don't remember what we said, but we'd walked along field paths and past Tankersley Old Hall before Towser could stop pinching his nose with his bloody hankie and talk in a normal voice again.

# NINE

There is, sir, an airey of children, little eyases, that cry out . . .
— William Shakespeare, *Hamlet*, 1599

A few weeks after my twentieth birthday in 1965, on a warm June evening I set off on a walk to Tankersley Old Hall. When I reached the crossroads at the centre of the village, instead of going straight ahead up Tankersley Lane I turned left and walked down the turnpike. It was up this hill that, in 1843, the last horse-drawn stagecoach had travelled through Hoyland Common. I knew this piece of history from talking to Arthur Clayton, a miner at Rockingham Colliery, who later became a published local historian and who I often came across in the village or when out walking. Arthur had discovered a newspaper advertisement from 1843, offering for sale the four horses that had pulled the mail coaches along this stage of the turnpike. Often Arthur was so fired up by his subject, oblivious to the cold, biting wind or the crack of thunder, that he would keep me talking when I was impatient to be off. Yet when the weather was fine I loved to listen to him, and the local history he taught me added interest to my walks. For example, as I walked down this section of the turnpike called Parkside, which still had an eighteenth-century milestone, I knew I was walking along the boundary of the medieval deer park which had once surrounded Tankersley Old Hall. That June evening as I climbed over a stile and into the parish of Tankersley and the fields which had once been the deer park, it fascinated me to think that in 1727, on his tour of Britain, Daniel Defoe had visited here and written that he believed the red deer in Tankersley Park were the largest in this part of Europe – before going on to make the exaggerated claim that one of them had been even bigger than his horse.

The land here had been divided by a stone wall into two fields. Early in spring, in the field to my left, lapwings had nested in scrapes of earth between green wheat shoots, and had risen and tumbled in the sky above my head, calling 'peewit . . . peewit . . .' as I'd walked along the path beside the stone wall. Now, in June, the corn was knee-high and had already begun to turn golden, and tall flowers – pinkish-purple foxgloves, white ox-eye daisies, red poppies – grew beside the stone wall. In the field over the wall to my right, black and white cows grazed and swallows flew low over the grass catching insects.

Soon the path led into Bell Ground Wood, its name derived from the bell pits that had been dug here for ironstone mining in the late eighteenth and early nineteenth centuries. Walking through the tall, mature trees of the wood, with shafts of sunlight pouring through the leaves of its green canopy, it was difficult to imagine that the ground under my feet had once been scarred by mining. Yet the evidence was there, a few yards off the path through the undergrowth. In the past miners had sunk a shaft into the seam of Tankersley ironstone, which was only a few yards deep, and mined ironstone within a five- or six-yard radius, which they had hauled to the surface using ropes on a pulley system. Now, well over a century later, as I stood on the edge of one of those collapsed shallow bell pits, it reminded me of a bomb crater. The magnificent trees which now grew in Bell Ground Wood, Arthur had told me, had been planted to conceal them.

Back on the path, I continued walking through the wood and as I came out on to a cart track opposite Tankersley Old Hall I saw John, the lad who'd brought me the young kestrel that had died. He had an air rifle tucked under his arm and was gazing across a field of buttercups at the ruins of Tankersley Old Hall. As I approached him he smiled, but his eyes didn't look pleased to see me. Maybe somebody had told him the fate of the kestrel.

'Getting a kestrel this year?' I asked.

'Don't know,' he said.

'Does tha know a nest? I want to get one.'

'Wait here.'

Curious, I watched John walk down the track. After fifty yards or so he stopped, aimed his air rifle and fired at the ruined Old Hall. Moments later a kestrel flew out and disappeared over Bell Ground Wood. There was a nest somewhere in the ruins, and John had fired close to the nest hole to scare out the kestrel. He was obviously trying to keep the location a secret, and hadn't wanted me to see the kestrel fly out. Yet by the time he'd walked back up the track to join me, it seemed to have dawned on him that even if I didn't know exactly where the nest was, I could find it by watching the parents fly in and out of the ruined Hall. Eventually he told me he'd been watching the nest for weeks, then, as he nodded towards the stone farmhouse which stood only yards away from Tankersley Hall, he said he was going to get a young kestrel late one night, when the farmer had gone to bed, and that I could go with him and take a kestrel for myself.

A few nights later, around eleven thirty, John called at our house and I stepped out into the June night to join him. New council houses were being built on allotments at the edge of the village. Stepping over a pile of canes left from the previous year, the dead runner beans still attached to them, we spotted a ladder leaning against the scaffolding of a half-built house. Lowering the ladder to the ground, we carried it out of the building site. The moon was large and bright and the occasional trail of white cloud was visible against a dark blue sky. Black and white cows watched us as we walked through the fields carrying the borrowed ladder between us. When we entered Bell Ground Wood John let go of the ladder, cupped a hand around his mouth and struck up a conversation with a tawny owl. His every 'Whoo ooo' returned from within the dark wood like a ghostly echo. To our relief the lights were out in the farmhouse next to the Hall; the farmer's dogs were silent. We clambered over the wall and headed across the field towards the looming ruins.

The last tenant to live in Tankersley Old Hall in 1654 was Sir Richard Fanshawe, a Royalist in the English Civil War. In her memoirs his wife, Lady Anne Fanshawe, writes, 'The house of Tankersley and Park are both very pleasant and good', and while there she and Sir Richard 'lived a harmless country life, minding only country sports'. Falconry was the rage back then. As an aristocrat Sir Richard would have been knowledgeable about the country sport of hawking. In her memoirs Lady Anne also says Sir Richard 'spent his idle hours' reading and that even when out walking he had 'some book in his hand'. I'd read a vivid description of how to hood a hawk that had been taken from Edmund Bert's 1619 book *An Approved Treatise of Hawkes and Hawking*, and I was fascinated by the thought that, over three hundred years ago, Sir Richard would have probably read those selfsame words.

As John and I placed the ladder against the wall, extending it so as to reach the kestrels' nest, I sensed a connection with Sir Richard across the centuries. He'd have known that hawks' nests were 'eyries', young hawks 'eyases', and that the correct term for fully grown feathers was 'hard penned'. I imagined that, rather than looking on us as trespassers, Sir Richard, despite holding kestrels in low regard, might have encouraged us to climb up to its eyrie, and told us how long it would be before the eyases' feathers were fully grown, and they would be ready to train.

I heard the 'kikiki . . . kikiki' of the young kestrels as John examined them at the top of the ladder in the moonlight. In a loud whisper he told me the kestrels were still covered in down, too young to take. So we made a plan to come back in a week or so, and carried the ladder back through Bell Ground Wood, across the fields, and into the building site where we'd found it.

The delay in getting my kestrel worked out well. I'd got a cardboard box ready to keep the young hawk in for the first night, but I hadn't had time to prepare the 'mews'. We weren't taught French at secondary modern school but from my reading I'd discovered *mew* means 'to moult', which, although I couldn't pronounce it, originates from the French *muer* – to change the feathers. In the past the mews was where you put your hawk to moult – there used to be a royal mews at Charing Cross until 1534, when the mews were converted into stables. Today a mews simply means the place in which you keep your hawk.

Standing in the doorway of our shed I gazed around in dismay at the chests of drawers, bikes and tools, wondering how I could turn the shed into a mews. I was considering moving all the clutter to one part of the shed and then partitioning off the remaining space, when I had an idea. I could ask Barry if I could use the Second World War air raid shelter at the bottom of his garden. Barry agreed and cleared out the shelter. It looked like a corrugated-iron tunnel. It was about ten feet long, around seven feet high; the back of the shelter had an arch-shaped brick wall, while its front brick wall had a door set in it. I sawed a window into the door, over which I fixed vertical wooden slats. In the wild, falcons stand on flat rock ledges so on the inside of the door, just below the slatted window, I fixed a shelf perch so the young hawk could enjoy the morning sun. At the far end of the mews, I also fixed up a perch wide enough for the kestrel to stand on without having to grip it with its claws.

Almost two years earlier, after I'd read about the equipment needed to train a hawk in *A Manual of Falconry*, I'd only examined the dog leads and leather bootlaces on the display in the cobbler's shop. Today, I placed a dog lead and a bootlace on the counter. Then I explained to Tommy, the cobbler, how, after I'd cut the swivel from the dog lead, I'd use it to fasten the end of the kestrel's jesses, and thread the bootlace through it so I could carry my hawk on the glove without it flying away. Maybe Tommy couldn't make head or tail of what I was trying to explain because he simply smiled. Like most shopkeepers in the village he knew his customers. He knew me, he knew my parents. Maybe it was this sense of being part of a community, along with his amusement at my youthful enthusiasm, that led to what came next. For when I reached into my pocket and asked, 'How much is that?', he replied, 'Nothing', as he put the two dog leads and the leather bootlace into a bag and handed them to me over the counter.

That evening I sat at the kitchen table with my mother's sewing kit. I'd already made the hawk's jesses; my mother didn't want to part with her best leather gloves, but she'd searched out an old pair for me to cut up. I was now making the lure, in the form of a small leather pad. I wasn't very handy with a needle but I'd managed to sew up three sides of the lure, and was pouring in sand to give it weight, when someone knocked on the door. When I opened it I was surprised to find John standing on the doorstep, days before he was expected.

'Are we going tonight?' I asked.

'I went last night.'

'Why didn't tha call round for me?'

'I did – there was nobody in,' said John, reaching inside his jacket and handing me a young kestrel.

My heart racing with excitement, I thanked John, then, with my thumbs across her back and my fingers gently pinning her wings by her side, I carried the young kestrel into the house. Her head and back were reddish-brown with dashes of black. Wanting to get a better look, I tilted her slightly and saw her large brown eyes. What struck me most was the colour of her 'cere' – the bare patch at the top of her curved beak – and the colour of her legs and toes. They were as yellow as buttercups.

'It's not unlike a throstle,' mother said, her eyes taking in the kestrel's speckled buff and black breast feathers.

A few weeks ago in early June, the hay meadow had been a pinkish haze of long grasses among which wildflowers bloomed: purple vetch, pink clover, buttercups. This evening swallows flew low, hunting insects over the freshly cut hay which had been raked into piles to dry. John's unexpected delivery of the hawk meant that I hadn't any food ready for her. It was legal to shoot sparrows in the 1960s and so, carrying my air rifle, I stalked the hedgerows. I wanted to give my kestrel the type of natural food she'd have been fed by her parents.

The dead body of the sparrow I'd shot was still warm, and its head lolled around when I knelt on the lawn outside the mews in Barry's garden, and placed it on an old bread board. To lessen the chances of anything sharp puncturing my young hawk's crop, I cut off the sparrow's sharp beak, then its lower legs, so she wouldn't swallow its claws. Using a hammer I then smashed the sparrow's thigh bones. Picking up my knife again I spread out the sparrow's wings on the bread board, pressed the knife blade down hard and severed each one from the shoulder joint. I didn't want her swallowing any large wing feathers. Plucking the sparrow carefully, I left some soft feathers attached to its breast so the young kestrel could regurgitate a pellet containing the feathers, along with any small bones that she did swallow. Finally, I cut open the sparrow's breast and stomach to encourage my young hawk to eat the innards.

I now needed help, so I fetched Barry from the house and we entered the mews. The young kestrel gasped and struck out at my hands as I reached into the cardboard box. Covering her back with a large white handkerchief to prevent damage to her feathers, I pinned her wings by her sides and then passed her to Barry to hold. Reaching into my pocket I took out the pair of jesses which I'd cut out from my mother's gloves. I'd practised fitting the jesses around a pencil, and although the young hawk tried to grab me with her talons, fitting the first jess and tightening the loop of soft leather snugly around her leg was easy. As I fitted the second jess around the other leg I told Barry I was going to call my kestrel Kessy. Holding her in front of his chest as I gently tightened the jess around her leg, Barry suggested I shorten the name to Kes. I agreed that the shortened version was better. So Kes it was, and with her newly fitted jesses dangling from her legs, Barry released Kes on to the perch at the back of the mews, then quietly left, leaving me to try and get her to feed.

Careful not to make any sudden movements that would spook the young hawk, I slowly reached into the falconer's bag hanging by my side, a canvas bag with a shoulder strap which I'd bought from the Army Stores. The warm, soggy thing I could feel in my bag was the sparrow I'd shot and cut up.

Sleek, her feathers held flat to her body in fear, Kes watched my hand move slowly towards her and place the opened-up sparrow on the perch. Nervously looking at me she showed no interest in it, so reaching out slowly I picked up the sparrow, entrails upwards, and held it in front of her feet. Shooting out a foot she grabbed it and watched me back away before she began to tear at the deep red meat with her curved beak, gulping down the sparrow's heart, and swallowing its gullet as if it was a string of spaghetti. The stomach was still attached and swung like a pendulum before disappearing down her throat.

Today, almost half a century later, I can order frozen hawk food on the internet and have it delivered to my door next day. Back then, in the 1960s, my decision to bring a wild young falcon into my life plunged me into a world where I had to become a provider of meat. As a result I spent large parts of my days searching the hedgerows for sparrows or starlings to shoot.

As the days went by, when the birds saw me wandering the hedgerows of the meadows and crop fields with my air rifle, they cottoned on to what I was up to, and often flew away before I could get close enough to take a shot. Early one sunny morning, when a warm wind rippled across the seas of golden wheat, I did manage to get close enough to line up some sparrows perched in the hedgerow in my sights. But in the breeze they swayed so much that when I fired I missed. Hoping for better luck I climbed over a gate into a meadow where the farmer was turning over a pile of hay with a pitchfork, checking if it was dry. I knew the farmer. He smiled as I approached but I could see the air rifle under my arm made him feel uncomfortable. When I told him about my kestrel, he seemed interested. Particularly when I told him that, while her feathers were still growing, I needed to feed her three times a day on sparrows or starlings, as any shortage of natural food could temporarily stop proper feather growth and leave 'hunger traces', which looked like razor cuts across the feathers and made the feathers liable to break. I also told him that, as feathers and beaks were both made of keratin, a lack of natural food could even cause cracks in the hawk's beak. I continued to stalk the hedgerows but didn't manage to shoot a bird before going to work.

At lunchtime I tried and failed again and had to feed Kes beef. Before returning to work I made myself a coffee and was sitting on the doorstep sipping it when my Auntie Gladys, my dad's sister, and her husband, Uncle Francis, appeared around the corner of the house, having driven all the way from Mirfield in West Yorkshire. I told them I was sorry but my mother wasn't in. Uncle Francis, with his moustache, sports jacket and tie, spotted my air rifle which I'd leaned against the wall beside me, and asked if I'd been shooting tin cans. I told him I was hoping to shoot a sparrow or starling for my young kestrel to eat. Uncle Francis went 'white around the gills', as my mother used to say.

'You shouldn't shoot birds,' he said.

I'd expected him to be interested in my kestrel and, taken aback, I said: 'I'm not doing it for fun.' To keep my hawk healthy, I added, I needed to feed her the kind of wild prey her parents would have fed her in the wild.

'You could feed it on other meats,' he said.

'Such as?'

'Rabbit.'

I'd seen rabbits running across stubble or ploughed fields suddenly brought down by a blast from a 12-bore shotgun, rolling over and over screaming piteously. To me, shooting rabbits would have been even more upsetting than shooting birds, but I suspected if I said this Uncle Francis would reply: 'If you feel like that, why did you get a hawk?' I would have struggled to answer, so I stuck to the facts, and explained that rabbit meat wasn't nutritious enough to sustain a young kestrel. Uncle Francis wasn't having it, even though it's true. Auntie Gladys, standing there in her flowered dress and cardigan, and not wanting to take sides with her husband against her brother's son, remained silent.

Uncle Francis and Auntie Gladys were two gentle, kind-hearted people, and I liked them, but as they now obviously saw me as a loutish, irresponsible youth, I brought the conversation to an abrupt end. Without inviting them in or offering them a cup of tea, I said I had to get back to work, locked the door and hurried up the path, leaving them standing in our backyard.

That evening found me stalking the hedgerows again with my air rifle. Already I feared that Kes would develop hunger traces across her feathers, or that her growth would be impaired. I desperately wanted her third meal of the day to be natural and nutritious, but it was getting dark and it increasingly looked as if I'd have no choice but to feed her up on the extra butcher's meat that I'd bought from the butcher's in Hoyland. Then, in a hawthorn hedge I saw a dark, sparrow-sized shape, fired and hit the poor thing. I always retrieved the birds I'd shot for hawk food tenderly, but once they were dead I wasn't squeamish about cutting them up. With a sense of relief at having managed to secure her a vitamin-rich last meal of the day, I put the sparrow's carcass on the perch beside her. Kes grasped it in the talons of one foot, lowered her head and began pecking out and swallowing chunks of dark red breast meat.

Two weeks or so later, at around eleven o'clock at night, I could just make out the rectangular bales of straw in the field. Under my boots I could feel the stiff, sharp stalks of stubble as I walked through the recently harvested wheat field. Opening a gate at the edge of the field I entered my brother's garden. Untrained hawks are calmer in the dark and tonight I'd come to check if Kes's feathers had stopped growing.

When I shone my torch through the slatted window of the mews' door, I saw Kes standing on a perch towards the back of the mews. I'd already made a couple of night visits and both times when I'd unlocked the door I'd been struck by the thought that the last people to have entered this air raid shelter at night would very likely have been anxiously listening to the German bombers flying overhead during the Second

World War. One of their targets was a tank-building factory on the northern outskirts of Sheffield, a couple of miles or so from the crumbling stone ledge at Tankersley Old Hall, where Kes had hatched. Closing the air raid shelter door behind me, I slowly approached her.

I switched on my torch, throwing shadows around the corrugated-iron walls of the mews. In the half-light my young kestrel remained calm, and carefully fanning out her tail I shone my torch on the bases of the feathers. A few nights earlier the shafts of the feathers had been soft and blue, still 'in the blood', but tonight I saw what I so desperately wanted to see: the shafts of the feathers were hard. She was ready to train.

I switched off the torch and could just make out the baking scales I'd commandeered from my mother, which were standing on the floor in a corner of the mews. I stood the scales on the shelf perch I'd fixed behind the door, then, pulling on my 'gauntlet' – a gardening glove – I walked back to Kes standing on her perch, the dark making her as docile as if she'd been drugged. I touched the back of her legs. I'm not sure why, maybe the pressure on the back of the legs makes a hawk feel slightly unbalanced, but just as my falconry book had suggested Kes stepped back on to my glove. Carefully taking hold of her jesses in my gloved fingers I carried her across the mews, gently pressed the back of her legs against the wooden perch I'd fixed on to the baking scales, and persuaded her to step backwards on to the scales. I shone the torch on the dial and saw the pointer had stopped just short of nine ounces. I knew from my reading that by reducing her meals from three to one a day I'd need to bring her down to a 'flying weight' of around eight ounces, and at this weight, in the words of seventeenth-century falconer Symon Latham, she would 'flie with spirit, courage and attention to the man'.

# TEN

MANNING, manned, making a hawk tame by accustoming her to man's presence.

— J. E. Harting, *Bibliotheca Accipitraria*, 1891

Most falconers blow a whistle to call their hawk, but football matches were played in the recreation ground a few fields away from where I flew my kestrel, and on match days I feared she'd disappear over the hedges and fly around the referee each time he blasted his whistle, so the whistle was out for me. In *The Goshawk* T. H. White had written 'his soul felt too poetical' to use a whistle and that his goshawk was 'too beautiful to be shrilled at with a . . . mechanical note'. Instead he called his hawk by pursing his lips and whistling Psalm 23, 'The Lord's my Shepherd'. I can't whistle so I simply used her name to call her.

'Come on, Kes,' I called, standing in the meadow holding a small piece of beef between my gloved fingers as I raised my arm.

Perched on a fence post, her breast looking creamy white in the evening sun, the black stripes beneath her eyes strikingly prominent, my young kestrel bobbed her head a few times, then launched herself into the air and flew fast towards me. Trailing behind her was a length of fishing line, a 'creance', to which I'd attached her jesses to ensure she wasn't lost while being trained. To my horror, after flying about twenty yards she suddenly halted. Wings pumping furiously, eyes fixed on the meat on my raised glove, she was stationary in mid-air a few feet above the ground. The creance attached to her jesses had caught on a rigid stalk of rough grass.

'Come on, Kes. Come on, girl,' I urged.

My hope was that if she kept flying the creance would come loose from the grass. It didn't, and despite her desperate wingbeats she remained at a standstill as if she was flying head first into a gale-force wind. Finally, confused and disheartened, she sheered away and pitched into the meadow.

A week or so earlier, excited and hardly able to believe I was going to do what I'd dreamed of for so long, I'd begun Kes's training. Calling her name and holding a morsel of meat, a 'bechin', in my gloved fingers, I'd tempted her to hop from her perch in the mews on to my glove. Later, after attaching a creance to her jesses, I'd flown her to the glove across the lawn in Barry's garden, increasing the distances until she flew ten yards to me the moment I raised my glove. Today she was fit and lean and at her flying weight of just above eight ounces. I'd brought her into the meadow to fly twenty-five yards, but now she was standing in the grass looking bewildered. Crouching, so as not to loom over her, I approached her slowly, offering meat on my glove, but instead of hopping on to the glove she flew off and fluttered around at the end of the creance, until I pulled the creance through my fingers and reeled her in.

Feathers sleek, looking around wildly, she now 'bated' off the glove and hung upside down at the end of her jesses flapping her wings and screaming with rage, 'kikiki . . . kikiki . . .' Placing my hand on her buff and black breast feathers I gently lifted her back on to my glove. In *A Manual of Falconry*, M. H. Woodford had reprinted a glossary of falconry terms from Harting's 1891 *Bibliotheca Accipitraria*. I knew it off by heart, and 'MAR-HAWK, one who spoils a hawk by clumsy handling' came to mind, neatly expressing my fears. I should have left Kes in the mews, come to the meadow beforehand, trailed the creance to check where it might catch and cut any long, tough bits of grass with shears. I should also have persisted longer in trying to get her to hop on to the glove, rather than reeling her in, upsetting her, causing her to hurtle off the glove in a crazy bate. I might have set her training back by days.

Now, with Kes standing on my glove, I unfastened the fishing line creance from her jesses, threaded the leather bootlace leash through the swivel and wrapped it around my glove. Suspecting my inept handling might have put her in too bad a mood to risk flying her again that evening, I decided to feed her up and take her back to the mews. But as I looked at her now, calmly standing on my glove, I wondered if my fears had arisen from remembering the raging mood swings of Gos, the crazy yellow-eyed hawk in T. H. White's *The Goshawk*. Reminding myself I was training a falcon, which, according to what I'd read, was less temperamental than a goshawk, and noting her sudden calm, I changed my mind and decided to fly her free.

I walked across the meadow, and when I'd reached the fence she'd flown from with the creance trailing behind her, I removed her leash and swivel, then tilted my glove and encouraged her to hop on to the fence. Standing there, her jesses hanging loose, her large brown eyes looking around the meadows and stubble fields, she was free. If she wished she could be off, her shallow wingbeats taking her over the hawthorn hedges and out of sight in seconds, never to be seen again by me. Heart racing, glancing over my shoulder, I walked away from her across the meadow. After twenty-five yards or so I turned and raised my glove.

'Kes . . . Come on, Kes.'

Without hesitation she launched herself off the fence. Eyes fixed on me, she flew a few feet above the recently cut meadow then curved upwards to land on my raised glove. Relieved, I let her tear off a couple of pieces of meat and swallow them. Then I carefully unpicked her talons from the piece of beef, pulled it through my gloved fingers, and concealing it in my hand put it in my falconer's bag. I headed back across the meadow and let her hop from my glove to stand on the fence, her jesses hanging free. Again I called her: 'Kes . . . Come on, Kes.'

Again she flew three or four feet above the grass then swooped upwards on to my raised glove to take her reward of beef.

The correct term for feeding a hawk is to 'Feede hir up', as George Turbervile explained in *The Booke of Faulconrie or Hauking*, published in 1575. 'Feeding up' my young kestrel on my glove, I walked across the meadow towards a group of bullocks standing at the other side of a five-bar gate. She stopped eating. I stood still watching her closely. Any hint that she was about to sleek her feathers to her body, which was a sign of fear, and I'd slowly move back, hoping to prevent a bate from the glove. There was no need, for after a momentary look at the young bulls peering over the gate she lowered her head and began tearing at the meat. Once again I slowly walked closer to the curious bullocks.

This was 'manning', making her tame by accustoming her to humans and their activities. At the start of her training, when I'd begun her manning, any sudden movement, such as the instinctive brushing away of an insect from my face, spooked her. Later when I walked the country lanes with her on the glove, the sight of a miner cycling to work or a car's sudden appearance around a bend would send her bating off the glove. Even a couple of evenings ago a bellowing cow running around in an adjacent field had sent her flying off the glove to hang upside down at the end of her jesses. But her daily manning was paying off. She was getting much tamer, and this glorious summer evening as she tore at the meat on my glove, she paid no attention to the young bulls looking over the gate. She didn't even bate when I attempted to stroke one, causing it to hurriedly back off and then stretch its head forward to wrap its rasping tongue around my outstretched hand.

Pleased her manning was coming on well, delighted she'd successfully flown free to the glove, I took a recently shot sparrow out of my falconer's bag, held it between my gloved fingers, and let her pluck and cast away the sparrow's breast feathers. As we headed back across the fields to the mews, she began tearing into the deep red breast meat.

Each morning before work, or at weekends, I called at the mews to check on Kes. This morning, the gate into the garden from the field had been left open and a lovely black and white calf stood on the lawn. Skirting around the calf, trying not to spook it, I took a small lump of soil from a flower bed and threw it up at the bedroom window. Barry pulled back the curtain. For a moment he looked as if he thought I was the bearer of bad news, but when I pointed to the calf he smiled. Arms out by my side I steered the calf through the gate and back into the field, then unlocked the mews.

Now she was being trained she needed to be secured to a perch with her leash, which allowed me to pick her up calmly, rather than be forced to chase her around in a flutter of wings if she decided to try and evade me. Unlike sparrowhawks and goshawks, which grip tree branches when perching, falcons have adapted to stand on flat surfaces such as rock ledges, and I'd made Kes a 'screen perch' – a flat four-inch-wide beam of wood with sacking hanging below. The sacking had a slit in it, through which I pushed her leash and fastened it to the perch. If she did bate off the perch, which she did very rarely, she was able to scramble back up the sacking. I loved opening the mews door in the mornings and seeing her standing contentedly on one leg on her screen perch, the other leg tucked into her buff and black breast feathers.

Falcons also need an outdoor 'block perch', which is a piece of wood in the shape of an upside-down cone with a flat top, with a metal spike sticking out of the bottom to push into the ground. Trained falcons have perched on block perches for centuries. I didn't know anyone who could make such a perch but I knew a lad who was doing metalwork with my old teacher, Wee Georgie, and I asked him to make me a metal one with a horizontal crosspiece for my kestrel to perch on, and a two-foot spike to stick into the lawn and tie her leash to. I have a photograph of Kes standing on that perch. For padding I have wrapped my dad's blue-checked pit scarf around the crosspiece and wound string around it to hold it in place. On fine days I put Kes on this perch on the lawn to 'weather', to make sure she got plenty of natural light so that when she preened her feathers she'd ingest the vitamin D and keep her bones healthy. I don't remember if I worried about my young kestrel standing on her metal perch, her claws grasping my dad's pit scarf instead of being flat on a block perch as they should have been, but I remember I feared her leash would come loose.

In *The Goshawk*, T. H. White describes how his hawk finally escaped from its outdoor perch into the surrounding woods, where, jesses entangled in a tree, his beloved Gos almost certainly ended up dead. Determined such a calamity wouldn't befall Kes, I practised my knot-tying many times. Opening Woodford's *A Manual of Falconry* I would place it on a dining chair and kneel down beside it. Then, with my left hand holding the end of the leash that would be attached to Kes's jesses, I would glance at the illustration of the 'falconer's knot' and, using only my right hand, practise tying the hawk's leash to the chair leg. I practised so often that when I did kneel on the lawn with Kes on the glove of my left hand, tying her leash was easier than I'd anticipated. In the end I stopped worrying that it would come untied.

My new fear was that she'd be attacked by a cat, or a dog leaping over the garden wall, or a fox sneaking in from the fields. So whenever I put her out to weather I stayed with her, sitting on the wall or the grass, only leaving her unattended while I made coffee in my brother's kitchen and watched through the window for danger.

One day a crow hopped across the lawn towards Kes as if intent on attacking her. I wasn't too worried, thinking I'd be out of the kitchen before any damage could be done by the crow's powerful beak. Then, to my surprise and horror, the crow, almost as if it was trying to liberate her, began pecking and pulling at the loop of the knot on Kes's leash. Imagining her disappearing over hawthorn hedges, doomed to die hanging upside down, her leash and jesses entangled in a tree or electricity pylon, I rushed out of the house and down the garden path clapping my hands. But not only did this scare off the crow, it also sent Kes bating off her perch, to stand on the lawn at the end of her – still luckily attached – leash. That brought home to me just how easily a hawk can be lost.

# ELEVEN

The word 'stoop' . . . and 'swoop' (Macbeth, 'at one fell
swoop'), signifies a rapid descent . . .

       – J. E. Harting, *The Ornithology of Shakespeare*, 1864

Earlier in the summer, before I got Kes, I'd been on holiday to Colwyn Bay in Wales with the sole purpose of
visiting the Welsh Mountain Zoo, the only place in Britain
where I could see a falconry display. I'd never seen a falcon
stooped to the lure and I desperately wanted to see how an
experienced falconer did it. Excitement had surged through
my body when I first spotted the falconer's hat, with feathers
in its headband, bobbing through the crowd. Yet when the
falconer entered the large grass display area with a tawny
eagle on his glove I was bitterly disappointed. I wouldn't
have gone there had I known all I would see was an eagle
flying to the glove. Eagles of all species are magnificent birds,
but I'd come all this way hoping to discover how falcons
were flown to the lure. I already knew how to fly a bird
of prey to the glove. This trip wasn't all bad, though, for
Towser, home from drama college, had come to Wales with
me. It hadn't worked out between him and Lynn, and while
we were there we met two girls from Wrexham – Gwen and
Pat – and had a great time, strolling through the amusement
arcades and along the seafront with our new girlfriends,

listening to Sonny and Cher's 'I Got You Babe' repeatedly playing on one of the girls' transistor radio.

One night, after an evening out on our own, my girlfriend Pat and I returned to find her guest house locked. We decided she would stay with me, but then discovered that my own guest house had been locked up for the night. Gazing up at the bedroom windows and satisfied I'd located my room, I climbed a drainpipe and clambered on to the slates of the sloping roof of a large bay window. The bedroom window was open just wide enough for me to get my fingers into the gap. I slid the sash window upwards a foot or so, where it stuck. I managed to pull my head, shoulders and chest through into the dark bedroom when, to my amazement, a light was switched on, and there before me, sitting bolt upright in their separate beds, were two women in nighties. Seeing me, they started screaming. One was an old woman, the other her middle-aged daughter. The old woman continued to scream, but recognising me from the breakfast room, her daughter stopped screaming and shouted: 'GET OUT'.

With my head, shoulders, chest and arms inside the bedroom I couldn't grip the windowsill with my hands and pull myself backwards.

'It's all right, Mother, it's all right,' said the daughter, before once again turning to me to shout: 'GET OUT.'

'I'm stuck.'

'GET OUT.'

By the time I managed to wriggle free I was in such a panic that I lost my footing and slid down the bay window's sloping roof, dislodging slates. As I slid over the edge, trying to halt my fall, I grabbed the gutter but my weight pulled it loose and it crashed down beside me as I hit the ground. Lights were now flicking on in the bedrooms of the guest house. As I scrambled to my feet I saw Pat running full tilt down the road.

Towser's had been a holiday romance but I kept in touch with Pat, and, as neither of us had a telephone at home, we wrote to each other a couple of times a week. In her letters she joked about her shock on hearing the women screaming in the bedroom, then seeing me sliding down the bay window roof before crashing to earth alongside falling slates and the bay window gutter. She also delighted in reminding me that next day, when I'd tried to apologise, the daughter of the old woman had said to me: 'I hope you realise you nearly killed my mother last night.' And she loved to tease me about the guest house landlady's response to my apology: 'I've never housed a savage before.' Yet she lived in Wales, and now that Towser was away at drama college for most of the year I needed to try and find other friends.

One evening after I'd fed Kes up, I went with three youths from our village for a drink in the Rockingham Arms, a country pub in the nearby village of Wentworth. They began to talk about local lads they knew who had a reputation for fighting. Finding the subject boring and wanting to move it on, I said that when playing rugby at grammar school I'd been battered plenty of times, and on one occasion I had been knocked unconscious. I then told them that when I'd been in the second year at secondary modern school, an older, much bigger boy, had grabbed me by the lapels and repeatedly banged my head against a wall, and how, in a temper, I'd swung my arm and landed a lucky blow, which to my surprise had sent him running across the playground holding his nose. I added that that was the closest I'd ever been to having a proper fight, and that fighting in fact scared me. One of the youths latched on to this comment and goaded me throughout the evening, mocking my cowardice. Unlike the rest of us, this lad was middle-class, with a father who ran a business. For some reason, he seemed to think he'd been offered an opportunity to win respect by acting tough and he began repeatedly asking me to step outside for a fight. Eventually I got fed up, and to his surprise, agreed.

It was still light, a lovely summer's evening, as we stood on the bowling green facing each other in the shade of a copper beech tree. The lad looked bewildered, as if it had just dawned on him he'd no grudge against me, no reason to try and do me harm, and not fired up by anger he looked scared. I could see his plan the moment he thought about it. He swung his right arm, I raised my left arm and blocked it, then grabbed his shirt, put my foot behind him, and pushed him over backwards. After a bit of wrestling, I sat on his chest, and, holding both his wrists with my left hand, I pinned his arms to the ground, then threw a few pretend blows with my right fist, stopping them inches from his face, while telling him if I wanted to I could smash his face in. When I offered the lad my hand and pulled him to his feet, to my surprise he began to cry. In the end I put my arm around his shoulder and walked with him across the bowling green and back into the pub.

Next day I popped out of the council housing department office and into the butcher's shop across the road from the Town Hall to buy two ounces of lean beef for Kes. The butcher usually asked about my hawk, and I was going to tell him about the next stage in her training, 'introducing' her to the lure, when he turned from the chopping bench behind the counter and said: 'I'm disappointed in you.'

I looked at him, confused.

'I saw you,' he continued, 'on the bowling green outside the Rockingham Arms – fighting.'

The butcher had told me previously he enjoyed going to Wentworth for a quiet civilised drink. He must have spotted me sitting on the youth's chest on the bowling green and thought that my pretend blows were real, because as he wrapped the lean beef for Kes in greaseproof paper he shook his head, and when he handed it across the counter and took my money he said: 'Fighting – I thought you were better than that.'

Embarrassed, I headed out of the butcher's shop, past a queue of women who now looked at me disapprovingly.

That evening I placed the sand-filled leather pad that was my lure on the shelf perch behind the mews' door. When I'd made the lure I'd threaded pieces of string through it. Using these strings I tied on a pair of sparrow's wings, which I'd saved from Kes's last meal, and then 'garnished' the lure by tying on scraps of raw beef. Kes was on her outdoor perch on the lawn. When I threw the lure on to the grass in front of her, curious, she tilted her head to one side and looked at it. When I jiggled the line to move the lure around on the grass she flew off her perch and was on it in an instant, gripping it in her talons, devouring the scraps of beef. She'd been 'introduced' to the lure. That was easy. What flummoxed me was how to go about getting her to 'stoop' to the lure. A stoop is a headlong dive, but I couldn't imagine how I would get Kes to do that.

In *A Manual of Falconry*, M. H. Woodford seemed to skip over the details of how training a falcon to stoop was done. Instead, after emphasising it required great skill, he suggested the best way to learn was to watch an experienced falconer. I'd never met anyone who had trained a hawk, nor heard of any falconers who lived nearby, so all I could do was to try and puzzle out the technique from the unclear, poorly written instructions Woodford did give: '. . . the lure is swung.' Do I twirl it above my head like a lasso? I wondered. '. . . the falconer swings it to and fro.' Do I keep my arm by my side, slowly swinging the lure backwards and forwards?

Having never seen a hawk fly to a lure, these were the kinds of questions I asked myself. After much rereading I found a phrase which gave a glimmer of what was involved – 'twitched it away from her at the last moment'. With that in mind, I took the lure I'd made into the backyard, to practise my lure swinging.

The lure line is a long piece of string which is attached to the lure by a swivel, and is wrapped around a short 'lure stick' when the lure isn't being used. Holding the lure stick in my left hand, I uncoiled a length of lure line. Holding the lure line in my right hand and not twirling it too fast, I swung the lure by my side as if marking out circles in the air. Then, aiming the lure at a small gap at the top of the coalplace door, I let the line slip through my fingers and lengthen, allowing the weight and momentum of the lure to send it speeding towards its target. At the last moment, pulling hard on the lure line, I twitched the lure away from the gap at the top of the door, as if keeping it out of reach of Kes's grasping talons.

I practised a lot. On my way across the fields to the mews I'd often stop beside a hedge, for instance, and aim the lure at a twig, or a leaf, or a berry. Just before it hit the target I'd twitch it away. At home I'd aim the lure at a vase on the sideboard, or at the clock on the mantelpiece, and not twitch it away until it was a fraction of an inch from sending them crashing to the floor.

Unlike twigs, or vases, or the clock on the mantelpiece, my young kestrel would be flying quickly towards me a few feet above the ground. The worry was that I might accidentally hit her with the lure. Following the instructions in my book on how to make a lure, I'd poured one and a half ounces of sand into it before sewing it up. It needed at least this amount to give the lure enough weight to enable me to swing it out to her as she approached. One and a half ounces seemed light but the weight of the lure wasn't far short of a fifth of my kestrel's body weight, and I worked out that if I accidentally hit her with it as she flew towards me this was the equivalent of me being hit with a bag of sand weighing around thirty pounds while running full-tilt. I also feared ensnaring her in the lure line and damaging her feathers as she chased the lure through the air.

It was an evening in July when I first put what I had learned into practice. The white clouds which minutes earlier had been sailing over the Pennine hills continued their eastward journey across the blue sky. Hawk on my glove, I stopped gazing at the clouds and with the wind at my back walked eastwards across the stubble to the edge of the field. There, Kes hopped from my glove on to the fence. Occasionally glancing back over my shoulder in case she set off before I called her, I walked into the middle of the field a hundred yards or so from the fence where she was perched. Taking the lure from my falconry bag, I unwound a length of lure line, leaving some wrapped around the lure stick. Then, gripping the stick in my gloved hand and holding the line in my other hand, I swung the lure in vertical circles, the attached sparrow's wings whirring.

'Kes . . . Come on, Kes.'

Now that she'd been 'introduced' to the lure she knew that her reward for catching it was a tasty snack of meat. So with her jesses trailing freely, she gained height as she flew towards me into the wind. Approaching fast she was almost upon me, a few feet higher than my head. Not yet. Not yet. *Now!* Then, after one last twirl of the lure, following the lure's ascending arc I threw my arm upwards, letting the lure line slip through my fingers as its weight and momentum propelled the lure up to the hawk. She tried to grab the lure with her talons. I twitched it away, pulled down hard on the lure line, and kept it just out of her reach. To my delight she stooped – that is, dived head first through the air, before levelling out and curving upwards and into the sky.

Having failed to grasp the lure and take her prize of beef she looked confused, unsure what to do.

'Come on, Kes . . . Come on, girl.'

Holding the lure stick in my gloved hand and pulling, I shortened the lure line, pulling it through the fingers of my lure-swinging hand, making it taut enough to swing the lure for a few twirls by my side, before throwing out my arm again and letting the lure line slip through my fingers as the lure's momentum carried it up to within a fraction of an inch of her talons. Again she stooped, flying in a headlong dive as I pulled down hard on the lure line. Then, as she followed its rising arc, her momentum propelled her into the sky. She was panting now, beak open. After twirling the lure by my side a couple more times I lobbed it up to her slowly, allowing her to catch it in her claws. Keeping the lure stick in my hand I kept hold of the line as she fluttered down into the stubble. As she took her reward of beef from the lure I pushed the pointed end of the lure stick into the ground, in case she tried to fly off with the lure. Then I knelt beside her and offered her meat from the glove. When she hopped on I was delighted with my young kestrel's performance. I fed her up on the glove as I walked across the stubble field and back to the mews.

Each evening I increased the number of stoops before letting Kes catch the lure and take her reward of beef. She became fitter, more cunning, varying her approach. Sometimes she flew in high, sometimes low. When she hit the lure with her outstretched talons, I'd reward my young hawk by letting the lure fall into the stubble for her to stand on and devour the attached beef, before flying her again. My lure swinging improved. When she flew in low over the stubble I became adept at throwing out the lure to her, then sweeping it in front of her before making it rise steeply, sending her shooting up into the sky, where she'd deftly flick her wings, turn over and stoop in a headlong dive. Evening after summer evening her pumping wings powered her downwards then upwards as she tried to get close enough to strike the arcing lure, which I kept tantalisingly just out of reach, until her momentum propelled her high into the air to begin another stoop. After a couple of weeks or so, she was on the wing and flying hard for up to fifteen minutes each evening before I let her strike the lure and take her reward. And so it went on throughout the summer and into autumn, my kestrel Kes hurtling downwards, before at the last moment arcing upwards from the golden stubble field and into the sky.

# TWELVE

Though that her jesses were my dear heartstrings, I'd whistle
her off, and let her down the wind, To prey at fortune . . .

— William Shakespeare, *Othello*, 1603

It was late September, and, as I had done each evening for
weeks over the summer and early autumn, I pressed the back
of Kes's legs against the wooden perch I'd fastened on to the
top of the baking scales and persuaded her to step backwards
on to them. Satisfied with her weight I took her up on the glove,
walked out of the mews, through the gate at the bottom of
Barry's garden and into the field, where I raised my glove. Her
large brown eyes surveyed the landscape, the stubble fields, the
cows in the meadows, and beyond these the colliery slag heap.
After I'd tilted my hand she flew off the glove and I walked
into the middle of the stubble field. Taking the lure out of my
falconry bag I unwound the lure line and looked up at the sky. I
can remember the lovely evening skies of that summer of 1965,
ribbed, high white clouds like seaside sand over which a retreat-
ing tide has rippled. But to my eyes the sky this evening was
empty. I had been expecting to see Kes's flickering wings and
shallow wingbeats, interspersed with glides as she circled above
me, waiting for me to begin swinging the lure. She was nowhere
to be seen. Had she disappeared over the hedges or the horizon,
never to be seen again? Heart racing, I looked around.

Eventually I spotted her perched on a fence post near the gate at the bottom of my brother's garden, back where I'd entered the field and cast her off the glove. Confused, I thought back to her previous evening's meal. Sparrow meat is more nutritious than beef, and when I'd first started to train her I occasionally gave her too much of it and would find that she was over her flying weight next day. When I'd weighed her this evening, though, her flying weight was spot on and her droppings, which falconers call mutes, looked healthy. I'd no idea why she was sitting on a fence post instead of flying above me looking forward to flying to the lure. Then I held a piece of meat on my glove and raised my arm to see if she'd fly to me, and she rocketed across the field and smacked on to my glove at what seemed to be twice her usual flying speed. She ate the meat so hungrily she looked as if she intended to go on to eat the glove once she had devoured the meat. Then, within seconds, her appetite had gone. She pecked at the meat very slowly; it seemed as if eating had suddenly become too much of an effort for her.

As I trudged back across the field my heart seemed acutely aware of how much the kestrel on my glove meant to me, and my brain flicked through the pages of my falconry books desperately searching for a diagnosis of her behaviour. *Croaks*? No. I would have heard wheezing. *Aspergillosis*? The hawk looked bright except for a shortness of breath. Could be that? No. The hawk refuses food or flicks it away with her beak. Suddenly I was overcome by dread. Just as T. H. White's inexperience had caused the death of his first hawk, so I feared my own inexperience as a falconer was about to bring about the death of Kes. I realised that I hadn't taken into account how her daily lure exercises would have built up her muscles over the weeks, and the weight she flew at when I started to train her, around eight and a quarter ounces, would now be too low. I should have increased her flying weight over the summer. It suddenly seemed so obvious.

Now I know that if a wild bird looks ill, its chances of surviving are poor because birds have evolved a way of concealing illness until they are almost dead, to avoid attention from other predators on the lookout for weaknesses. Back then I didn't know why, but through my experience of finding wild birds I knew that any bird showing signs of illness would struggle to survive. Searching for such signs as I put Kes on her perch in the mews, I convinced myself that her usually round, bright eyes had become dull and oval-shaped. I began desperately to hope that I'd misremembered what I'd read, but I feared she might have used up all her fat reserves and would now be converting her muscle into energy. If that was the case her weight might suddenly drop and despite my frantic efforts to feed her up it would be too late. Kes would die.

That evening I fed her up on small pieces of meat offered in my fingers. Next morning I was up at dawn, jeans drenched with dew as I walked quickly through the fields. I looked through the slatted window of the mews fearing she'd be dead beneath her perch.

Two or three minutes later, she was standing on my glove tearing at the meat with her usual enthusiasm. I gave her three meals a day for the next few days. Once I'd raised her weight I fastened the creance to her jesses and began to test her keenness by swinging the lure a couple of times, before throwing it on to the lawn. If she refused to fly to it, at her next meal I slightly reduced the amount I fed her, until I found the highest weight at which she would fly. I don't recall the precise weight but it was only fractionally more than her previous flying weight. Above this, in the words of the falconer Symon Latham: 'her stomacke [appetite] be colde and dull' and she would 'flie wilde and carelessly . . . stooping here and there without care and respect for her keeper'.

A few weeks later, on a Friday morning in October 1965, I found myself standing in the foyer of Sheffield station waiting to meet Pat, my girlfriend from Wrexham, who I had met in Wales in the summer. The announcement of the arrival of her train echoed around the station and when I saw her innocently handing in her ticket to the ticket collector I felt awful. My timing was terrible. Just two days earlier I'd met another girl, Jackie, in Barnsley town centre, where, recognising me from the village, she'd said hello then blushed when I asked her if we knew each other. We travelled back to the village on the bus together. It was the day after her eighteenth birthday. She was a student at Barnsley Art School, was a fan of Howlin' Wolf's blues and had been wearing a purple dress that she'd designed and made herself. Then, last night, we'd been to the pub together, got on well and discovered our shared interests in literature, cinema, animals and birds. Mobile phones didn't exist back then and as neither Pat, my Welsh girlfriend, nor I had a telephone at home, it had been too late to write and tell her to cancel her trip and now here she was, with her short black hair and lovely, trusting face smiling as she ran across the station foyer to greet me. On the bus to our village, as she talked excitedly, I decided the only fair thing to do was to make sure that she had a nice weekend and then write to tell her when she'd gone home that it was over.

Soon after we arrived at our house, looking for something to eat she took a paper bag out of the fridge and opened it before I could warn her. Screaming, she threw it down. Inside was a dead sparrow I'd shot. It was a beautiful warm autumn day and robins were singing in the hedgerows as we walked to the mews. Pat didn't seem interested when I showed her Kes, and she looked bored as she stood in the field of stubble watching me fly my kestrel to the lure. Her earlier excitement had deserted her. Maybe she was disgusted by the thought that, after I'd flown her, my kestrel would eat the sparrow she'd discovered in the fridge, but I suspected that she'd sensed something was wrong.

The train began to move as I walked along the platform beside it. The plan had been that Pat would return home on Monday, but I couldn't keep up my act for long and, with genuine sorrow, I'd apologised and called it off between us. So here we were back at Sheffield station on the Saturday morning, only a day after she'd arrived. My heart ached as she looked at me through the carriage window, tears rolling down her cheeks. For a moment I thought about opening the carriage door and asking her to jump off the moving train and continue her stay. For weeks she'd been telling family and friends she was going to visit her boyfriend in England. Now she faced the humiliation of explaining why she'd returned home early, why her hopes had come to nothing.

I was upset when the train left taking the poor lass back to Wales, but my sorrow didn't last long. When I got back to the village I hopped off the bus and went to see Jackie. She was small, with short, straight dark brown hair and brown eyes. On our first date in the pub I'd been struck by how shy she was, how softly spoken, how hesitant her speech was as she weighed her words. Yet when she began to talk about art, she suddenly became eloquent. Passing garden borders full of pink and yellow autumn flowers – Michaelmas daisies, chrysanthemums – I hurried up the path of Jackie's parents' council house. Jackie blushed when she answered the door but seemed pleased to see me and invited me in. She'd been making a new dress and as she cleared away her sewing I looked at the beautiful pencil drawings in her sketchbook, moving from a nude model sitting on a chair, to an architectural detail from an ancient church, and then brambles in a hedgerow. She had her own bird, a budgerigar, which earlier she'd let out for a fly around the room. Later, after she'd carried her budgie on her finger and put him in his cage, she came with me to the mews. There she watched fascinated as I weighed Kes on the baking scales, then flew her to the lure in the stubble field.

After I'd flown the hawk we walked through the fields to my home, where I persuaded Jackie to test my knowledge of hawking terminology. Book open, she searched for questions to ask me from the glossary of Harting's *Bibliotheca Accipitraria*.

'What's jouketh mean?'

'Sleep.' Not content, I made Jackie laugh by adding a quotation and a source: 'Your hauke jouketh and not slepith – the *Boke of St Albans*, 1486.'

Smiling, Jackie looked down at the book and found another question to ask: 'Cadge? What's that?'

'The wooden oblong square frame, on which hawks are carried hooded to the field,' I told her.

'What's a cadger?'

'The person who carries the cadge: hence the abbreviated form "cad", a person fit for no other occupation.'

The next day, Sunday, when I called at Jackie's house I discovered I'd already met her parents. Her dad, a bricklayer, had once stopped to ask me about Kes when he'd seen me 'manning' her. And her mother worked in a local fish and chip shop and had served me many times over the years. That day was warm despite the sun being a ghostly white disc through high mist, and later, as we walked hand in hand through Hoyland Common, Jackie and I passed the stone-built infant school we'd both attended. When we reached Calvert Street, three streets away from where I lived, Jackie pointed out the small brick terraced cottage in which she'd been born and had lived until the age of eleven, when she'd moved with her parents into their council house. Moments later, we passed the junior school where we'd both been pupils.

I'd been in a class two years above Jackie; even so we'd have sat in the same assemblies, played in the same playgrounds. Yet we didn't remember ever having seen each other. As we headed up Tankersley Lane, and along a path that led to Tankersley church, I asked Jackie about her life.

She'd been confined to bed with rheumatic fever and hadn't attended junior school for the whole year before sitting her eleven plus. The result of her exam wasn't straightforward. She'd been a 'borderline case' and had to wait weeks for the final decision as to whether or not she'd passed. The decision went against her, and Jackie ended up at Kirk Balk Girls' Secondary Modern School, which was on the same site as the boys' school I'd attended, but was segregated from it and had a different head teacher. In her final year there, at the age of fifteen, and when it was time to think about finding a job, she'd been taken on a school visit to a 'typing pool' in a Sheffield factory. Row after row after row of women sat all day tapping away on typewriters. She didn't fancy that. In fact she'd no idea what she wanted to do. Then art came to her rescue. Curiously, Jackie's mother hadn't noticed her daughter had an aptitude for art, but when a friend of Jackie's pointed this out to her, her mother went up to school to see the art teacher. Soon afterwards, carrying a folio of her work, Jackie was on her way for an interview at Barnsley Art School. She was accepted. She'd already taken Art and Craft O levels, as well as other O levels which had been taught in classes at Barnsley Tech. Now she was working on her A levels at the art school.

By now, as I listened to her story, Jackie and I had passed Tankersley church and were walking down the lane which led to Tankersley Old Hall. When we got there, I pointed out the nest in the ruined wall from which Kes had come.

After that Sunday walk, Jackie and I spent our evenings and weekends together. On some evenings, as Jackie sat at a table doing her work for art school, I'd sit on her bed listening to pop songs on pirate Radio 270, which was broadcast from a ship moored off the coast of Scarborough. One evening I asked about an old black and white photograph on a chest of drawers, which showed an old man sitting in a field with a sheepdog lying beside him. This was her grandad, her mother's dad, with his dog, Fly, Jackie told me, then went on to explain that he had been a tenant farmer in nearby Wentworth, where her mother was born. I was intrigued, so the following Sunday afternoon we walked the couple of miles or so to Wentworth village, and through the fields in which, as a girl in the 1920s, Jackie's mother had taken beer and sandwiches to her dad for his lunch at harvest time. And where, later in autumn, Jackie's mother, along with her own mother, Jackie's grandma, had gleaned wheat seeds from the stubble to make bread over the winter, and where, in spring, Jackie's grandad had walked behind his shire horses, holding and guiding the plough they were pulling as it turned the earth into long, straight furrows.

One evening as Jackie worked on her art, I found myself sitting on her bed looking through her four *Flower Fairies* children's books. She'd had these books since infant school, and each illustration showed a fairy with a pair of butterfly's wings, dressed in clothes the colour of the wildflower the fairy was holding. As a child, she had used these books to teach herself to identify wildflowers. I discovered that not only did Jackie know the names of most wildflowers, she also knew where they grew. She had a particular fondness for spring wildflowers, and on our next walk together she pointed out the places where some of her favourites would flower next spring: yellow cowslips in the uncultivated field beside the old turnpike road; dog violets the other side of a stile leading into Bell Ground Wood; pink purslane just off the path opposite Tankersley church.

We visited the pubs in our village but on some evenings we walked through the countryside to the Rockingham Arms in Wentworth. We loved sitting in that country pub with its stone-flagged floor and blazing fire, Jackie with half a pint of beer, me with a pint, as we tucked into a cold roast beef sandwich and talked. Maybe it was because of our shared pit village background, or perhaps because of our shared love of nature and the countryside. It could have been because we'd both been scarred by our experiences of being dumped in a secondary modern school at the age of eleven, which had resulted in shared feelings of awkwardness and low self-esteem. Whatever the reason, almost from the moment we'd met we'd both felt an affinity. We just seemed to like each other, both of us accepting the other as they were, and not expecting or wanting them to be something they were not.

It was the end of October, when the hedges and cobwebs glistened with dew.

Kes had been born in the wild, and I believed it was now time to release her back to where she belonged. Or, to use the falconry term, I'd decided to 'hack her back' to the wild. After she'd eaten her fill of meat on my glove I cut off her jesses and raised my arm. I was struck by her beauty, her curved beak, her large brown eyes calmly looking around the stubble fields and meadows, her buff-coloured breast feathers with dark streaks, her yellow legs and toes with their black talons gripping my glove. I imagined when offered her freedom she might fly straight to a fence post, or land unsurely in a hedge, but she flew off my glove and powered into the sky.

That wasn't the last time I saw Kes, for the next day at the same time I was back in the field swinging the lure. She must have flown low across the field behind me because I was only aware of her presence when she seemed to appear out of nowhere and snatch the lure. I let the lure fall to the ground and she devoured the meat fastened to it. When 'making in' – approaching her when she was eating on the lure – I always took great care, offering her titbits of meat, and crouching down so I didn't seem like a threat by looming over her. I was proud she had never 'carried', flown off with the lure grasped in her talons, but today, after only twenty-four hours of living in the wild, instead of hopping on to my glove to eat the meat I offered her, as she had all summer and autumn, she tried to fly off with the lure. I held on to the line, but she wouldn't let go, and for a few moments it must have looked as if I was flying a fluttering bird-shaped kite at the end of a string. Finally, I threw the meat I'd been holding to the ground and she dropped the lure, grabbed the meat and carried it to a fence post to eat. I was struck by how quickly she'd forgotten the lessons I'd taught her, how wild she'd become.

Witnessing how quickly Kes had reverted to the wild brought home to me the appeal of hawks, why I was obsessed with them. They have no understanding of hierarchy, of social subservience; it's not in their make-up to be herded and controlled. Shouting or bullying or using physical force won't make a hawk submissive. I love their wildness, how they can't be domesticated, how their will can't be broken by cruelty or violence. One of my favourite quotes came from *The Goshawk*: 'The mishandled raptor chose to die.' Yet over my summer flying Kes, I'd shown how a hawk's intractable nature can be won over. I loved the advice given by Nicholas Cox in his 1674 *The Gentlemen's Recreation*: 'You must by kindness make her gentle and familiar with you.' I think it was this wisdom, passed down the centuries, which made hawks so appealing to me, this insight that an intransigent hawk, whose wildness is never lost and always resides just beneath the surface, can be reached, not by force, but by gentleness and kindness. It intrigued and delighted me that by treating Kes kindly while keeping my side of the bargain to provide her with food and fly her free in the fields, I'd been allowed to spend a summer and autumn in her presence.

Each day, at the same time, I returned to the field and swung the lure. Some days she would turn up to grab the meat I threw out for her and eat it on a fence post a couple of fields away, and on other occasions she would disappear over the hedges carrying it in her talons. Increasingly there were days when she didn't show up until, finally, after she hadn't returned for over a week, I stopped going into the field to swing the lure. Kes had been 'hacked back'.

For the rest of autumn and over the following winter and spring I keenly watched any wild kestrel that I came across when out walking. Maybe it was because I was worried how Kes would survive in the wild, but for the first time I noticed how many times kestrels miss when hunting. I'd watch them hover, drop into the grass, and more often than not, fly up clutching a clump of grass or a twig, rather than the vole at which they'd presumably aimed. I knew that even if the wild kestrel I was watching was the one I'd trained, there would be no sign of recognition. Even so, after glancing around to make sure no one was working the land or walking the field paths nearby, I'd look up at the wild kestrel hovering or flying overhead and call: 'Kes . . . Come on, Kes.'

# THIRTEEN

Alas! . . . That we should live to see our noble falcons gibbeted, like thieves, upon 'the keeper's tree' . . .

         – J. E. Harting, *The Ornithology of Shakespeare*, 1864

I'd hacked Kes back to the wild, but my passion for hawks remained undiminished. Flying my kestrel was only half of it, for I delighted in the ancient language of the books. There seemed to be a term for every movement my kestrel had made:

FEAKE . . . said of a hawk when she wipes her beak on the perch after feeding (J. E. Harting, *Bibliotheca Accipitraria*, 1891).

MANTLE, said of a hawk when she stretcheth one of her wings after her leg . . . (Nicholas Cox, *The Gentleman's Recreation*, 1674).

WARBLE . . . when she . . . bryngith booth her wynges togeder ouer hir backe, ye shall say youre hawk 'warbellith hir wynges' (Juliana Berners, *Boke of St Albans*, 1486).

Falconry history fascinated me, and at work, as I wrote down a property repair requested by a tenant, or handed someone a form to fill in to get on the council house waiting list, I'd tell them stories from falconry's past. Such as how the Bishop of Ely threatened a medieval thief with excommunication for stealing a monk's sparrowhawk from the cloisters of Bermondsey Abbey. I must have driven my Town Hall colleagues crackers. I'd walk into the finance department, forget my errand and keep them from their work by telling them about the medieval nuns who were reprimanded by the bishop for taking their hunting hawks into church. Or I'd tell them how a woman farm labourer on Salisbury Plain in the late 1880s had refused to kowtow to the toffs of the Old Hawking Club when a crow, being pursued by their trained falcon, dropped out of the sky and took refuge under her long skirt. Despite threats to push her over if she didn't drive the crow out, the woman had only hitched up her skirt and let the crafty crow fly free after the falconers had called their peregrine down to the lure and ridden off.

Even out on my work visits I'd steer the conversation around to hawks. One day I visited a woman whose name was nearing the top of the council house waiting list, who lived in a tiny brick terraced cottage. I found it embarrassing having to look through the rent books of tenants living in rented private property, to check if they were in arrears with their rent. Once when a woman who hadn't been able to pay her rent for the last couple of weeks clung to me, crying and begging me not to report this to the council and ruin her chance to escape her awful damp rented property, I perjured myself by noting her rent book was all paid up. That day's private tenant didn't mind when I flicked through her rent book, and she smiled as I glanced around the room checking the house was clean and tidy, before writing my findings in a notebook. Put at ease by her friendliness I told her how my kestrel had come from a nest, but how in the past falconers preferred to fly 'passage hawks', which were trapped as they followed flocks of migrating birds in the autumn. As I spoke, the woman, who was about twice my age, stood looking at me smiling.

'You remind me of my brother when he was young,' she said.

Encouraged by her interest I told her how generations of the Mollen family, who lived in Valkenswaard in Holland, used to trap hawks for falconers by hiding in a turf-covered hut from which they pulled several lines to trigger a trap. I was about to explain how they tethered a grey shrike to a perch so that its alarm call would alert the trapper to an approaching falcon, when I realised that although looking up at me fondly, the woman wasn't listening to a word I was saying. Before I could get back to talking about her prospects of getting a council house she said: 'Can I ask you something?'

'Yes.'

'Kiss me.'

Taken aback and embarrassed, I gave the woman a quick kiss on her cheek, gave her an idea of how long she and her family would have to wait for their council house, then hurried out of the door.

Working in the council housing department was a worthwhile job, for we were helping provide a decent home for people who couldn't afford to buy their own. I also found meeting people interesting. Once a woman mysteriously shouted 'Stop wiping your feet' at me as I wiped them on the doormat. Then she began to sob, and continued to sob and sob and sob as she told me her partner, before going to work, had forced her to have unprotected sex with him. When I returned late to the office and explained how the poor woman, desperate for someone to talk to, had delayed me, the housing manager forcefully told me I wasn't paid to be a social worker. Yet, talking to council house tenants and people on the waiting list was what I liked best about my job: telling them my falconry tales, hearing their stories and sorrows. Unfortunately the bulk of what I was paid to do didn't interest me, particularly the office work. I seemed to spend hours pulling out drawers and then sliding them back into filing cabinets, as I filed repair work cards or other information into the file of each individual council property. I also had to update a ledger called the rental register. Council house tenants could request improvements to their house and pay extra for them on their rent – a new fireplace, say, for a shilling and six pence a week – and I had to write these rent increases into the rental register and make sure the various columns of numbers added up. I dreaded the audit at the end of the financial year.

Bored with office work I took to pranks to liven up my days. One day, for instance, I was working in an upstairs office that was once a bedroom in the converted cottage. From downstairs I heard a woman from the finance department asking a colleague if she knew where I was, as she wanted to ask me a work-related question. My colleague told her I was upstairs. The woman asked if she was sure and said somebody had said they thought they'd seen me go out, perhaps across to another department in the Town Hall. My colleague must have been irritated that her word was being doubted.

'He's upstairs,' she said in a sharp, bossy voice.

Annoyed by her manner, I hurried across to the upstairs window, opened it and climbed down a drainpipe. When I came in through the front door my colleague was amazed, and apologised to the woman who'd been looking for me, who was now coming back down the stairs after finding the upstairs office empty.

Another day I went into the public health department and handed the chief public health officer a jar of Colman's mustard. I'd just bought it, I told him, but there was something wrong with it. Sitting at his desk, he held it up and examined it.

'It looks as if the vinegar's run,' he said.

'I don't think that's the problem,' I said. 'It smells awful.'

Looking puzzled, he unscrewed the lid. A green snake rose out of the mustard jar emitting a shrill scream. Horror-struck, he leapt backwards, his glasses slipping down his nose, his chair scraping on the floor as he threw the mustard jar and snake on to the desk in front of him. I laughed as I concertinaed the green paper and wire snake back inside the jar, and screwed on the lid, but the public health officer was understandably furious.

That evening after work, as my mother prepared my tea, I told her about the prank. I thought she'd laugh, or at least smile, but she was terribly angry. Raging at me as she put my favourite meal of chips and egg on the table, she said, 'You're not right in the head, Richard', then went on to tell me that I'd not only 'shown up' myself with my stupid behaviour, but that I'd 'shown her up' as well. Finally, she told me that I'd end up getting sacked from my job.

Maybe I was subconsciously trying to get myself sacked. In a few months, in May 1966, I'd be twenty-one and I still had no more idea of what I wanted to do with my life than I had when I'd left secondary modern school. One thing I did know. I didn't want to study for the professional qualifications I needed if I was ever going to be promoted to assistant housing manager, or even a housing manager. So, one day, while working on the rental register, I decided to jack in my job. I'd had summer holiday jobs while at Barnsley Tech and grammar school, working as a labourer for the council hous-ing maintenance department. I'd quite enjoyed that work, so unsure of what else to do I had a chat with the housing manager, who was surprised, but after I'd persuaded him this was what I wanted to do, he rang the foreman at the build-ing repairs yard, who took me on as a labourer. Sometimes I worked as a plumber's mate, other times as a bricklayer's labourer. Each morning, wearing a pair of recently bought workmen's boots, I rode into the council yard on my bike at about quarter past seven, and waited for the foreman to tell me which tradesman I was working with that day.

Then, one night in the pub, a teacher friend of Barry's told me a teacher training college was starting a new course in Environmental Studies. It suddenly struck me that if I studied that subject, I could use my obsession with hawks, along with my anger that they'd been trapped, shot and hung on gamekeepers' gibbets for centuries, and were now being wiped out by agricultural pesticides, to land myself an interesting job as a teacher.

It was a warm spring day when I went for my interview, and, shielding his eyes from the sun as he looked up at me, the student pointed across the campus of Leicester Teachers' Training College. I walked on past other students sitting or lying on the grass, chatting or reading. One group sat around a table outside the bar, as elsewhere music drifted out of the open windows of a hall of residence: Dusty Springfield, the Rolling Stones. I liked the feel of this place. When I'd applied for my job at the Town Hall I'd been interviewed by a panel of officials and councillors, but in this interview a woman admissions officer simply called me into her small office and invited me to sit down. My passion for my subject must have shown because after we'd shaken hands and I was opening the office door to leave, she suddenly decided to tell me there and then that I'd been accepted, and she was looking forward to seeing me in the autumn.

My fascination with hawking had sparked a voracious appetite for reading and knowledge. Like Sir Richard Fanshawe, the last tenant of Tankersley Old Hall, I always had 'some book in hand'. I'd read late into the night, I'd stop to read while out walking and sometimes I'd sit reading on the bench beside Tankersley church. On one occasion as I sat in a meadow of buttercups I looked up from my book to see a kestrel hovering nearby; as Jackie drew landscapes in her sketch book, I lay in the grass beside her reading a book.

The bell tinkled as I entered the Barnsley bookshop, where, three years earlier, I'd ordered my copy of M. H. Woodford's *A Manual of Falconry*, which had arrived a couple of weeks later. Today, I'd rung from a telephone box to order the book I'd come to collect. It was the newly published 1966 edition of *A Falcon in the Field* by J. G. Mavrogordato, a famous falconer known as Jack by falconers. Mother was house-proud and our house was spotless; yet when I got home I wiped the table down with a clean tea towel, just in case, before unwrapping *A Falcon in the Field* and carefully placing it on the table. It was one of the most beautiful books I'd ever seen. On the cream cover was a magnificent pencil drawing of a gyr falcon's head. Opening the book I carefully lifted the protective cellophane inserts to view the illustrations: an eyas peregrine on a block perch, a lanner falcon perched on a desert rock, to name but two of them.

Mavrogordato had trapped and flown desert falcons in Sudan, and his book, with its references to desert falcons and Arab falconry, led me to *Seven Pillars of Wisdom*, T. E. Lawrence's account of his experiences when he led the Arab revolt forces against the Turks in the First World War. Lawrence fascinated me, not least for his anti-establishment ways. Robert Graves and Lawrence were friends. In Graves's First World War memoir, *Goodbye to All That*, he describes how once, when visiting Lawrence in his room at All Souls College, Oxford, Lawrence opened a window on to the quadrangle and rang a large bell that he'd commandeered from a railway station in Arabia. When Graves told him he'd wake the whole college, Lawrence replied that it needed waking up.

Lawrence was also responsible for an event that had never happened before in Oxford University's centuries-old history: organising a strike of the College servants and winning them better pay and hours. When I saw the film *Lawrence of Arabia* I loved the scene in which Lawrence, much to the disgust of his snobbish fellow British officers, takes an Arab friend into the officers' mess to report that he and the Arabs have taken Aqaba.

One day, when I was working in a council house with a plumber called Jimmy, I watched as he removed the S-shaped waste pipe from under the kitchen sink, showed me where it had been leaking, and then said: 'It's had it. Ride up to the council yard on thi bike and ask Mick in the stores to give thi a new S-bend.'

As I stood at the counter in the stores, and Mick the storekeeper searched among the shelves stacked with plumbing and building materials, I told him that I was reading *Seven Pillars of Wisdom*. Mick didn't answer and I thought he wasn't interested, until he plonked a new S-bend on the counter and said: 'I knew Lawrence.'

It turned out that Mick had been in the Royal Air Force as a young man, and he told me he'd met T. E. Lawrence when Lawrence joined the RAF. He said although he'd changed his name to Shaw everyone knew he was Lawrence of Arabia. Mick said he was a 'surly bugger' and had one close mate, and that he would talk to Mick and the other airmen only about technical things – motorbikes, aeroplanes, things like that – and would never speak about his experiences in Arabia. I was in the stores listening and asking questions for at least half an hour. Carrying the S-bend, I climbed on to my bike, rode back to the council house where we were working and hurried into the kitchen where Jimmy was standing waiting, a spanner in his hand.

'Where's tha been all this time?' he asked.

'Talking to Mick in the stores . . . he knew Lawrence of Arabia.'

'Bugger Lawrence of Arabia. Give me that S-bend,' said Jimmy.

On my bookshelves I still have the 700-page Penguin Modern Classics edition of *Seven Pillars of Wisdom*, which I read all those years ago. It cost me ten shillings and sixpence. Even now I can remember the thrill of coming across a sentence in which T. E. Lawrence described an Arab carrying a saker falcon. Later I flicked through Mavrogordato's *A Falcon in the Field* and found his assessment of its qualities: 'The saker's character is complex; intelligent, even cunning, suspicious until her confidence is gained.'

In *FALCONRY. Notes on the Falconidae used in India in Falconry*, published in 1871, the author, Lieutenant Colonel Delmé Radcliffe, tells how in the heat of India the army marched at night. On one particular moonlit night the bugles had been sounded and the camp was being dismantled. Tents, cooking equipment, all the baggage of camp life was being loaded on to the backs of bellowing bullocks, grumbling camels and trumpeting elephants, to be transported to a new camp. Amid this din, added to by men talking and calling to each other, Colonel Radcliffe shouted an order to someone. A few seconds later he heard the cry of a hawk, looked up and saw his goshawk flying around him. He raised his hand but the goshawk 'blundered in the moonlight' and landed on the baggage piled high on a nearby camel's back. After telling the camel driver 'to make the beast kneel' he took up his goshawk on his fist. On hearing and recognising Colonel Radcliffe's voice the goshawk had 'bolted away from the man who was carrying him', and finding itself free, after its jesses had slipped through the hawk carrier's fingers, had flown to seek its trainer.

This story's location also fascinated me. Except for Jack Mavrogordato, who was a barrister when he'd trapped and flown falcons in Sudan, most writers on falconry seemed to have been army officers who'd served in foreign lands, in India, the Middle East or Africa, in the days of the British Empire. I remember thinking how remarkably fortunate these army officer falconers were, to live overseas in exotic places where they could trap and fly hawks. Such experiences were beyond my reach, utterly unattainable.

Or that's how it had seemed, until one day I read in a newspaper about an organisation called Voluntary Service Overseas – VSO – a London-based charity which sent volunteers overseas, on one- or two-year contracts, to work in developing countries. The newspaper article said they were looking for volunteers with 'professional expertise'. My problem was I wasn't professional, having abandoned my office job and a chance of studying for professional qualifications, and as a building labourer I hadn't any expertise. Even so I became taken up with the idea of living abroad in a country where, unlike Britain, hawks were still common. Realising that I could defer my teacher training course for a year, I sent in an application form, expressing a particular interest in the Middle East and, I'm ashamed to say, exaggerating my 'expertise' in building.

Each day at lunchtime I cycled home from work to make myself a sandwich. One day I leaned my bike against the wall, unlocked the door and was beside myself with excitement to discover a letter which told me that the VSO had invited me to attend a 'board' in London. I'd never heard 'board' used in this context before but it seemed that I'd been asked to come for an interview. The tradesmen that I worked with were now surprised by my sudden interest in building as I asked them one question after another. Most of these men had only ever worked on building repairs, but Jackie's dad was a bricklayer who had built houses and office buildings for years, and I now bombarded him, too, with questions, and borrowed his building books and manuals.

The foreman gave me the day off work and it was pleasant travelling to London on the train, looking out at the passing woods and fields, searching the sky for hovering kestrels. I'd stayed with Barry in his flat in Hampstead when he'd taught in London, so I found my way around easily on the Tube. As I sat waiting in the VSO headquarters, through a partially open door I could see five or six men and women taking their places around a table. After looking at the papers in front of them, one of them got up, opened the door and invited me in. To my relief it seemed no one on the interview board knew much about building and I was answering their questions well until one man, for no apparent reason, suddenly seemed to become angry. Had they brought in a building specialist after all?

'Come off it, Richard,' he said.

My heart raced, fearing he was going to out me as a fraud, and he did, but not in the way I was expecting.

'You're not interested in being a volunteer, are you? You just want an all-expenses-paid adventure, don't you?' he said, glaring.

Taken aback, I was about to confess that what he said was true, as well as admit my lack of building experience. Perhaps, I thought, I should also admit the only reason I'd expressed an interest in the Middle East was because of my fascination with Lawrence of Arabia and Arab falconry. Controlling my panic, however, and telling myself this would be my only chance to live overseas and to fly a hawk like the army officer falconers did in the days of the British Empire, I tried to convince the interview board that

I had something to offer as a volunteer. At the end of the interview they all smiled and thanked me, and I them, but my heart was aching. Convinced that they'd found me out, I headed home to my job as a building labourer, consoling myself that at least I'd be starting at teacher training college in September.

# FOURTEEN

As the ox hath his bow, sir, the horse his curb, and the falcon
her bells . . .

– William Shakespeare, *As You Like It*, 1623

In the summer of 1966 I trained another kestrel, which I
also named Kes, and like my first she came from the nest
at Tankersley Old Hall. In May, on my twenty-first birthday, I unwrapped a present from Jackie to find she'd made
me a falconry gauntlet of leather so thick an eagle's talons
wouldn't have pierced it, never mind a kestrel's. I'm still in
possession of that gauntlet, and I also have a photograph
of me wearing it in 1966 while holding my second Kes by
her jesses. Within a couple of weeks of being 'hard penned'
this new young kestrel was flying to the lure each evening,
performing stoop after spectacular stoop.

On my way to work each morning I would call in at Barry's
garden and open the mews door to see my second Kes standing
on one leg on her perch, the other leg tucked into her breast
feathers. While there I checked for signs of illness. Nictitating
membranes are translucent third eyelids which clean the
hawk's eyes and protect them from sharp stems of grass, thorns
or claws, as they catch their prey. If the third eyelids are
permanently visible, say half covering the eyes' surface, this is a
bad sign, signalling the hawk could be dangerously ill. So on each

morning my first job was to check that Kes's eyes were round and bright. The next thing to examine was her mutes. I much preferred the falconry term 'mutes' to droppings, and on occasions I'd find myself quoting from the 1486 *Boke of St Albans*, 'And ye shall say that your hauke mutith', as I checked Kes's mutes were a healthy white with a clot of black. Hawks can't digest bones and feathers, so these are regurgitated in a pellet. If Kes had been fed wild prey the previous evening, I would pick up the pellet from beneath her perch and check it was firm, dry and oval-shaped. If the weather was fine I put her on her block perch on the lawn to 'weather' and stayed with her a while, before returning her to the mews and heading off to work. Then, in the early evening, calling 'Come on, Kes', I stooped her to the lure, keeping her on the wing for fifteen minutes or so, only letting her strike the lure when she had her beak open, panting.

One evening after I'd flown my kestrel and put her away, I came out of the mews to see Barry walking down the garden path towards me, the sleeves of his V-neck sweater pushed up to his elbows.

'Hey up,' I said.

To my surprise, as I locked the mews door Barry told me his next novel, his second one, was going to be about a kid who trains a hawk. I didn't think that sounded a promising story, but rather than say so I asked: 'What kind of hawk?'

'A kestrel,' Barry replied.

To me, having the lad fly a hawk despised by the medieval falconers seemed like a bad idea, and I told him: 'I wouldn't give him a kestrel if I was thee, I'd let him find an escaped imported goshawk to train.'

Barry wasn't impressed. He'd already decided on a title for his novel, *A Kestrel for a Knave*, the name of the lad, Billy Casper, and the name of the kestrel he was going to train, Kes.

I'd usually been on my own when weighing, flying and feeding Kes but now Barry came out to watch. Some evenings he made notes as I flew her to the lure. On another occasion I recall he stood beside me with his notepad as he watched my hawk eating a sparrow on my glove. All the time he scribbled notes on how she plucked and scattered the feathers, pecked the skin on the sparrow's head to reveal its fragile skull, gulped down its intestines, and, grasping the sparrow's leg in her claw, pecked the meat off its tiny thigh.

On Saturday mornings it was our practice to meet up soon after dawn to walk together through the fields and woods around the village. Barry had seen me flying my kestrels, but on our walks he now asked me about my falconry experiences more generally. I told him how I was refused permission to take out Woodford's *A Manual of Falconry* from Barnsley Library, and had then gone to the bookshop to try and buy a copy. On another early morning walk we traced the route on which John and I had carried the ladder on that June night the year before, and I described how the cows lying in the grass were clearly visible in the bright moonlight, and how in Bell Ground Wood John had cupped his hand around his mouth and called to a tawny owl. Later, as we stood together gazing up at the nest hole in the ruins of Tankersley Old Hall, I explained how we'd come at night to avoid being caught trespassing by the farmer, and how we'd clambered over the wall and hurried across the field to climb up to the nest.

*A Kestrel for a Knave* had scenes set in the countryside, and during that summer, as he prepared to write those scenes, our usual fast walking pace was often slowed as we waded through tall grasses in meadows full of ox-eye daises, yarrow and purple vetch. When we came across anything that we didn't recognise, Barry would pick a single flower or a stalk of grass and carefully put it in his pocket for identification when he got home.

Barry's first novel, *The Blinder*, was about a boy who, like him, was a good footballer. I wondered why Barry hadn't once again used his own school experiences, and had instead chosen to have Billy Casper attend secondary modern school. He told me that while he'd been teaching in secondary modern schools in London and Barnsley, he'd come across lots of clever kids who'd failed the eleven plus exam, and that he wanted to produce a book that was critical of an education system which wrote off the majority of children when they were eleven years old. I was surprised. I'd never heard him fuming about the iniquities of secondary moderns when I was a pupil in one. Still, he was younger then. He summed up the idea of his new novel: 'I want to give the education system some stick.' I was all in favour of that.

One day that summer I visited the annual Game Fair at Chatsworth Park in Derbyshire. For today my falconry hero Jack Mavrogordato, whose books I loved, was scheduled to give a falconry display. I'd got to the display area early and I was now in the front row of a crowd of people surrounding a large area of grass. I saw the crowd moving apart but couldn't see Jack until he appeared in the flying area. I'd never seen a falcon other than a kestrel before, but, instead of focusing on the lanner falcon on his glove, I couldn't take my eyes off Jack himself. A man of around sixty with a neatly trimmed beard, he was much smaller and slighter than I'd imagined. He cast off the falcon, which then flew, with shallow wingbeats, within a few yards of me on its circuit around the flying area. What struck me forcibly was the sound of its bells. I'd read about bells and 'bewits', the strips of leather used to attach bells to a hawk's legs. According to M. H. Woodford the best bells were made by 'some ancient process' in the Lahore region of Pakistan, but I'd never guessed what a beautiful sound they made.

I'd never seen anyone stoop a falcon to the lure, and the unclear instructions in Woodford's *A Manual of Falconry* made it hard to picture. I'd done my best to work it out, but until now it hadn't really mattered whether it was correct or not. The fact that Barry was now writing about falconry and using my technique as a model changed that. I didn't want Barry to be made to look foolish by getting his description of stooping wrong.

I was apprehensive when the lanner flew in fast towards Mavrogordato as he swung the lure by his side. 'Now,' I whispered, and as if he'd heard me Jack threw out the lure to the lanner, twitched it away at the last moment, and then somehow brought the lure behind his back. Looking for the lure the lanner rose into the air, then stooped as Jack once again swung the lure by his side and then threw it out for the hawk to pursue. My heart was racing, for this wasn't how I flew Kes: my technique was to sweep the lure in front of me in a downwards then an upwards arc to send her shooting high into the sky to begin another vertical stoop. I blamed M. H. Woodford's indecipherable instructions. I reckoned I'd let Barry down. I watched the lanner put in two or three stoops, circle around the display area, then fly in again to Jack's swinging lure to stoop a few more times. As I watched I began to think perhaps things weren't as disastrous as I'd first thought. Reasoning that I'd taught myself lure flying from a book, I told myself it was feasible that Billy Casper would fly a hawk to the lure the way I did. After all, in Barry's novel Billy teaches himself falconry from a book.

Early one morning I wheeled my bike up the path beside the house and mounted it in Tinker Lane. Wearing my work clothes and workman's boots, I was about to ride off to work when the postman handed me a letter. It had a London postmark. Standing astride my bike I tore open the envelope. It couldn't be. I'd written that off. But it was; the VSO had written to tell me I was to go overseas for a year in the autumn. Later that morning, with my hands smudged with soot from carrying a fireplace from a council house, I rang from a telephone box and arranged for my college place to be delayed for a year.

That evening, sitting at home, I flicked through the pages of *A Manual of Falconry* and stopped at a photograph of a saker falcon. It had white breast feathers speckled with dark brown, and had its head turned to one side showing a large dark eye and a ferocious-looking curved beak. Turning over a few more pages I found a photograph of a lanner falcon. It had more splashes of dark brown on its breast feathers than the saker, and had a dark vertical stripe under each eye. The history of those two falcons fascinated me. They had probably been introduced into Britain in the Middle Ages by knights returning from the Crusades in the Middle East. In Abbess Juliana Berners' 1486 *Boke of St Albans* the saker was allocated to a knight: 'Ther is a Sacre and a Sacret [the female]. And theis be for a knyght.' The lanner was held in less esteem, and in her book the Abbess allocated it to a knight's attendant, the squire: 'Ther is a Lanare and a Lanrell [the female]. And they's belong to a Squyer.'

I'd first gazed at the photographs of those two falcons in Barnsley Library, when copying out Woodford's book. Back then I couldn't have imagined that three years later I would be hoping I might have the chance to fly a saker or a lanner in the Middle East or Sudan. If I was posted to India or Pakistan the falcon I'd fly there would probably be a luggur. I hadn't seen a picture of one, but, according to Jack Mavrogordato in *A Falcon in the Field*, although it resembled a lanner in 'size and build, though not colour' it was an 'inferior alternative to the lanner' because of its lack of 'courage and drive', and was held in such low esteem it could be bought from a hawk trapper for a few rupees. I'd prefer to train a saker or a lanner, but, despite the disparaging remarks, Mavrogordato made a comment about the lugger, 'Tame and placid . . . it is a . . . falcon for the inexperienced falconer', which suggested it could be the most suitable hawk for me.

Wherever I landed in September, the young hawks would have fledged the nest. I'd no idea if I'd be able to buy a hawk from a trapper, and that evening I continued to look through my falconry books, searching for information that would help me trap a hawk myself. The most dramatic and surprising method used in the desert was to drive a falcon off its prey, then bury yourself in sand with your hand below the falcon's prey and just your nostrils showing. When you felt the falcon return to continue its meal, you grabbed its legs, then rose out of the desert, spitting sand with the flapping falcon in your hand.

Other trapping methods included the 'Arab net' and Indian 'do gazza', which use a caged decoy bird such as a pigeon to lure a falcon into a net, where it becomes entangled and is then picked up by the falconer. The method that appealed to me most, because of its historic origin and simplicity, was that described by Abbess Juliana Berners: 'Looke where an hawke perchith for all nyght . . . And softely and layserly clymbe to her with a . . . lanterne in . . . yowre hande and let the light be towarde the hawke so that she se not yowre face and ye may take her by the leggys . . .'

It was early September 1966 and the dew glistened on the hedges. When my second Kes had eaten her fill on the glove I cut off her jesses and raised my arm. After looking around for a few moments she launched into flight, and, as I watched her shallow wingbeats take her high above the golden stubble fields, meadows and hawthorn hedges, I wondered if next year I'd be releasing a luggur or maybe a lanner, or even a saker, into a very different landscape.

When I learned the details of my posting, though, it wasn't quite what I expected.

# PART TWO

# FIFTEEN

And kites
Fly o'er our heads, and downward look on us,
As we were sickly prey . . .

– William Shakespeare, *Julius Caesar*, 1599

Clouds of red dust billowed up behind us as we travelled in a Land Rover along a road through a landscape of reddish-brown earth, straw-coloured scrub and the occasional green thorn tree. On the front seat, between the driver and me, were a couple of women wearing colourful wraparound dresses and headscarves. In the back seat were another two women along with two men wearing white kaftans and white caps, and a child or two. We journeyed through villages and towns with markets and flat-roofed mud houses, passing bleating goats and braying donkeys. At one point I watched transfixed as, kneeling beside a river, a group of women pounded their washing on rocks, all of them keeping the same rhythmic beat as they sang.

I'd hoped to follow the journey that my hero T. E. Lawrence had made to the Middle East, but following Jack Mavrogordato to Sudan would have been equally exciting. Both these places had a history of falconry. India, where Colonel Delmé Radcliffe's goshawk had sought him out in the moonlight, and where you could buy a luggur falcon for a few rupees, would also have been wonderful. Instead, VSO had posted me to Nigeria in West Africa, a former British colony, which as far as I knew had no history of falconry. At first I'd been disappointed, until I took out a map and looked up my destination in the north of the country. To my delight I saw it was semi-desert not far south of the Sahara, the type of open landscape suitable for flying a falcon.

The Land Rover was taking me to Potiskum, a town where I was to work as a volunteer for the Ministry of Agriculture in the 'tsetse fly eradication unit'. Although I was relieved VSO hadn't found me a building project and discovered I was a fake, I hadn't received any information as to what the job would involve. From my reading I knew that the tsetse fly looked like a housefly, fed on the blood of humans and animals and passed on disease. The illness it caused, called 'sleeping sickness' in humans, attacked the nervous system and brain of both humans and animals, and caused lethargy and weakness and often resulted in death. Of course I'd no idea of what to expect, but that didn't stop me imagining what I hoped the job would be.

From childhood I'd watched benign images of the British Empire on cinema newsreels, on television and in films: the Queen waving to smiling natives; white expats in khaki shirts and shorts working on African game reserves helped by smiling black men. Earlier this year in a cinema in Barnsley, Jackie and I had watched the film *Born Free*, the story of a white couple who released a lioness back into the wild. My mind fuelled with images from film and television, I imagined the job which awaited me in Potiskum. My dream would have been to assist an expat vet, dressed in khaki shirt and shorts, as we visited farmers. Sometimes we'd travel in a Land Rover, other times fly in a small plane, as we helped reduce the devastating effects of disease. I was brought out of my thoughts by a loud noise coming from the Land Rover's engine.

A little later, as I stood beside the driver as he worked on the engine of our broken-down Land Rover, another one pulled up beside us in a cloud of red dust. Inside were a white couple in their fifties dressed in khaki, precisely how I'd imagined such people would look. The woman lowered the window. I thought she was going to ask if they could help, or perhaps offer a lift to the women and children who had climbed out of our Land Rover to sit beside the road. Instead she asked where I was going. When I told her, she said they would take me to Potiskum. I'd enjoyed my journey so far, laughing and talking with my Nigerian travelling companions, who spoke good English even though it was their second language. So I thanked the woman and politely turned down her offer. To my amazement, after glancing disdainfully at the Nigerian families sitting beside the road, she said, in a strikingly posh English accent, 'These people shit in the bush'. Then they drove off before I could think up a reply.

The driver eventually fixed the engine and we all clambered back into the Land Rover. I don't recall where all the people packed in there were going, but they had a little more room when the driver dropped me off at the 'Government Rest House', which was located in scrubland a mile or so outside the town of Potiskum. In the days of Empire, Government Rest Houses existed throughout the British colonies. In this one, from 1900 until 1960, when Nigeria gained independence from Britain, government employees would stay for a night or two, breaking their journey across this vast country. The rest house included a single-storey building, with a large room which served as both a bar and a restaurant. Behind the bar, which was also the reception desk, was a door which led to the kitchen. There were no bedrooms in this part; guests slept in chalets, which surrounded a reddish-brown sandy square. What had struck me most as I'd walked into the bar/restaurant were the small green lizards, at least four or five of them, scuttling across the floor and along table tops, running a short distance, stopping dead, running again. After signing in I was served a meal of chips, eggs and chicken, and, as I sat at a table eating, I watched the lizards and at one point was delighted by the sight of a large green frog, which had hopped in from outside through an open door.

In Northern Nigeria the sun rose around 6 a.m. and set around 6 p.m. By the time I'd finished my meal it was dark, so, holding a paraffin lamp, I walked out of the restaurant into the warm starlit night and made my way across the sandy square. The lamp cast shadows around the single room, which had a bed curtained by a white mosquito net. After placing the lamp on a chest of drawers, I clicked open the locks on my suitcase and opened the lid. Lying on top of my folded clothes was my falconry equipment: the glove Jackie had made; the pairs of jesses I'd made; sheets of tracing paper on which I'd copied hood patterns so I could make a hood for whichever hawk I managed to trap. Back home, when I'd dreamed of living overseas and flying a falcon, it had never crossed my mind that VSO would put me up permanently in a hotel room where I wouldn't be allowed to keep a hawk. Flying a hawk had motivated me to come overseas, and perhaps it was this overpowering disappointment that suddenly drained me of all the excitement I'd felt up to this point on my travels. For, as I put the falconry glove Jackie had made into a drawer, I remembered it was Saturday. I imagined how Jackie would have spent her afternoon in her bedroom, painting or drawing, and I desperately wished I was home with her, sitting on her bed, listening to pop songs. Jackie's mother had told me how upset Jackie was that I was going away, but Jackie hadn't said this to me. Instead, she'd encouraged me to go overseas, and when I suddenly wished I wasn't leaving, as we said goodbye, fighting back tears, she had said a year would soon pass. But, as I glanced around that drab chalet room with its mosquito net, in the dim light of a paraffin lamp, the thought of spending a year here on my own, without even the chance of making a telephone call, was awfully daunting.

Still. No one had made me come here. It was my choice. So, next morning, after a breakfast of chips, eggs, baked beans and fried bread, I forced myself to cheer up, and sat in a chair on the porch of my chalet watching six or seven black kites, which, with their broad wings and long tails, looked like hawks, as they soared in the sky. Later, still sitting on the porch of my chalet, I wrote to Jackie, telling her what I'd seen on my 170-mile journey by Land Rover from Kano airport. Cloudless blue skies; women with babies tied on their backs; people on bicycles and on foot balancing things on their heads – large bowls, trays of bread, rolls of cloth. I told Jackie how I'd seen men with long sticks walking beside their herds of white cattle through the scrub, how each time we'd driven past a river I'd spotted white long-legged egrets wading in the reeds, and that the starlings were a metallic blue. I didn't mention the bad news, that where I was accommodated meant I couldn't keep a hawk, but I did tell her about the awful woman who'd insulted my Nigerian travelling companions. Had I not already sealed the envelope, the following day I could have told Jackie of another incident involving a white expat.

On Sunday I was eating my lunch of chicken and chips when I was joined in the restaurant by an Englishman in his sixties, who'd stayed overnight in one of the guest house chalets. After lunch we had a drink together, and as he talked nostalgically about his time in India during the British Raj, a Nigerian waiter put a drink he'd ordered down on the table. Holding up a shilling 'dash' – as the Nigerians called a tip – the man said: 'Kiss my feet.'

To my amazement, the waiter did just that, lowering himself on to his knees and kissing the man's shoe. He was given the shilling. Disgusted by the man's behaviour, and annoyed that the waiter hadn't thrown the drink in his face, I left. I'd only met three white British expats, but my expectations of them being khaki-clad, smiling, good-natured sorts were already unravelling.

My boss at the tsetse fly eradication unit was Ian, an Englishman in his early fifties with a small moustache, dressed in a khaki shirt and shorts. On Monday he picked me up from the Government Rest House in his Land Rover and drove me to work. On the way I asked what my job would involve and he said I'd be working in an office. Trying to conceal my dismay, and to keep the conversation going, I asked what method was used to eradicate tsetse fly. The answer shocked me. 'We spray them with chemicals, mostly DDT,' Ian told me. The dreadful irony of it! I couldn't believe how gormless I'd been; reading my falconry books back home and dreaming romantically of flying a falcon in an unspoilt, pesticide-free country. It hadn't occurred to me that the chemicals used here to spray insect pests like the tsetse fly might be the very same that had virtually wiped out hawks in Britain. The poisoning of my beloved hawks by agricultural chemicals was a scandal to me. I'd secured myself a place at teacher training college by my informed rage against the practice. Yet here I was, about to start work for a department of the Ministry of Agriculture which poisoned the African soil with the very same chemicals. But what could I do? Ask to go home?

Stunned into silence, I gazed out of the Land Rover window. Noting the number of kites soaring in the clear blue sky I tried to cheer myself up. I reminded myself that kites eat carrion, and then reasoned that if their prey had been poisoned they wouldn't be so numerous. So, I told myself, things here might not be as bad as they were back home. There still might be hawks around.

Ian drove the Land Rover through two open gates into the tsetse fly eradication unit, which looked like a works depot. A high wire fence surrounded a large square in which were parked a few Land Rovers. At one end of the square was a sizeable corrugated-iron shed, into which Ian took me to show me the offices and stores. My first job was to do a 'stock check', and I grumbled to myself as I noted every item on row after row of shelves in the stores: spray guns, face masks, Land Rover parts. I told myself if I'd wanted to work in an office I would have stayed at Hoyland Town Hall, where the work was much more interesting than this. I was so bored that, had I not been opposed to it, I'd have asked to go out in the Land Rovers with the DDT sprayers.

Occasionally, my boss Ian took me in his Land Rover on work-related trips to other towns. One night as we crossed a bridge over a river, thousands of fireflies lit up the night. Then there was the day when we drove around a bend in the road and there, perched in a tree, its yellow eyes staring wildly at me, was a goshawk. Almost as exciting was the sight, another time, of a sparrowhawk flying from one boulder to another across the scrub. Unfortunately, I didn't see any falcons on my journeys in the Land Rover. A falcon, such as a saker or a lanner, is what I'd dreamed of training in Nigeria. Yet the African species of goshawk or a sparrowhawk would have been fine, if only I'd somewhere to keep one.

One day, amid the colour and bustle of Potiskum market, beside the live hens and ducks for sale, I spotted something I could use as a decoy, or 'barak', to trap a falcon. It was a black kite, imprisoned in a small wire cage. Kites evolved to hunt small prey, such as lizards, and to feed on carrion, and for this reason they are unsuitable for falconry. Instead, Arab and Indian trappers used them to trap falcons. The way they did

143

this was to attach a bundle of feathers covered in small nooses to the legs of a kite and then release it. Wild falcons often attempted to steal prey off other raptors. So, if things went to plan, a wild falcon would think the kite was carrying prey, but when it tried to steal it, the falcon's talons would become entangled in the nooses, bringing both it and the kite tumbling to earth. The trapper would then untangle them, release the kite unharmed and keep the falcon to sell to a falconer.

I didn't need the kite to trap a falcon, but, feeling sorry for the poor thing, I decided to buy it and release it into the wild. The market trader took it out of its cramped wire cage and passed it to me. With my thumbs across its back and my fingers pinning its wings by its sides, I examined it. It was bigger than a kestrel, had brown eyes, a curved beak, and, although called a black kite, its feathers were mostly dark brown with streaks of pale brown, and it had black on its wings. I noticed that some of its breast feathers were soiled with white droppings. Seeing a chance to barter down the price, I pointed this out to the market trader. To my fury he grabbed the soiled feathers and yanked them from the kite's breast, then told me that the bird looked in good condition now. I paid up.

When I released the black kite I discovered it would have been useless as a decoy. It couldn't fly. Instead of powering upwards to soar in the cloudless African sky as I'd imagined, it hopped and fluttered along the ground, disappearing into the parched scrubland. When I'd examined it I couldn't see anything which suggested it might not be able to fly, and now I could only console myself with the faint hope that the kite might manage to avoid predators and live off carrion and lizards.

A few days later Ian picked me up from my chalet at the guest house in the Land Rover as usual, except today he took a different route to work.

'Where are we going?' I asked.

'You'll see,' he replied, driving up a sandy track until we stopped outside a lovely thatched bungalow. In a day or two, he told me, when it had been cleaned up, I was to move out of my chalet at the Government Rest House and into this bungalow. I was delighted. I'd have a place of my own where I could keep a hawk in a spare bedroom.

The thatched cottage had been built in the days of the Empire, and that first evening, as I sat with a glass of beer in an armchair on the veranda, I imagined that the army officers who'd flown hawks in the British colonies would have spent their evenings like this. All I needed to complete the scene was a hawk or falcon on a perch in the light of the setting sun. Although they catch their prey almost exclusively by flying fast and low, hawks do occasionally soar or fly high, just as falcons do. With this in mind I often glanced up, hoping I'd see a circling falcon or a soaring hawk in the clear blue sky. I'd only seen kites. Yet, the fact that kites hadn't as yet been poisoned by pesticides convinced me that there must be hawks and falcons in the vicinity, too. That weekend, I'd look for the distinctive splashes of white mutes and regurgitated pellets of feathers and bones that indicated a roost in a tree. If successful in my search, holding a torch to dazzle it, I would climb up one night and grab the hawk by the legs. Although he'd used a long pole with a torch and a noose attached to the end, rather than climbing the tree, Jack Mavrogordato's falconer friend William Ruttledge had trapped five sparrowhawks on their night roost in Sudan in the 1940s. If I couldn't find a roost, I'd search for scattered feathers from earlier kills, which would alert me to the haunt of a hawk, where I could set up a 'do gazza' net trap. That night as I fell asleep my mind was full of hawks.

I awoke suddenly in the early hours of the morning. Through the mesh of the mosquito net I saw a black shape about the size of my hand flicker across the dark room, then another, and another. The almost pitch-black room was alive with flickering shapes. I reached for the torch beside my pillow and clambered out from under the mosquito net. As my torch beam swept around the walls and ceiling I stood there transfixed. Dozens and dozens of bats poured out of the open bedroom door, into another room, then back into the bedroom again, flying in front of me, above me, behind me, past my legs, flickering away at the last moment when it seemed they were about to crash into my head or body. Whoever had cleaned the house before I moved in must have cleared up the bat droppings because next morning the bedroom was covered in them. The bats roosted in the thatched roof and it was too unhygienic to live in the bungalow. I'd hoped to move back in, after the bats had been cleared out and the place had been done up properly. Unfortunately, Ian told me it was cheaper for me to go back into a chalet at the Government Rest House.

One evening a Nigerian waiter brought a paraffin lamp to my chalet and told me I was the only guest staying in the chalets at the Government Rest House. So early next morning I was surprised to hear English voices and occasionally an African woman's voice talking earnestly as I walked across for breakfast. Sitting around a table in the restaurant were Ian, my boss, and another Englishman I didn't know, who to my surprise had a Nigerian wife. Wondering what had prompted them to leave their homes and meet up here so early I walked across to join them. As I sat down, the man I hadn't met before said in pidgin English: 'Plenty palaver.'

Confused, I looked at him, then he told me that last night a mob of northern Nigerians, who were from the Hausa tribe, had roamed the town searching for eastern Nigerians from the Igbo tribe. And that they'd found six Igbos, dragged them out of their homes and killed them. Ian butted in, saying if the mob had come anywhere near his bungalow carrying their flaming torches and machetes he'd have come out with his double-barrelled shotgun and blasted a barrel over their heads. And if that hadn't stopped them he'd have blasted the other barrel into the mob before reloading. Turning to me, Ian then said: 'You're lucky they didn't make it up here.'

'What?'

He told me the mob were on their way to the Government Rest House to search the chalets for more Igbos to kill, but that when they were a couple of hundred yards or so away, the police had managed to turn them back after persuading them there were no guests staying in the chalets.

There was one guest staying in one of the chalets fast asleep and unaware. Me.

Pointing at me, the Nigerian woman began to laugh.

'Look at his face,' she said.

I was terrified, as I imagined what might have happened: being woken by voices; the door crashing in; being dragged out of the chalet; the seething resentment against arrogant white expats being directed against me by machete-wielding men in the light of flaming torches.

That afternoon Ian needed to go to the bank in Potiskum. I went with him, and as the Land Rover inched along behind a herd of bleating goats, he filled me in on the recent events which had led to last night's trouble. He told me there had been retaliatory massacres earlier in the year against eastern Igbos, when Igbo plotters had killed northern leaders in a government coup in which General Ironsi, an Igbo, had taken power and become President of Nigeria. Through the windows of the Land Rover we could see, plastered on the mud walls of flat-roofed buildings, posters of Colonel Gowon, who had recently taken over as President in a counter-coup. Nodding towards one of the posters, Ian told me he had been surprised by last night's massacre of Igbos in Potiskum now that Gowon, who was from the northern region, was in power.

Later, I was sitting in the parked Land Rover waiting for Ian to return from the bank when four young Nigerian men approached. Three of them carried a machete each; the other had a club-shaped stick. Scared, I wound up the open window next to me. Passing by threateningly close, the four men stared in at me. Avoiding their gaze I looked down at the long blades of their machetes glinting in the sun, and saw that a nail was protruding from the club-shaped stick.

Thousands of people were killed throughout Nigeria in 1966: there were massacres of Igbo in the north by the Hausa and retaliatory massacres of Hausa in the east by the Igbo. But after that awful night when six Igbos were dragged from their homes and killed, no more Igbos were murdered while I was in Potiskum after the Emir had said, at Friday prayers, the killings were wrong and must stop.

Those four young men in town armed with machetes and the spiked club had terrified me, yet I found the Hausa people open and friendly. On one occasion Jahid, a Hausa friend in his twenties, invited me to his home for lunch. With him in his white kaftan and white skullcap, and me in shorts and a short-sleeved shirt, we sat in the open air on mats in his compound – a small backyard enclosed by high mud-coated walls. His wife, dressed in a colourful wraparound dress and headscarf, brought out the food then sat with us and joined in the conversation. I recall eating with my right hand and dipping yam into a sauce. After the meal Jahid told me they'd bought a drink especially for me, and his wife went inside and returned carrying a tin of Ovaltine. I'd no idea why they thought this bedtime drink was special. But sitting there under a cloudless African sky, drinking the milky chocolate-coloured drink I'd last had as a child wearing pyjamas, I suddenly missed home and those carefree days in our mining village when I was little and Dad was alive.

On a different occasion, Audu, another Hausa friend, invited me for an evening meal. We sat on mats inside his flat-roofed mud-walled home. As we chatted, at one point I thought he'd asked me if I liked beetles. Fed up of the chips, beans and fried bread served at the Government Rest House, and suddenly excited at the prospect of eating an exotic indigenous dish, I replied yes. My host stood up, walked across the room, pulled back a cloth to reveal a record player, and put on a record.

'A Hard Day's Night' blasted out of the speakers.

As we listened to the Beatles, who I loved, my friend's young wife brought in the meal, crouched down and put it before us as we sat on the floor. I hoped that she'd stay with us to eat and join in the conversation. But after she'd put down the food and stood up from her crouching position, to my astonishment and dismay she bowed to me before shuffling backwards, repeatedly bowing to me until she was out of the room.

Seeing a friend's wife bow her way out of the room simply because I was white upset me. I'd begun to wonder if my African friends really felt at ease with me and if my friendship was an imposition. Feeling isolated and lonely, and fed up with my job, I desperately wanted to move from the tsetse fly eradication unit. So, although I'd only worked there for a couple of months, I told my boss Ian that, having been accepted at teacher training college, I'd be interested in teaching. Ian contacted someone from VSO who found me a post as a volunteer teacher in Kano.

# SIXTEEN

Checke, or to kill checke, is when . . . other birds coming in view of the Hawke, she forsaketh her natural flight to flie at them.

– Symon Latham, *Latham's Faulconry, or The Faulcon's Lure and Cure*, 1615

My job in Kano was to teach English in a technical school, where teenage boys from all over Nigeria lived in dormitories and were taught trades such as motor mechanics and plumbing. The bungalow in which I lived in Kano didn't have the romantic charm of the isolated thatched bungalow in Potiskum. Roofed in corrugated iron, my new home sat between similar bungalows where the white teachers lived. Unlike the thatched bungalow and my chalet at the Government Rest House, which were lit by paraffin lamp, this bungalow had electricity. What had caught my eye when I first arrived was the fridge; there would be no problem keeping hawk food fresh here. Then, through the back window, I spotted the school field: perfect for flying a falcon to the lure. But once again hawk-keeping was impractical. There was no garden in which I could build a mews. Nor was there a spare bedroom in which I could keep a hawk. Here in Kano, I shared the bungalow with Tom, a tall, thin American Peace Corps volunteer teacher.

Yet the impossibility of falconry here meant I could direct my energy into my English teaching job. I'd read lots of books on teaching for my Leicester Training College for Teachers interview the year before, and once I arrived in Kano I spent hour after hour in the school library, preparing lessons and reading about teaching methods. Even so, I did worry about my lack of teaching experience. Occasionally I asked a couple of other qualified teachers who also taught English if I could look at samples of their students' written work. To my relief it seemed my students' work was on a par, or at least not far behind the work of their students. This might not have had anything to do with my teaching, of course. The only thing I remember from teaching an actual lesson is a lad called Aliyu saying how strange it was that in English we say someone sleeps '*in* a bed' rather than '*on* a bed'.

My airmail letters home to Jackie were full of my new experiences. In one letter I told her how, when I'd moved into the bungalow in Kano, I'd been taken aback to discover that we had a cook. He was a small Nigerian called Sali, who, despite being around my mother's age, and despite my protests, embarrassed me by insisting on calling me master. I went on to tell Jackie that we also had a Tuareg night watchman to guard our bungalow. Unlike his camel-riding desert ancestors, he was no longer a nomad. Instead, he slept on a mat in the garage in the day and guarded our bungalow at night, sitting cross-legged on our veranda, his long sword tucked into his waistband, with only his eyes visible through a slit of the dark blue wrap wound around his head. In another letter, I told Jackie that to beat the heat we started work at 8 a.m., and how each morning, dressed in a short-sleeved shirt, shorts and sandals, I rode the short distance to the technical school on my bike. And how, when the sixteen-year-old lads I taught, who were Muslim, went out to pray, a small flock of tiny brightly coloured finches would fly in, hop around the floor and on the desks, and then all take off together and fly back out through the open classroom door.

Most of the teachers were white, but there were also two or three Nigerian teachers, and one day as I was sipping my tea one of them called across and told me someone wanted to speak to me. When I walked to the door, there, standing outside in the corridor, was our cook, Sali. He looked upset.

'Come home, master,' he said.

'What's wrong?'

'Thief man.'

Sali told me that he'd put a pile of my shirts on the ironing board in the kitchen to be ironed, but when he returned after doing something in another room they were gone. Rushing to the open kitchen door, Sali had spotted the thief running across the school sports field with half a dozen of my shirts in his arms. Sali went on to tell me that he had run to the garage and woken up our Tuareg night watchman, who, sword in hand, had raced across the field and caught the shirt thief and was now holding him prisoner on the veranda, awaiting my return and the arrival of the police.

I rode the few hundred yards home on my bike, amused by the image I had in my mind of the thief running across the school sports field with his arms full of my shirts. Making my way through a small crowd of Nigerian cooks who'd hurried out of the other bungalows on hearing Sali shouting, my mood changed to horror. Sitting on the concrete veranda floor with his back against the bungalow wall was the thief, a thin old Nigerian man. Running down his forehead and down the side of his nose and on to his cheek was a deep wound. The night watchman had slashed him across the face with his sword. He also had a sword wound across the top of his arm. Showing me the palms of his hands, the old man looked up at me and quietly pleaded, 'Let me go'. The sword cut on his face wasn't bleeding much, but I gave him my handkerchief to press on the wound on the top of his arm to stem the bleeding. Sali was annoyed with me for showing concern for the thief, and, as the wounded man sat on the veranda holding out his palms begging me to let him go, Sali and the small crowd of Nigerian cooks abused him in Hausa. When I told Sali he shouldn't have called the police and that I didn't want to press charges, the cooks from the other bungalows turned their anger against me. Sali and his fellow cooks got their wish. The old man was taken away by the police and I never heard what happened to him.

Later, I asked Sali why he and the other cooks had been so angry. 'Thief men' jeopardised their jobs, he told me, because in their experience if anything went missing from a white man's house the cooks tended to be blamed and got the sack. I shook my head, smugly thinking that I wasn't implicated in any such arrogant behaviour. I'd even befriended a group of beggars in Kano. One had all his fingers missing on both hands. Two or three of them had been crippled by polio and pushed themselves around on home-made trolleys, and others couldn't find a job. Whatever their woes, it didn't seem to affect their sense of humour. They thought it amusing that I rode a bike and were always asking me how come I, a white man, a 'baturi', hadn't enough 'kudi' – money – to buy a car. I usually gave them money, but one day, for a bit of fun, I told them that I rode a bike because I was hard up. To my amusement they had a whip-round for me, each of them taking a few coins out of his begging bowl and throwing them into a white cap. But one day I discovered that not all Nigerians were so amused by baturis.

I was fetched from the staffroom by a student who told me a fellow teacher needed to speak to me. He wouldn't say why, and I innocently followed him back to the classroom where minutes before I'd been teaching.

'Wipe it off.'

'What?'

'You wrote it. You rub it off,' said the Nigerian teacher as he held out a board rubber and pointed to the white chalk writing covering the blackboard, which I'd forgotten to wipe off. Taken aback by his aggression and bad manners, I glanced at the students sitting in their rows of desks, looking for support, but I couldn't see any of the lads I taught, or any of the lads I took for football training. These were students I didn't know and there was no support there. All too used to seeing white men ordering Nigerians around, this was probably the first time they'd seen the tables turned. There was silence as the students waited to see how I, the baturi, would react. I sensed they were willing my humiliation, willing me to do as their Nigerian teacher had ordered me to do, willing me meekly to wipe the blackboard clean under their sneering gaze.

'Come on. Clean the blackboard,' the Nigerian teacher said, even more aggressively, as he stepped forward holding out the board rubber. I couldn't understand such seething hostility, and my surprise turned to anger. As he stood there offering me the board rubber, I wanted to shout in his face. I wanted to tell him he wouldn't have picked on me if I'd been older and had a little moustache and an authoritative presence like many white expats. Hurt and rendered inarticulate by anger, I responded like a child.

'Wipe the blackboard yourself,' I said and stormed out of the classroom.

Having so far found the Nigerian people I'd met welcoming and friendly, I was left shaken and upset by this episode. That night, unable to sleep, it dawned on me that since arriving in Nigeria I'd never done a menial task. The clean white sheet I was lying on had been washed by Sali; the clothes I'd worn at school earlier that day had been washed and ironed by Sali; tomorrow morning's breakfast would be cooked by Sali. I started to see the classroom incident in a different way. Rather than thinking I'd just forgotten to wipe the blackboard clean, maybe the Nigerian teacher had seen it as typical white expatriate arrogance, left over from the days of Empire; a manifestation of an attitude that lowly, menial tasks such as cleaning a blackboard were below me, and that like all baturis I expected some Nigerian to clean up behind me. The 'glories' of the British Empire had been instilled in me by my 1950s education and the jingoistic cinema newsreels of the time. When I'd read tales of army officers flying hawks in the Empire, and longed to follow in their footsteps, I'd never thought about the lives of those colonised. As I lay there in the hot night, recalling the rows of black faces in the classroom, I realised their seething rage against me was most likely rooted in the fact that, even now, six years after independence from Britain in 1960, the Empire's legacy still permeated northern Nigerian life.

Next morning as Sali greeted me with a cheery 'Good morning, master', I was acutely aware that, despite my liberal sentiments, I was part of this legacy. Like all white expats I was a member of Kano Club, a legacy of Empire, with its tennis courts, playing fields and golf course. I played cricket at the club, and most days I swam in the outdoor pool. On Saturday evenings I went to Kano Club's open-air cinema to watch films shipped out from England, and one evening I watched Noël Coward's *Blithe Spirit* performed on stage by the club's drama group. Until my dressing-down by the angry Nigerian teacher, I hadn't really noticed that the only black faces in the club belonged to the waiters. At the first opportunity I asked the club secretary if membership was open to anyone. He said it was, and had been since independence. Then he added that the vast majority of Nigerians couldn't afford the subscriptions and as a result the club didn't have any Nigerian members – as a VSO volunteer I paid a special reduced rate.

Now a disagreement over the cleaning of a blackboard had made me much more aware of the demeaning legacy of

British rule. For instance, in the bar at Kano Club the white manager of a groundnut company told me that some of the many job applications he received began: 'Dear Sir, I humbly and respectfully beg . . .' And each time I went out in Kano, at least one Nigerian man would hand me a reference from a previous British employer, then stand beside me smiling as I read it, desperately hoping the comments on his cooking, ironing and honesty would impress me enough to employ him. On one occasion, a young man whipped off his skull cap and gave my shoes a quick polish, then asked me for a 'dash'.

I'd planned to apologise to my Nigerian colleague for forgetting to wipe the blackboard but when I saw him in the staffroom he looked so unfriendly that I decided against it. Nonetheless, I began to see the world through his eyes, and to understand his anger at this legacy of deference and humiliation. I came to admire the way he had confronted me, and demonstrated to his students that they could call baturis to account. But my favourite act of resistance against we baturis took place every Sunday around 5 p.m., when I played cricket at Kano Club. Two Tuareg night watchmen, dressed in their dark blue head wraps, flowing clothes, and with swords in their waistbands, walked very slowly across the cricket field on their way to work. They would cross the wicket between the stumps, infuriating the white cricketers who stood there in an impotent rage as the Tuareg held up the cricket match. Perhaps they had no idea it was sacrilege to walk across the wicket, but I strongly suspected that their slow walk was an act of defiance. They may have worked for us, but, jobs aside, they were still proud and noble desert nomads, who kowtowed to no one.

Ironically, I had come to Nigeria full of admiration for the falconers of Empire, and yet, rather than flying a hawk myself, I had begun to question my naive view of that very Empire.

# SEVENTEEN

Few peregrines are left . . . they may not survive. Many die on their backs, clutching insanely at the sky in their last convulsions, withered and burnt away by the filthy insidious pollen of farm chemicals . . .

– J. A. Baker, *The Peregrine*, 1967

It was the beginning of July 1967. Up early, and delighted to be home again, I was once again walking my old haunts, walking through green fields with grazing cows, through woods, the trees heavy with green leaves.

I walked past Tankersley church, with its square Norman tower, and down the lane to Tankersley Old Hall, where I stopped dead in my tracks. Side by side and all facing the same way, five beautiful young kestrels were perched on the roof of a hen hut in the field in front of the ruined Hall. They had hatched from their reddish-brown mottled eggs on the same crumbling nest ledge as the two Keses I'd trained over the previous two summers. Had I not gone to Africa, one of those kestrels would most likely have been in the mews, and later today would be flying across the meadow to my glove, a creance trailing behind it.

The young kestrels took flight from their perch. One landed on a telegraph pole across the field, the others found perches on the crumbling sandstone ledges and the ruined walls of Tankersley Old Hall. After I'd watched them for a few minutes

I turned into Bell Ground Wood and headed for home. Two summers ago, when John and I had walked this path with a ladder on our shoulders, the moonlight hadn't penetrated the foliage and underfoot the path had been pitch black. This morning as I walked through the wood strong sunlight threw shadows and speckled the path with dark leaf patterns.

One morning I returned from a walk and found a blue airmail letter on the table. It had two Nigerian stamps, three pence and six pence, and a postmark which read: 2pm, 26th July, 1967, Zaria. I still have the letter. Turning it over, I read the back and saw it was from Aliyu A Sani, the lad who'd thought it strange that we say 'in a bed', rather than 'on a bed', who had returned to his home town for the school holidays. I carried the letter outside and sat on the doorstep in the backyard to read it, my heart racing. To my surprise his letter began: 'You left us with heavy hearts of loosing such a very good teacher . . . thank you for your kindness and the hard work you did . . . Nigeria is very greatfull for your help . . .'

Aliyu went on to say: 'We shall never forget you, especially I, the writer of this letter.'

Aliyu's kind words brought home to me how irresponsible I'd been. While in Nigeria I'd done my best for Aliyu and the other lads I'd taught. Even so I was a secondary modern school write-off and grammar school dropout, and I'd kidded my way into VSO under false pretences for no better reasons than that I wanted to experience life beyond the pit village, and fly a falcon I couldn't fly at home. As I sat on the doorstep with the blue airmail letter in my hand I felt I'd let down Aliyu, and all the other multilingual, clever, well-mannered lads I'd taught in Nigeria.

A week or so after I'd flown home from Nigeria, I'd been sad to read that civil war had broken out after the Eastern Region split from the Northern and Western Regions to become Biafra. Learning that a murderous machete-carrying mob were on their way to the rest house where I was sleeping, or being glared at by four men carrying machetes and a club, weren't the only terrifying experiences I'd had in Nigeria. On my way to Kano to begin my teaching job, the Land Rover I was travelling in was stopped at a bridge, where a soldier with bloodshot eyes and sweat running down his face held a rifle to my chest through the open window, then demanded I open my suitcase so he could search it for ammunition and explosives. Yet, except for those awful moments, I hadn't had experiences that suggested war had been brewing. Aliyu's blue airmail letter ended: 'Please, sir, pray for the returning peace and unity for my beloved country NIGERIA.'

Before signing off: 'Your obedient student, ALIYU A SANI.'

When I'd returned home, Jackie had travelled to London overnight to meet me off the plane at Heathrow airport. As we travelled in a taxi to the railway station, holding hands, smiling, talking, it was as if we'd never been apart. I'd bought her a present from a street trader in Kano. Later, at home, when I rummaged around in the suitcase and handed it to her, she ran her finger over the bands of tiny metal studs beaten into the golden brown-coloured bone bangle. Then she noticed the parts worn smooth over the years, maybe over the centuries, by brushing against other bangles worn on the wrist. As Jackie examined the bangle then slipped it on her wrist, we thought about the generations of women in colourful wraparound dresses who'd worn it, carrying water from the well, pounding grain with a large pestle, pounding clothes on a rock beside the river.

Over the summer of 1967, while waiting for my Environmental Studies course to begin, I worked as a building labourer, and in the evenings Jackie and I walked the countryside surrounding the village, then called in at the pub, where Procol Harum's 'A Whiter Shade of Pale' played repeatedly on the juke box. It was good to be home, and when the robins sang in September and the grass and the bushes sparkled with dew I didn't want to leave. But then I read J. A. Baker's *The Peregrine*, which had been published that year. I was gripped by this beautifully written elegy to what at the time seemed a lost species of falcon. Baker also mentions sparrowhawks, writing that they 'were hard to find . . . being so few and so wary'. Somehow, having seen a sparrowhawk flying across scrubland in Africa seemed to emphasise its absence back here, and brought home to me that I might never again see one of that 'banished race of beautiful barbarians', which were virtually extinct in Britain. As for the peregrines' plight, it seemed they were doomed, on the verge of being wiped out by poisonous agricultural chemicals, and that I'd never see the 'Fawken gentill' and 'Tercell gentill' of the *Boke of St Albans* fly over our moorlands and cliffs. My enthusiasm reignited by Baker's book, I couldn't wait to go to college to begin my research. I had decided to write my dissertation on the fall from grace of hawks and their destruction by pesticides.

# EIGHTEEN

Whosoever hee bee that can flye his Hawke every day, shall
have every day a good and perfect Hawke.

– Symon Latham, *Latham's Faulconry, or The Faulcon's Lure and
Cure*, 1615

At college in Leicester I lived in halls of residence in term
time. Some weekends Jackie visited me, and on others
I came home to see her. In the spring of 1968, one Friday
evening when home for the weekend, on my way to see
Jackie I called in at Barry's house to see if he fancied an early
morning walk next day. He was in the garden, sitting on a
kitchen chair and reading. When I approached, he looked
up, smiling.

'Hey up.'

'How do,' I replied, nodding at the buff-coloured book.
'What tha reading?'

He turned the title towards me: *A Kestrel for a Knave*. It
was a proof of his soon-to-be published novel. Turning the
pages, he found what he was looking for near the front and
held it up. On an otherwise blank page, I read:

To
RICHARD

I realised that he'd dedicated the novel to me.

On Saturday I finished reading the novel in one sitting, delighted by the way that my hawking experiences had helped Barry's fiction: Billy Casper being refused permission to take a falconry book out of the library; Billy conversing with a tawny owl in the wood, just as my friend John had on that night we'd carried the ladder to climb up to the kestrel's nest; Billy taking his young kestrel from a nest in a ruined Hall at night to avoid being caught by the farmer. Like me, this Billy was a school write-off who taught himself falconry from a book and trained a kestrel called Kes, but there the similarity ended. I found myself engrossed. As I read on I was carried along by the way that Barry had told this powerful story of the fifteen-year-old; a boy neglected by his single mother and bullied by his older brother, a miner. His brother's name was Jud. When he discovered Billy hadn't placed what would have been a winning horseracing bet, as he had been asked to, and instead had spent the stake money on fish and chips, Jud killed Billy's kestrel and dumped it in a dustbin.

One weekend, when I called around for him to go on a pre-arranged walk, Barry was sitting outside on the step putting on his boots. As a youth, when he'd jived to rock 'n' roll in his fingertip-length jacket and narrow-legged trousers, Barry looked flamboyant. In fact he was the opposite: reserved, quite shy really, and he spoke in an understated way and disliked exaggeration. So that morning, when I excitedly told him about a newspaper review of his newly published novel, *A Kestrel for a Knave*, in which the reviewer had called his book a masterpiece, he looked up from tying his bootlaces and said: 'That's a bit of a hyperbole.'

On another weekend, as I passed Barry's house on my way to see Jackie, I saw him brushing his black and white collie, Bess, outside the kitchen door.

'All right?' I asked, as I walked up the drive.

'Not too bad.'

As we stood talking, in his low-key manner and without a hint of excitement Barry said: 'A producer wants to make *A Kestrel for a Knave* into a film.'

'Wow. That's brilliant,' I said, delighted for him.

'I'll believe it when it happens,' he replied.

A few months later, on a sunny morning in late June, home from college for the summer holidays, I was carrying an empty cardboard box as I walked through meadows full of buttercups on my way to Barry's house. It seemed the film was about to happen, and what was wonderful for me was that Barry had asked me to be the film's falconer. But for that we needed kestrels, and the plan this morning was for Barry to hold the ladder while I took the young hawks I would need to train for the film, before carrying them home in the cardboard box.

When I opened the door and stepped into the kitchen, Barry's collie dog, Bess, ran up to me wagging her tail. Bending to stroke her, I called: 'Anybody in?'

'Hang on,' Barry replied, before coming through the door looking pale-faced and ill.

'What's up?'

'Film's off,' he said.

'What?' I asked.

'Let's go in there,' he said, pointing into the lounge.

The Hollywood company that had agreed to fund the film had pulled out. I was devastated. It wasn't just that I would now have to spend my summer holiday from college working as a building labourer, rather than training kestrels for a cinema film; it was much more. I'd been a school write-off, I'd jacked in my office job at the Town Hall and I'd kidded my way into a voluntary job in Nigeria. But this summer, finally, I'd been offered a job I was passionate about, which required skills I'd taught myself. Finally I'd landed a job I could be proud of.

'I don't know what to do about the kestrels,' Barry said. I looked at him.

'How's tha mean? We won't need any kestrels now.'

'We probably won't. But there's a slight chance it might happen – Tony's still trying to raise the money to make it,' Barry told me.

I understood Barry's worry. The kestrels would soon fledge their nest at Tankersley Old Hall, and even if Tony Garnett, the producer, did raise the money to make the film it would only have to be cancelled again because Billy Casper wouldn't have a kestrel to train. Back then, hawks had to be taken from the wild, unlike today, when they are bred by falconers and can be bought. I told Barry I'd take the kestrels anyway, and if the film wasn't made I'd fly them in the evenings when I came home from my labouring job, and hack them back to the wild in the autumn, before I returned to college. Still feeling ill with worry, Barry went to bed to recover and carrying the cardboard box I went to find Jackie.

To prove what I was about to do was legal, I'd brought the government licence I'd been granted to show the farmer at Old Hall Farm. As we walked through Bell Ground Wood together, I took it from my pocket and gave it to Jackie to read. She was surprised when she saw it authorised me to take three kestrels 'for the purpose of falconry'. Having read *A Kestrel for a Knave*, Jackie assumed I would only need to take one kestrel. But it had dawned on me that one hawk might become ill or lost, and that by taking three I'd be able to prepare them to fly at different times. This would allow filming to go on longer and make filming them easier, assuming, that is, that different hawks could be cut into a sequence of shots to give the impression that just one hawk was being trained. Two kestrels would be too few, I reasoned, and four difficult to find enough food for, and too time-consuming to train. So I'd applied for a licence to take three.

In 1965, when my friend John and I had leaned a ladder against the moonlit ruins of Tankersley Old Hall, we were trespassing. As if that wasn't bad enough, we didn't have a licence. This sunny morning three summers later, Jackie and I carried a ladder across the field of buttercups and leaned it against the Old Hall with the permission of the farmer; in fact it was his ladder we'd borrowed.

When I reached into the kestrels' nest hole I looked down at Jackie in dismay.

'What's wrong?' she called up from the foot of the ladder.

'It's empty.'

Reaching in up to my shoulder, I felt around the crumbling sandstone ledge. I heard a gasp from inside the nest then something sharp raked across the back of my hand. Talons! Relief surged through me as I reached into a crevice, put my hand around the young kestrel's back, pinned its wings down to its side and gently eased it out.

Jackie held the cardboard box while I put in the young hawk. Its large brown eyes were bright and clear, a sign of good health. It still had a few specks of down on its head, and its black-barred reddish-brown tail feathers were almost fully grown. It was at the perfect age to take. I closed the lid, and Jackie and I walked through Bell Ground Wood without saying a word. My mind was racing. Last summer five kestrels had hatched in the nest. I'd been expecting there to be four or five young in the nest this year, but someone must have got there before me. One kestrel wasn't enough. As we walked I racked my brains desperately, wondering where I could get two more kestrels. Keith, I suddenly thought. Keith, who had lived in the village before becoming a gamekeeper in Wentworth.

A few days later, as I was kneeling on the lawn cutting up hawk food on the chopping board, Keith walked down Barry's garden with a box. He was telling me how he'd taken the two young kestrels in the box from an old crows' nest their parents had taken over, when Barry's sheepdog, Bess, ran down the garden followed by Barry. Bess was usually friendly, but today she barked wildly at Keith, and when he reached out his hand to befriend her she raised her top lip and snarled; she'd caught the scent of the fox Keith had sat up all night to shoot after it had killed his pheasants. Holding her by the collar, Barry led Bess back into the house while I carried the box containing the two young kestrels down to the mews, then eased my way sideways through the door and closed it behind me. The two new young kestrels gasped as I took them out of the box and put them on a perch. One had an exceptionally bright yellow cere – the bare patch above its beak – and I named it Yellow Cere.

For the purposes of the film, all three kestrels would need to respond to the name Kes when called to the glove and lure. Yet they also needed individual names. One day when out with my airgun searching for hawk food, the sight of the colliery slag heap reminded me of a story Dad had told me. He said three miners at his pit were best mates, inseparable, and that one day when they'd walked into the canteen a fellow miner had shouted, 'Here they come, Freeman, Hardy and Willis', the name of a chain of shoe shops. I liked the names. So the kestrel I'd taken from the Old Hall became Freeman. Yellow Cere became Hardy and the other hawk which gamekeeper Keith had brought became Willis.

Just a few days later, in early July, holding Freeman firmly in my hands, I found myself on the platform of a hydraulic crane as it was slowly raised up the ruined wall of Tankersley Old Hall. The film, which would later be called *Kes*, was going ahead. Barry had told me that Tony Richardson, the legendary producer/director who'd made one of my favourite films, *The Loneliness of the Long Distance Runner*, had rung United Artists in Los Angeles and raised the money on behalf of Tony Garnett and Ken Loach. So here we were, about to film. In Barry's novel Billy Casper discovers a nest when he sees a kestrel fly out. After being refused permission to take out a falconry book from the library, he steals one from a bookshop, then takes a young kestrel from the nest in a ruined hall. Today, I was helping in the filming of the scene where Billy Casper, played by fourteen-year-old David Bradley, takes his young kestrel from the nest.

As the platform of the hydraulic crane was slowly raised up to the nest hole, standing beside me was Ken Loach, the film's director. Ken, who was slim and wore glasses, a leather jacket and jeans, seemed too polite and reserved to be a director. Yet he was friendly and had a quiet authority. Also on the platform, holding the film camera, was Chris Menges, who had dark hair and a beard, and who, like Ken, was polite and reserved. When we reached the nest hole I carefully put Freeman into the nest I'd taken her from a few days earlier. Chris then filmed David as he climbed the wall and reached into the nest and took the young kestrel out again. I knew that Freeman should have been in the mews for at least another week, for her feathers were 'in the blood', which is to say still soft and blue at the bases of their shafts, and they could easily be damaged. Yet if we'd waited until her feathers were 'hard penned', moments after I'd put her in the nest hole she would most likely have flown out again and disappeared over Bell Ground Wood. I was relieved after David had taken the kestrel from the nest hole without mishap, then dismayed to discover that it was just the first take; and so it went on, with me putting the young hawk back into the nest hole, David climbing up and taking her out again, Ken Loach calling 'cut', and David passing the hawk to me to replace in the nest yet again. Eventually Ken was satisfied with what had been filmed, and we were lowered back down in the hydraulic crane.

Stress can cause 'fret marks' on feathers still 'in the blood', which, like hunger traces, manifest as razor-like cuts which weaken the feathers. So after the young kestrel had been put in and taken out of the nest time after time, and been raised and lowered in the hydraulic crane, I was keen to get Freeman back into the cardboard box so that the darkness would calm her. Just as I was about to do this, I was approached by the sound recordist who told me he needed 'wild track' – non-synchronised sound – to be used over the shots of David taking the hawk from the nest.

Out of the wind and well away from the noise of the film crew, I crouched behind a stone wall holding the young kestrel firmly in my hands. I'd been worried about her developing fret marks through fear, and here I was tilting poor Freeman from side to side, deliberately making her call out in alarm, 'kikiki . . . kikiki . . . kikiki'. Crouched beside me, the sound recordist was holding a microphone, recording her cries. I understood he needed to do his job, but after a few alarm calls I insisted on returning the frightened young kestrel to the cardboard box.

David Bradley, the boy who played Billy Casper in the film, was small for a fourteen-year-old. With his short hair and fringe, he looked like the waif and stray I'd imagined Billy to be when reading Barry's novel. I have a photograph from that summer of 1968 in which David has the young kestrel Willis on his glove. I'm standing beside him hiding a piece of meat in my hand, ready to take over should the hawk begin to bate. In the photograph the top of David's head barely reaches my shoulder, and over his head and behind him is the brick-fronted air raid shelter mews in Barry's garden. The wooden laths I'd fixed into the sawn-out window in the door were still intact, but the coat of paint I'd put on three years earlier, in 1965, is peeling and rain and damp have creased and curled the piece of plywood that I'd nailed across the top of the door to strengthen it. The terrible state of the mews door embarrasses me, but my neglect went much further than not repainting the door. I should have worked out how to fix an extra door, so I could close the first door behind me, before opening the second. But I didn't and paid dearly for my carelessness.

A few days before the three young hawks' feathers would be fully grown, I plucked and cut up their food and put it in my falconry bag; then, after carefully opening the door of the mews a few inches, I eased my way in sideways. To my horror Hardy – the hawk also known as Yellow Cere – flew straight at me, eyes staring wildly, and in a blur of flapping wings she was up and over my shoulder through the gap at the top of the door. Distraught and fuming at my stupidity for not fitting an extra door, shuffling sideways I eased my way back out of the mews and closed the door.

I couldn't see the young kestrel anywhere – not in the garden or perched on the house, nor at any of the neighbours'. Running up the drive, I stared wildly at walls, fences, bushes, trees and the rooftops of the houses opposite, then I ran back down the garden and through the gate into the fields. As I wandered the stubble fields and meadows the sense of loss was added to by the futility of my search, by the senselessness of it. For if I did see her, I wouldn't be able to capture her and bring her back. She was untrained and completely wild. I was nothing to her, I had no hold over her, I couldn't call her name, call her to the glove, call her to the lure. She didn't yet associate any of these actions with food, and so she was lost, irretrievable. Yet I continued to wander the fields desperately looking for her, reminding myself that when she'd escaped her jesses were hanging loose. Unlike T. H. White's doomed goshawk, she had no leash trailing behind, but still she was unable to fend for herself and so would probably die of starvation. And that was entirely my responsibility.

I was in despair. I hadn't even started training the hawks and I'd already lost one, nor had I any idea where I could find a replacement, as the other young kestrels that Keith had left in the nest would have fledged. A few days later I heard that Towser's younger brother, Chris, was rearing a young kestrel. There still might be unfledged kestrels in the nest he had taken his from, I thought, so I headed over to Chris's house. As I walked along the street where he lived he appeared around the corner of a house with his kestrel on his fist. Seeing its feathers were fully grown, I knew this hawk's nest mates would have fledged the nest weeks ago. I stroked the breast feathers of Chris's kestrel with my finger as I told him my woes. Chris listened sympathetically, and then with amazing generosity said I could have his kestrel as a replacement for the lost Hardy. Later that day, he released her into the mews to join Freeman and Willis and so she became the second Hardy. I never saw the original again.

By now, the field of wheat had been cut and as I made my way across, towards Barry's garden, a black flock of rooks and jackdaws rose up out of the stubble. A week or so earlier I'd walked this field at night, sneaking into the dark mews to shine a torch on Freeman and Willis to check if their feathers were still 'in the blood' or 'hard penned'. On those starlit nights I was aware of the sharp stubble crunching under my boots. This morning my attention was caught by the twitter of swallows, a skylark singing, and, a couple of meadows away, the lowing of a cow.

One of the carpenters who worked for the film's art department had made me a long perch that stretched the length of the mews. Peering in through the wooden slats on the mews door, it was lovely to see the three kestrels perched side by side, each contentedly standing on one leg. As had become my routine, I pushed the spikes of the three block perches into the lawn, carried each kestrel out of the mews, and, one by one, let her hop from my glove on to her perch.

Occasionally the three young hawks would 'rouse' – raise their feathers, shake them, then allow them to drop back into place: a sign of contentment. Other times, cocking their heads to one side, the three young hawks watched as swifts flew high in the sky above the garden. Seeing the kestrels, I was struck by how different they were. Freeman, who'd come from the nest at Tankersley Old Hall, looked like the pictures of kestrels you see in books, for she was handsome with her head in perfect proportion to her body; Willis, who'd been reared by her parents in an old crows' nest, had a small head, large eyes and a really long, curved beak; and Hardy, who Chris had brought me, was noticeably smaller than either Freeman or Willis. Her wings drooped down by her sides, quite unlike the other two, who crossed their wing tips neatly across their backs as they perched on their blocks.

A wild screaming hawk, hanging upside down from the glove, wouldn't have done David or the young kestrel's confidence any good at all. To try and prevent this from ever happening, I decided to man, train and fly the kestrels twice a day myself, to make them tame and amenable before I introduced them to David. Freeman's training was well on its way, for she was already flying free to the glove. Willis had become hard penned a few days after Freeman, so her training had begun later and I was still flying her to the glove on the creance, but before I flew those two hawks this morning I needed to see what my new kestrel, the second Hardy, could do.

Head lowered, tail fanned, Hardy now tugged at the raw beef held between my gloved fingers as I walked through the stubble field. To my dismay her tail feathers had 'hunger traces', or maybe they were 'fret marks' caused by stress. The location of the damage, halfway down her tail, suggested that the lack of nutrition which had temporarily thwarted feather growth had happened while she was still in the nest. Noticing small feathers from a previous meal still on her beak, I took a closer look and saw that her beak was also cracked and that the feathers had become stuck in the crack. Whatever had taken place in the nest to cause her temporary starvation or heart-racing stress, it seemed the same thing had also damaged her beak.

Leaving the field of stubble, I walked across the meadow and tipped my glove, encouraging Hardy to hop on to the fence. As the young kestrel perched there, bits of feathers still stuck in the cracks in her beak, her wings drooping by her sides, I thought what a poor little thing she looked. I suddenly feared she might not be a good enough flyer to appear in the film.

With Hardy still perched on the fence, I turned and walked back across the meadow. As male and female juveniles have identical plumage, I hadn't known whether they were hes or shes, but I'd called both my Keses she. Initially I'd imagined Freeman, Hardy and Willis as males, and had only begun to call them she when I remembered that Billy Casper called his hawk a she in Barry's novel. Whatever Chris had called Hardy – 'he' or 'she'– before he'd passed her on to me, didn't seem to matter.

'Come on, Kes,' I called. 'Come on, girl.'

And she was off the fence in an instant, flying fast and powerfully across the meadow to my raised glove, the creance trailing behind her. Delighted, on her next flight I untied the creance from her jesses and flew her free.

Later that morning, leaving the streets of stone-built terraces, I walked past the red-brick council houses at the edge of the village. It was when these houses were being built that John and I had borrowed a ladder and carried it to Tankersley Old Hall in the moonlight. Three summers later, one of those houses was being filmed as Billy Casper's home. Behind it there was a patch of spare land where the catering van was parked. Having flown the three hawks, as I did each morning, I was on my way to have lunch. Barry spent his days with the film crew, and now, carrying my tray from the catering van, I joined him and David Bradley at one of the trestle tables to tell them how the hawks had flown.

After lunch, I wandered off to look at the hawk's mews which the film's carpenters had built on the spare land behind the garden of the house. They had used planks of wood and fitted a metal-barred window in the door. Opening the door, I saw the screen perch inside, then I looked into the shed they'd built beside the mews, which had a bench on which Billy could cut up the hawk's meat and fasten it to the lure. Further across the spare land, the film's carpenters had built a large, ugly shed. Inside, the film's art director held out a can of paint he'd just mixed and asked Ken Loach if that was the shade he wanted. The shed's interior had been made up as Billy Casper's living room and I was surprised how realistic it looked, with its tiled coal fireplace and wallpapered chimney breast. Through the large window I could see a hedge, and beyond that a field where David Bradley would fly the kestrels. I was worried that dozens of people would pour out of the houses to watch David as he flew the hawks, distracting them and sending them off in search of their usual flying ground back on the other side of the village. But there was nothing I could do except hope.

The day after, returning from a search for hawk food, I was walking through the stubble field with my air rifle under my arm when Barry and Ken Loach came through the gate from Barry's garden into the field. Barry had told Ken about my worries that we might lose the hawks if David flew them in the field behind the film set, and Ken had come to see if this was a suitable alternative. He gazed across the fields, then after what seemed ages said he liked the fields, the fence posts, the telegraph poles, the pit slag heap in the distance, and said he'd film the hawk flying scenes here. I was delighted.

# NINETEEN

The fierce and eager hawks down thrilling from the skies
Make sundry cancelleers . . .

– Michael Drayton, *Poly-Olbion*, poem, 1622

For most of the hawking scenes to be shot over the summer, all three hawks would be needed. After each flight for the camera, the kestrel would be given a small reward of beef, which would eventually dull her appetite and reduce her keenness to fly. The next hawk would then be brought on, then the last one. This significantly extended the length of time the hawks could be filmed. In the completed film, of course, the flights of the hawks were edited to give the impression of a single hawk. Today, the hawks were to be filmed flying on the creance. The night before, on receiving the call sheet with the details of today's filming schedule, I'd calculated each hawk's food so it would be at its flying weight when today's filming was due to begin. This morning I'd nervously carried each kestrel from the screen perch to the weighing scales on the shelf behind the mews door, and with great relief discovered that each hawk's weight was spot on. Now each kestrel was on her block perch on the lawn, slowly flapping her wings each time I passed, showing she was keen to fly.

Raising his glove, David called: 'Come on, Kes.'

Freeman launched herself off the fence. Untroubled by all the unfamiliar things around her – the camera, the boom swinger's large grey furry microphone, the crew or the creance trailing behind her – the kestrel flew fast and low across the meadow and up on to David's glove. David walked to the fence, let the hawk hop on to it, then walked back to the middle of the meadow and called her again. Again she flew fast and low and up on to his glove. As David walked back to the fence to give Freeman her last flight, I gave Barry a piece of beef from my falconry bag and asked him to go and fetch Hardy from her block perch in the garden.

After Freeman's last flight I'd unfastened the creance from her jesses and was feeding her up on my glove when Barry walked across the field with Hardy on his glove. Barry handed Hardy over to David. I handed Freeman over to Barry, then fastened the creance on to Hardy's jesses. As David walked to the fence with Hardy on his glove Barry looked upset.

'All right?' I asked.

'Yeah,' Barry said unconvincingly.

'What's up?'

'Hardy tried to gulp down a big piece of beef. I tried to take it off her but she bated and hung upside down at the end of her jesses screaming.'

'Did she swallow any meat?' I asked, panicking.

'Yeah – a great lump. After I'd managed to get her back on the glove.'

I was so angry with Barry, he later told me I'd looked at him as if he wasn't fit to have a hawk on his glove. It was my job to prepare the hawks for filming, and I was convinced Hardy would still be in a rage, and that, with the edge taken off her appetite, she would embarrass me on the first day of filming by refusing to fly.

David had walked back into the middle of the meadow.

'When you're ready, David,' Ken Loach called.

David raised his glove.

'Come on, Kes . . . Come on, girl.'

Hardy was off the fence immediately and flying fast across the field. Barry and I looked at each other and blew out a sigh of relief. After her next flight I stayed with the camera crew and David, while Barry took Freeman back to the mews and fetched Willis for the creance flying scene.

Standing in the middle of the field David raised his glove. 'Come on, Kes,' he called . . . And called . . . And called . . .

It looked as if I was going to be embarrassed on the first day of filming after all. Large eyes bulging out of her small head, Willis prepared to launch herself into flight, but, racked by indecision, she turned and walked along the fence, stopped, prepared to fly but again, when tantalisingly close to taking off, she turned and walked back along the fence, the creance trailing behind her. And so it went on, her hesitation becoming unbearable to watch. I was about to tell David to go and pick her up, and suggest to Ken Loach that he abandon filming, when the young hawk suddenly took flight. Flying high and fast, she looked as if she would overshoot David but she braked, hovered over David's head and flew back to the fence. David called the young kestrel again and she was just as hesitant, walking up and down the fence. When she eventually took to the air, once again she hovered over David's head, ignoring his upheld glove. With her training appearing to have gone backwards, I decided not to fly Willis for the camera until she improved.

The next morning I carried Willis into the field. I attached the creance to the swivel on her jesses, put the young kestrel on the fence, then walked into the middle of the field and raised my glove.

'Come on, Kes.'

She didn't move. I called again and again, encouraging her, pleading with her, willing her to take flight. She wouldn't, and I moved in closer, wiggling the meat around in my gloved fingers to tempt her to launch herself off the fence. She just stood there, until, overcome by frustration and fear that I wouldn't get her trained in time, I'm embarrassed to say that I did something stupid; futile. I shouted at her. This was definitely not the gentleness that it takes to redeem a hawk, and I had to calm myself, lowering my voice back to gentle, encouraging calls before she eventually took wing and flew across the field. To my dismay, just before she reached me she slowed, rose into the air, hovered a moment, and then sheered off with the creance trailing behind her until it caught on the fence. I hauled her in, flapping around in panic. She looked bewildered as I carried her on the glove across the field and back to the mews.

I decided to try and make Willis tamer by bringing her into contact with more people. After spreading newspapers on the floor, I put her on a perch in Barry's house so she'd see people from the film's production department traipsing in and out to use the telephone. Years later, on reading a translation of *D'Arcussia's Falconry*, written in 1643, I smiled to discover it had been the practice in seventeenth-century France to keep goshawks tame by placing them on a perch in the kitchen, which in those days would have been the busiest room in the house.

I also manned Willis by walking around the village carrying the nervous kestrel on my glove. One day a man I knew, referring to the title of Barry's novel, jokingly shouted across the road: 'Are tha the knave?'

Grinning, I walked on. Another day when I walked around the village with Willis, David joined me with Hardy on his fist and we called in at Jackie's house. Her mother spread out newspapers to catch the mutes and invited us to sit down. Rather than enquire about David's life as a 'film star', she asked him how he was 'getting on' at school. In the end Willis became so content when being carried on the glove that she occasionally fluffed her feathers, tucked one leg into her breast feathers and stood on the other.

Yet Willis's flying did not improve. She only flew to the glove when I approached to within a few yards. I'd thought it was just nervousness that made her reluctant. Now I began to wonder if her flying weight was too high and decided to feed her smaller meals. So I kept up the extra manning, reduced her flying weight from seven ounces to six and a half, and within a couple of days she flew across the field three or four times on the creance the moment I raised my glove. A day or two later Willis flew free to the lure but, with her eyes staring wildly, she hovered above me once again, too nervous to grab it until I let it fall on the grass. Then, like a wild kestrel which had spotted a field vole, she closed her wings and dropped on to the lure.

One day I found myself tramping across fields up to an area that until very recently had been farmland. Now it had been turned into a new, recently seeded playing field for the secondary school where I had been a pupil. It was only a few fields up the hill from the field in which I flew the hawks, but from here I could see the village below, and, beyond the village, Tankersley church with its square tower. Barry would be teaching kids games on this field in a few weeks' time as he was about to start a new job at my old school. His reasoning for leaving his job in Barnsley was that this new job, only a short walk from his house, would allow him more time for writing in the evenings. In *A Kestrel for a Knave*, Barry fictionalised a story I'd told him about how my eccentric headmaster, Ben, had mistakenly caned a boy who'd done nothing wrong and had only come to Ben's office with a message from a teacher. Although entertained by my tales of Ben, Barry wouldn't have applied for the job had he still been headmaster of the school. But things had moved on since 1960. Now, eight years later, the school had a female head teacher who frowned on corporal punishment, and it would later become a successful mixed boys' and girls' comprehensive. The kind of school I would love to have attended, where every child walked through the same school gates full of hope, having not been led to believe they were already failures at the age of eleven, and where we all had the opportunity to take exams and even apply to college or university.

This July morning in 1968 I was on my old school's new playing field for educational reasons. Freeman had taken to landing on fence posts after one stoop to the lure, and I was looking for a new flying ground without fence posts. The playing field looked promising. First of all it was the summer holidays and it wouldn't be used for sport until autumn. It was also well away from the school – a five-minute walk – in a quiet location hidden from the road by a row of bungalows. On another side was the old graveyard of Law Hill church, and on the other two sides were a field of barley and a potato field. As I stood looking around the distant perimeter I was unable to see any tempting perches, and I decided this was going to be the new flying ground.

Barry wasn't meeting up with the film crew until later, so, rather than taking the hawks to the flying ground one at a time, as I usually did, I asked him to help me carry Freeman and Hardy to the school field along with their block perches. We walked down the garden to pick up the hawks, which were on their perches on the lawn, but when I offered Hardy my glove she refused to hop on to it from her block perch. To my horror I noticed that her normally round eyes were oval-shaped and that her nictitating membranes had moved across each eye and given them an ominous grey colour. Crouching on her perch, she looked half dead, her wings drooping by her sides, her eyes half shut. Unsure what to do, I decided to leave her on her perch in the morning sun, fly Freeman, and then consult my falconry books. If I couldn't find a cause for Hardy's symptoms I'd ring a vet immediately.

With Freeman on my glove and Barry beside me, we trudged through the fields up to the new flying ground on the school playing field in silence. Barry's face was white with anxiety. The problem was that Willis was still refusing to chase the swung lure, hovering above me and only landing on the lure when I threw it to the ground. This meant that if Hardy was dying, which seemed very likely, the film's success would depend on Freeman, who was currently stooping to the lure only once before flying off in search of a fence post to land on. If I couldn't get her flying to the lure properly, the film would have to be called off. Finding another kestrel to train this late in the year would be impossible.

Standing in the middle of the school field I took the lure out of my falconry bag and began to swing it in circles by my side.

'Kes . . . Come on, Kes.'

Standing at the edge of the field, Barry raised his arm and cast off Freeman. Eyes fixed on me, she flew low and silently over the grass. I increased the speed of the swinging lure then threw out my arm, letting the lure's weight and momentum carry it into the kestrel's path. When she tried to grab it, I twitched it away and swept it in front of me. Instead of following its rising arc into the sky she flew straight on, looking for somewhere to land – but all she could see were distant crops and back gardens.

'Kes . . . Come on, Kes.'

As she turned back and flew in low, I threw out the lure and swept it in front of me again. Again she pursued it, then flew on as if looking for somewhere to perch before returning and flying in to try and grab the lure. By now Freeman seemed to be thinking that the only way she'd get a rest was by catching the lure. Her circuits around the field were less far-ranging and she was flying with more determination. When she flew in for the fifth time I lobbed the lure out for her to catch. Beak open, panting hard, she stood with her prize on the newly sown grass.

Relieved, I decided to fly her again. Barry cast her off from the edge of the field. By the time she reached me she was panting hard and flying so low that she was almost brushing the grass. Realising she was exhausted, I threw out the lure for her to take. She had flown so close to the ground and so slowly Barry said it was almost as if she'd been walking.

Twenty minutes later, with Freeman still feeding up on my glove, Barry and I returned to his garden. I'd feared finding Hardy dead on the lawn beside her block perch, but, to our delight, her eyes were now round and bright again and she was ready to fly.

'Kes . . . Come on, Kes.'

Stepping forward with my right foot, I threw the lure into Hardy's path as she approached fast and low across the playing field. But instead of trying to grab it, wings pumping she curved up into the sky. Shortening the lure line by pulling it through my fingers, I swung the lure in circles by my side while looking up at the kestrel above me. She flicked over. I threw the lure up to her. Head first, wings beating furiously, she pursued it, twisting two or three times in the air as she hurtled downwards. Then, as she levelled out at the last moment, she tried to strike the lure with her talons, missed, and curved back up into the sky, flicking over to begin another corkscrewing vertical stoop, or cancelleer.

Just over half an hour earlier Hardy had seemed on the edge of death. Now she performed stoop after stoop, some with two or three twists, as she descended head first out of the sky. I leaned backwards, almost falling over as I threw up the lure and swept it downwards and upwards. Soon I was panting, and I felt relieved when she flew off on a circuit around the field. When she returned this time she flew in high and descended in a vertical stoop the moment she was above my head. I just about managed to throw out the lure and get the line tight enough to keep it tantalisingly out of her clutches as she plummeted downwards and then broke her descent by curving upwards to begin yet another stoop. When at last I let her catch the lure, Barry approached with a smile as I fed up Hardy on the glove. She had been flying for ten minutes, he told me, and had done ten consecutive stoops before her first circuit of the field. Overall she'd stooped to the lure an astonishing sixty or seventy times.

Next morning an awful thought crossed my mind as I walked through the fields to put the hawks on their perches on the lawn. Had I made the same mistake with Freeman as I had with my first kestrel, Kes, and flown her at too low a weight? Was that why she was so exhausted? Leaving Hardy and Willis on their perches in the mews, I put Freeman on the scales – she weighed six ounces – then took her into the field and called her to the glove from a fence post. She rocketed across the field and on to the glove, where she began to devour the meat hungrily. But suddenly she lost her appetite: tearing and swallowing the meat seemed to have become too much of an effort. She was dangerously underweight. I hadn't flown her to the glove for a while, only the lure, and stupidly assumed her slow eating after flying to the lure was because she was unfit and exhausted, rather than a symptom of being underweight. Berating myself for my stupidity, I increased her daily food ration.

Three or four days later, Freeman weighed six and a quarter ounces, an increase of a quarter of an ounce on her earlier flying weight. Up on the school field at this new flying weight she had much more energy and had developed her own flying style. With shallow wingbeats, she flew in fast and low over the grass. I threw the lure into her path, and keeping it just out of her grasp swept it in front me as she pursued it, sending her curving up into the air, where, continuing to gain height, she flew out towards the potato field at the edge of the playing field. When she'd reached thirty feet or so she turned and flew back towards me, gradually losing height until she was once again skimming just above the grass, her eyes focused on the swinging lure.

# TWENTY

The falconer's primary aspiration should be to possess hunting
birds that he has trained through his own ingenuity . . .

> – Emperor Fredrick II, Emperor of the Romans, King of
> Jerusalem and Sicily, *The Book of the Divine Augustus*,
> circa 1250, translated by Casey Wood, 1943

One day at lunch at the catering van, Ken Loach
approached me and asked: 'Know any tough lads,
Richard? I'm looking for somebody to fight Jud in a pub
scene?'

'I've got a mate I could ask,' I replied.

So that evening I found myself walking along a street of
1930s brick council houses on my way to see a childhood
friend.

The last time I'd seen Budgie was in the pub with Towser,
five years earlier, when he'd bought us hot dogs and made us
laugh when he told us he'd been sacked from the colliery for
threatening to throw his boss down the pit shaft. All three
of us had been in the same class at junior school. There was
never any doubt that Budgie was cleverer than either Towser
or me, but he seemed to get fed up with school and began to
mess about. When we had all moved up to secondary modern
school he was put in the next-to-lowest ability stream. After
that we hardly saw him any more.

A sharp bark brought me out of my thoughts. A black Labrador was trotting up the path towards me, wagging her tail. There in the garden was Budgie, kneeling to feed his ferrets in a hutch, his sleeves rolled up to his elbows revealing tattooed forearms. When we'd run into him five years ago he had shoulder-length bleached blond hair. Now it was short and its original natural sandy colour.

'Hey up . . . What tha doing here?' Budgie said, smiling. Standing up, he looked at his Labrador and said: 'Fetch mi cigs.'

Wagging her tail the dog trotted into the house.

'Does tha fancy a part in the film of our kid's book?' I asked.

'Me?' he said laughing. 'The last part I played was a clown in that play in junior school, when tha was Father Christmas.'

'And tha got thrown out of that, didn't tha?' I said, grinning.

'I did – replaced by that lass who went to ballet classes.'

When the dog trotted up, Budgie gently took the packet of cigarettes from her mouth then said: 'Matches.'

By the time his Labrador was trotting back down the garden with the matches, I'd explained he'd play a character who fought Billy Casper's bullying brother, Jud, and that he didn't need to act, just be himself, and as Budgie bent to gently remove the box of matches from her mouth he said he'd give it a go.

So, a few days later, I found myself standing with Budgie as the crew prepared to film a fight scene in a Barnsley pub. Tony Garnett walked up to us, and, nodding across the room towards Freddie Fletcher, who played Billy's bullying brother, Jud, he leaned in towards Budgie and said: 'That big-headed bastard has it coming to him . . .' and went on to tell Budgie that Freddie needed a good hiding. Of course Tony was only psyching up Budgie, and his tactics perhaps worked too well. For when the sound and camera rolled and Ken Loach said 'OK, lads', Budgie attacked Freddie with such ferocity that Ken had to rush in and pull him away, and remind him that he was only meant to be pretending. Sadly the scene didn't make the final cut, but a few years later Budgie got another small part, this time as a miner arguing with a journalist in the television film *The Price of Coal*, written by Barry and directed by Ken.

Tony Garnett always looked cool, with his black-framed glasses, black polo-neck sweater and black raincoat. He had produced critically acclaimed drama films, such as *Cathy Come Home*, yet he was a modest man who made everyone feel valued. Once, for instance, he introduced me to someone by saying, 'This is Richard – a friend of mine', which surprised and moved me. Yet, although Tony was friendly he had presence and honesty; nor did he hang back from telling you what he thought.

One morning, for example, I'd been standing on the lawn in Barry's garden with my gloved hand raised high above my head. Hardy flew up vertically from the lawn, landed on my glove and took a small piece of meat, a 'bechin'. I then placed the hawk back on the grass, put another bechin into my gloved fingers, raised my arm as high as I could, and, once again, her wings flapping, the kestrel rocketed vertically up to my glove and ate the small piece of meat. It was at that point that Tony came walking down the garden path with a couple of visitors. When he asked what I was doing, I told him I used these 'high jumps' to exercise the hawks in addition to flying them to the lure, and I went on to explain I'd got the idea from the book *A Falcon in the Field* and that its author, Jack Mavrogordato, had been taught this technique by a well-known Pakistani falconer called Sheik S. M. Nasiruddin . . .

'Too esoteric, Richard, too esoteric,' Tony said, cutting me off in mid-flow.

Tony's response to my geeky reply amused me but a comment he made on another occasion took me aback. I was standing outside the mews with Tony and Barry, while someone was peering in at the hawks through the laths on the window in the mews door – I think it was a BBC drama producer friend of Tony's. It was then that Tony said: 'Barry's training the kestrels – and Richard's helping him.'

Amazed, I looked at Barry. I had expected him to put Tony right. Instead, looking ashamed, Barry raised his finger to his lips.

Later, I asked Barry about it. Looking embarrassed, he admitted, thinking only one hawk would be needed for the film he'd rashly told Tony he'd be able to train the kestrel. I was astounded. Barry had read T. H. White's *The Goshawk*, and he'd watched me train my kestrels and had borrowed my copy of *A Manual of Falconry* while writing his novel. But he'd never trained a kestrel; he hadn't even held a hawk on his glove until filming began. How he could have believed he'd be capable of training even one hawk for the film, while at the same time teaching himself and David Bradley how to do it, was beyond me. My reaction went deeper than not being recognised for the work I was doing. Tony's misapprehension had somehow unearthed feelings that I didn't even know I had. Barry had always been good at athletics and football, he'd always been my hero. I used to drive other kids crackers, forever telling them about his achievements. When I played sport or did athletics at school, the comments were always 'You're not as good as your kid'. I didn't mind, and was proud of him becoming a successful writer. The only thing in my life I'd done reasonably well, after lots of research and effort, was to train kestrels. Not much of an achievement compared to Barry's, but even so I was proud of what I'd learnt and done. Training hawks was my thing, my passion, but it seemed I still couldn't escape Barry's shadow. Now it seemed that whenever Tony was around I would be expected to keep quiet about the only thing I'd done in life of which I was proud.

It felt as if Barry had stolen my identity. That hurt must have turned to resentment, because one morning when he came to watch me fly Hardy, rather than carry her on the glove to the flying ground as I usually did, I cast her off as soon as we'd passed through the garden gate into the fields. As we walked through the stubble Barry looked up at the kestrel soaring high above my head and worriedly said: 'You'll lose her.'

'She'll be right,' I said, ignoring his pleas to call her down to the lure.

Looking back across the forty or so intervening years, I don't know if I was subconsciously trying to sabotage the film, or just demonstrating to Barry how much he depended on me. Later, recalling Barry's anxious, pale face as he looked up at the kestrel circling above, I felt guilty for deliberately upsetting him.

It seemed that Barry hadn't only told Tony he would train the kestrels, it turned out he had also been commissioned to write a book proposal about the hawk training for the film. He suggested we both make notes, he as an observer and helper, me as the falconer. I liked the idea of a joint book and in his first notes he often mentioned how I was progressing with the training. But as his notes advanced, I became irritated at the way he increasingly included himself in my falconry decisions and actions by writing 'we'. When I asked him about it, he said it wouldn't work as a book if he kept writing 'Richard did this'. I knew he'd landed himself in the embarrassing position of being commissioned to write a book proposal which the publishers thought was about him training the hawks for the film. I understood his problem, although I became furious when, at one point, a few lines of his notes gave the impression that Barry alone was the hawk trainer. It turned out my anger was unnecessary, for the proposal was turned down.

In Barry's defence I discovered he'd been using his book proposal fee to pay me to train the hawks, and later, after he'd seen how upset I was by Tony Garnett's misunderstanding, he told me he'd spoken to Tony and made sure I'd get a credit on the film as falconer, and had arranged for me to be on the film company's pay roll. From that point onwards, he went out of his way to tell everyone working on the film what a good job I was doing, and I was grateful to him for that.

# TWENTY-ONE

... fowle weather ... will breed offences [in] divers waies ...

– Symon Latham, *Latham's Faulconry, or
The Faulcon's Lure and Cure*, 1615

One morning David, as Billy Casper, was filmed 'manning' his kestrel as he walked through Barnsley town centre with her on his fist. Later, as we returned to the village in a taxi, Hardy bated off the glove and broke a feather at one of the slashes that had been caused by stress or hunger in the nest. She'd already broken two feathers at those weak points, which, like this new break, hadn't snapped off the feather completely, and she now had three feathers hanging loose. After this latest mishap, although I'd never done it before, I'd need to 'imp' Hardy's broken tail feathers before the filming of the crucial lure-flying scene.

Rolling up an old cardigan, I placed it on the wide shelf on the inside of the mews door. Holding Hardy firmly, thumbs and fingers across her back, Barry placed her feet on to the cardigan so she'd have something to grip. Ideally, I would now have deftly slipped a leather hood over her head to keep her in the dark and calm, but as I didn't have a hood I covered her head with a tea towel. Set out on the shelf beside her were three tail feathers that I'd received from a museum, along with a razor blade, a tube of glue and three-inch-long 'imping' needles. Proper imping needles are triangular shaped with three flat sides, and are filed to a point at the ends. Mine were ordinary needles from my mother's sewing kit.

Using the razor blade I cut a V shape in one of Hardy's tail feathers at the point where the shaft had broken, and removed the broken part of the feather. I then trimmed a new feather to fit into the V of the original tail feather, still attached to the young kestrel. Dabbing a touch of glue on the imping needle, I pushed it into the shaft of the new feather, leaving about half an inch sticking out like a strut. Then, after putting a spot of glue on this part, I pushed the exposed half of the needle into the shaft. The new feather fitted snugly into the original feather and gave the impression the young hawk had miraculously grown a new tail feather.

Like hair and fingernails, feathers are made from the protein keratin, and imping is painless for the hawk. But Barry winced, because despite the tea towel over her head, Hardy wriggled. When he was adjusting his grip, she grabbed his finger and sunk in her talons. Next she reached round and pecked his fingers. I wondered if she would be upset after her ordeal, but when Barry released her on to my glove she simply shook herself and began to feed, while we admired her three new tail feathers.

One evening, as Freeman flew in low and silently towards him, David Bradley let the lure fall on the grass and turned his back on the approaching hawk. It seemed he'd suddenly become frightened of her. Later, as we walked back across the fields to the mews, David told me that flying a hawk to the lure was ten times harder than anything he'd ever done. That worried me. Scheduled to be filmed at the end of the week was a scene in which Billy Casper stoops his kestrel to the lure watched by

Mr Farthing, his supportive teacher. If it was to work, David needed dramatically to improve his lure-swinging skills.

It had been misty and drizzling when I'd flown the three hawks up on the school field in the morning, more like November than August. That evening, when David arrived by taxi for his lure-swinging practice, a howling wind had got up. I wasn't sure what to do: risk a hawk being blown away and lost or jeopardise the film's credibility by failing to ensure that David developed the skills he needed. Eventually I decided it was worth the risk of flying Freeman on the old flying ground with the fence posts, which was more sheltered than the school field.

'Kes . . . Come on, Kes,' David called as he stood in the middle of the field, almost being blown off his feet as he swung the lure. Standing at the edge of the field with Freeman on my glove, I raised my arm, and the wind tipped her forward off my glove and sent her hurtling downwind towards David. Despite the hawk's speed he managed to throw the lure into her path and twitch it away, sending the kestrel speeding past. She turned and, battling with the wind, tried to fly back to David, but the wind was too strong and she sheered off and landed on a fence post, her feathers buffeted as she faced into the wind. Realising David wouldn't get much practice in this weather and that I was on the verge of losing a kestrel, I hurried across and picked her up off the fence post, and, shielding the hawk with my body so she didn't get blown off the glove, we headed back to the mews.

Next day the wind had dropped, but the clouds were dark blue and the rain so heavy that I didn't fly the hawks in the morning. When David and Barry arrived after filming had finished for the day the rain had stopped and I decided David should try and fly Hardy, our star performer. So with Hardy on my glove, David and Barry beside me, and Barry's collie,

Bess, running around in front of us, we trudged through the sodden fields up to the school field. When we arrived it began to rain heavily and as there was nowhere to shelter on the large field, within a couple of minutes all of us – humans, dog and hawk – were saturated. David badly needed to practise his lure swinging, so I told him to run into the middle of the field, swing the lure and call Kes to see if she would fly. When he swung the lure and called, she refused to leave my raised glove. She just stood there, drenched, her wings drooping.

So for the second evening running I trudged back through the fields, frustrated that David's lure practice had been thwarted by the weather. If things didn't improve he would never make a convincing falconer. On top of that I had a bedraggled hawk on my glove. Hawks often catch colds in stormy weather, experiencing watery discharge from the 'nares' (nostrils) and 'sniting' (sneezing), and I needed to keep Hardy in top condition. Today I would dry her feathers using a hairdryer, but back in the 1960s the falconry book's advice was to keep an electric light on in the mews – I'd have had to use a candle – so the hawk can rouse and preen rather than stand there immobile, wet and miserable in the dark. Barry had a better idea. After David had gone home to learn his lines, and after I'd fed up the hawk, Barry and I carried a small portable screen perch made by the film's carpenters into Barry's house, and left Hardy drying off on the perch in the bay window of the sitting room, while we went off to the cinema in Barnsley to watch the rushes – scenes which had been filmed the previous day and been sent off to be developed and were now ready to be assessed by the director and film crew. David Bradley, a polite, pleasant lad, with no previous acting experience, was the perfect choice to play Billy Casper. I laughed as up there on the cinema screen in his role as Billy he told outlandish lies as he tried to persuade the librarian to let him join the library and take out a falconry book. Then my heart jolted when he raised his glove and called 'Come on, Kes', just as I had when calling my two Keses.

Next morning, as each kestrel hopped from my glove on to the weighing scales, the rain was once again beating on the corrugated-iron roof of the mews. Each hawk was at its flying weight, but as I looked out through the barred window at the pouring rain and dark clouds, I knew I wouldn't be able to fly the kestrels. Instead I'd have to feed them up on half rations so they'd be ready to fly when David came over for his evening practice. It should have been pleasant sitting on an old kitchen chair in the mews, with a hawk tugging at the meat on my glove. Instead I was deeply worried. The scenes of David flying the kestrels to the glove on the creance had worked well, but anyone could manage that. To be convincing as a falconer he needed to be able to fly his kestrel skilfully to the lure. If things carried on like this I'd fail in my job and David would look incompetent. Later in the day I voiced my concerns to Barry. He told Ken Loach, and the filming of the crucial lure-swinging scene was put off until early the following week. It would give David more time to work on his technique.

To my relief, the rain had cleared by evening. Although the filming had been put back a few days, it was frustrating watching David fly Hardy. He was whirling the lure so close to his body that Hardy was unable to get in a clear stoop, and was hovering and flying around above his head. I was so stressed by David's lack of progress over the last few days that I lost my temper. 'Throw the lure out to her, David, throw it out!' I shouted.

Barry usually kept his emotions to himself, but my mood must have infected him because he joined in, shouting at David to get the lure away from his body.

Even the hawk seemed annoyed with poor David, and flew off on a circuit around the field before flying in fast and low.

David threw out the lure, twitched it away, then, keeping it just out of her reach, he swept the lure in front of the kestrel, sending her curving into the air. This was more like it. She stooped, and again he kept the lure just out of the hawk's grasp and sent her surging upwards. The next time Hardy plummeted out of the sky she caught the lure.

So I retrieved her and, standing at the edge of the field, I raised my glove and cast her off again. Gaining height, she was soon hovering thirty or forty feet above David's head, looking down on him. Looking up while swinging the lure, David ran across the grass, but she just followed, keeping directly above him before closing her wings and plunging down in a vertical stoop. To my amazement and delight he kept the lure out of her grasp and sent her arcing into the sky to stoop again, then once more managed to send her curving into the sky as she pursued the arcing lure. She caught the lure on the next stoop, but it was a very promising perform-ance. With David's confidence boosted and his eye now in, he flew Freeman even better than he'd flown Hardy. As we walked back across the fields to the mews, the dark clouds threatened more rain. Tonight I didn't care. David was getting the hang of it and if he continued to improve, next week's filming of the lure-swinging scene could be spectacular.

# TWENTY-TWO

He lures, he leaps, he calles, he cries, he joyes, he waxeth sad,
And frames his moode, according as his hawke doth well or bad . . .
    – George Turbervile, *The Booke of Faulconrie or Hauking*, 1575

The day's filming – David pretending to shoot a bird, David and Colin Welland, who played the teacher, discussing Freeman as she stood on her perch in the mews – had taken hours. It was after five o'clock in the afternoon when we arrived at the flying ground. I hadn't wanted to dull Freeman's appetite by feeding her scraps of beef, so her weight was below her usual flying weight. Last time she'd been so low, she was soon exhausted and had sought out fence posts to rest on, and although there were no fence posts on the school field I feared that she might pitch down on to the grass and refuse to fly. Racked with anxiety, I stood with Freeman on my glove as I waited for David to get into position. When he was ready, Ken Loach gave me the nod and I raised my glove and cast off Freeman from the edge of the field. My worries about her low weight and lack of energy were unfounded as she rocketed off my glove and towards David. Maybe he was as nervous as I was, because he didn't swing the lure immediately, or call 'Come on, Kes'. Perhaps Freeman was put off by the bright orange sweater of the sound recordist standing close to David. Whatever the reason, flying powerfully and gaining height, she ignored the swinging lure and continued flying until she disappeared over the edge of the field. Annoyed with David for not swinging the lure in time, I raced across the field in front of the surprised camera crew, snatched the lure off David and went in search of the lost hawk, eventually finding her perched on a fence post in a nearby field. Luckily, she came to the lure the moment I swung it. When I returned, Ken described her disappearance as a 'very nasty moment'.

It certainly was, and when I raised my glove to cast her off again for another take I was terrified she'd once more ignore David's swinging lure and fly out of sight. But to my relief, instead of gaining height quickly, she reverted to the way that she'd flown over the previous weeks, flying in low over the grass. David threw out the lure, swept it in front of her and sent her out towards the potato field where, after gaining height, she turned back to fly in fast and low. Again David kept the lure from her grasp. After the third or fourth such circuit around the field, the kestrel came in so fast that she managed to strike the lure with her outstretched foot, and David let her take her reward.

I walked towards the middle of the field to congratulate David and pick up Freeman. Things looked good. She was flying well and after a few more flights like this I'd bring on Hardy to perform her breathtaking vertical stoops. As I headed back towards the edge of the field with Freeman on my glove, I saw Ken and Chris and other crew members looking up at the sky. When I reached them the filming equipment was being packed away. The light had changed, which meant any further footage wouldn't cut together with what had just been filmed. To my dismay, filming had been called off for the day.

Next morning it was warm, with hardly a breath of wind, with white fine-weather clouds sailing slowly across the blue sky. By nine o'clock Freeman, Hardy *and* Willis were perched on their blocks at the edge of the school field. The first scene due to be filmed was one in which Billy Casper is annoyed when his kestrel Kes grabs the swinging lure, after he's been distracted by his teacher, Mr Farthing. Over the last week or so, Willis had begun to put in a few stoops as she tried to grab the lure, and this scene seemed a good opportunity for her to make an appearance in the film. As David swung the lure and Willis flew towards him across the field, Colin Welland, as Mr Farthing, shouted 'Casper', to let him know he'd arrived to watch. David, being a good actor, fumbled his swinging while swearing to himself. But instead of being on to the lure in an instant, as she should have been for the scene to work, Willis reverted to her old ways, and with her eyes nearly popping out of her head she hovered over David before sheering off. Perhaps using Willis hadn't been such a good idea. Once again I was expecting to be involved in an embarrassing chase, but Willis had spotted her block perch at the other side of the field and landed on it. In the end, the scene was reshot using an impeccably behaved Freeman, who kept to the script and grabbed the lure at just the right moment.

The next scene was to be the culmination of my summer's work: the one where Billy Casper stoops Kes to the lure while Mr Farthing watches. As before, both Freeman and Hardy were to be filmed and cut into a sequence. The brilliant flier Hardy was on her block perch across the field, but it made sense to continue flying Freeman, who was raring to go having just caught the lure a couple of times.

I could feel my heart racing as I cast Freeman off the glove. Calling 'Come on, Kes' and judging her approach perfectly as she flew in low over the grass, David threw out the lure.

Keeping it just out of her grasp, he swept it in front of her and sent her curving up into the air and out towards the potato field. Flying leisurely, with flickering wings and glides, she circled the school field, then, with her jesses trailing behind her, she flew in fast and silently just above the grass in another attempt to grab the lure. And so it went on, circuit after circuit, as David skilfully kept the lure out of her grasp. On some circuits she reached a height of seventy or eighty, maybe even a hundred feet, before circling around and gradually losing height, until she was skimming silently over the grass, her eyes fixed on the swinging lure. On another circuit she flew so close to the camera that a crew member holding a clipboard had to pull her head back as the hawk's wing tip flicked by her face. When David finally let Freeman catch the lure, I was so delighted that I ran across the field to congratulate him.

It was after lunch when the star performer, Hardy, got her turn to stoop to the lure. I'd weighed her in the lunch break and at six ounces her flying weight was now spot on. When I approached her on her block perch at the edge of the field she slowly flapped her wings, showing how keen she was to get on to my glove and get flying. I was delighted Freeman had flown well, but my hopes were pinned on Hardy flying her brilliant best and I had reason to be optimistic. It was a fine day with hardly a breath of wind, and on previous calm days like this she'd always put in up to sixty or seventy vertical stoops, often corkscrewing as she plummeted earthwards. David had got his eye in, flying Freeman earlier, and if he could keep that up and keep the lure out of crafty Hardy's grasp there was a good chance she would put on a spectacular show for the camera.

So, with Hardy on my glove, I stood at the field's edge behind the camera as David walked into the middle of the field. She was so keen to get cracking that she was bating off the glove. I turned my back, shielding the young hawk so she couldn't see David, but she kept trying to fly over my shoulder before he was ready. After what seemed ages, David eventually called: 'Come on, Kes.'

I turned to face him, raised my arm, let go of Hardy's jesses and cast her off my glove. She flew in low. David threw out the lure but she ignored it and curved upwards sharply and in an instant was twenty or thirty feet above David's head. Almost falling over backwards as he looked up, he pulled the lure line through his fingers, but before he could get it taut enough to twirl the lure and throw it up to her, the kestrel plummeted earthwards in a corkscrewing vertical stoop and struck the lure with her outstretched talons. David had no choice but to let her take her reward.

After tying new pieces of beef on to the lure, I took Hardy from David, trudged to the edge of the field and when the sound and camera were rolling cast her off my glove a second time. Again she flew in low, ignored the lure, and shot upwards, until she was directly above David's head. As he looked up and fumbled with the lure, she did a corkscrewing stoop and grabbed it. After tying more scraps of beef to the lure, I cast Hardy off for the third time. Once again she ignored the lure, and in seconds was above his head and plummeting earthwards before David could pull the lure line between his fingers, and get it taut enough to twitch the lure away from her grasp.

I surprised myself by calling out: 'She's making an idiot of him.'

Some of the crew laughed. Not me. As I ranted at Ken, telling him the stooping would look rubbish and Billy incompetent, he tried to calm me down, telling me they had already got some good shots of Freeman flying to the lure and that they'd be able to cut it all together into a good sequence.

David was a hundred yards or so away in the middle of the field, but perhaps he'd heard my ranting and this had upset him, for he called a halt, saying that he wanted a break and that he had blisters on his fingers from the lure line. Plasters were found, but, ashamed of myself and fearing my bad mood and anxiety might put him off even more, I stood at a distance from the group clustered around David. Barry and Ken were in that group and later, as I was heading back across the field to cast off Hardy for another take, Barry joined me. He told me that as David was having the plasters put on his fingers, Ken had said 'Three nil to Hardy'. David hadn't looked best pleased.

Poor David. Even if I'd been in a better frame of mind, I don't think I'd have been able to give him advice on how to respond to Hardy's tactics. He had done well. Earlier he'd flown Freeman marvellously but he hadn't had enough practice to fly Hardy when she was in this mood. If Hardy continued curving upwards into an awkward position directly above his head, and then plunging on to the lure in a vertical stoop, all her training would have come to nothing. It was beginning to look as if only the shots of Freeman would be useable for this scene.

Throughout the summer I'd imagined her brilliant flying would provide the most spectacular falconry scene in the film. I raised my arm and cast Hardy off the glove for the fourth time. Miserable, frustrated, and anticipating what would happen next, I watched gloomily as David threw out the lure to the fast-approaching Hardy. To my surprise, she didn't curve upwards; instead she carried on in level flight and tried to strike the lure. This time David managed to twitch it away from her, and keeping the lure just out of her reach he swept it downwards then upwards, and her momentum as she chased it sent her arcing high into the air, which gave him time to pull in the lure line and twirl the lure a couple of times by his side, before throwing it up into her path and sweeping it down in front of her. Wings pumping furiously, she descended in a vertical stoop, then, just as it looked as if she was about to crash head first into the grass, she pulled out of the stoop and followed the arcing lure skywards. Her momentum carried her so high David had plenty of time to pull in the lure line, twirl the lure by his side a few times and once again throw it up and keep it just out of the young kestrel's reach as she hurtled earthwards, before curving upwards to begin another stoop.

Later, each with a half-finished pint of Barnsley Bitter in front of us, Barry and I stood at the bar of our local pub, The Star.

'Is it the beer, or are you glowing with pride?' Barry asked, pointing at my face.

'Must be relief.'

Delighted for me, Barry said, 'David and the hawks did your work justice.'

'Eventually,' I replied, smiling, before adding, 'Just the hawks to hack back now.'

Looking back to that summer of 1968 I can recall one sunny day when it suddenly struck me how my love of hawks had changed my life. That morning, the crew had been filming a scene where Billy Casper discovers the kestrels' nest at Tankersley Old Hall. Leaving the hawks in the mews, I had walked through Bell Ground Wood to join the film crew and actors for lunch at one of the trestle tables which had been set up on the cart track opposite the ruined Hall. It was at this very spot, three summers earlier, when I was twenty, that I'd come across my friend John and discovered that kestrels nested here. I can remember thinking how, had I not met

John that evening and got my first Kes, I wouldn't have become so obsessed with hawks and wouldn't have applied for the Environmental Studies course. I wouldn't have travelled to Africa and I wouldn't have been sitting here eating lunch with a film crew, nor working as a falconer on a film. As I watched the swallows fly low over the buttercups in the field and around the Old Hall, I could hardly believe that my fascination for hawks had led to all this.

Two years later, in the spring of 1970, home from college for the weekend, I walked into the house to be greeted by my agitated mother.

'Have you seen it?' she asked.

'What?'

'The poster. I daren't show my face in the village.'

When I'd worked out what she was on about I walked up to the main road, and there on a large hoarding was the source of her embarrassment: a massive film poster advertising *KES*. On it David Bradley as Billy Casper glared defiantly out while giving a V sign to all passers-by, including local churchgoers and members of the Women's Institute.

I know the date on which I saw the film: Wednesday, 25 March 1970. I even know that the film was shown at 8 p.m. I've found my invitation from United Artists Corporation, which requested 'the pleasure of the company of Mr. Richard Hines & Guest at the World Premier of "KES" at the "ABC" Cinema in Doncaster'. The invitation is printed on white card in fancy looping writing. Although this is the first time I've looked at it in over forty years, I can recall being concerned when I read the words 'Black Tie' printed in the bottom right-hand corner. It seemed strange to me telling people what colour tie to wear, so, suspecting there might be more to it, I checked the dictionary and discovered it meant formal evening dress. The nearest thing I had to formal clothes was a tweed jacket which had spent a year hanging in wardrobes in Africa, and had never been worn since. As I tried on the jacket and smoothed it down I felt a lump in the lining. Using her sewing scissors, mother cut a small hole in the corner of the inside pocket, then put her fingers through it while I worked whatever it was in the lining up towards them.

'Got it,' she said, and raised her hand in triumph.

Then her face turned to disgust as she threw on to the carpet a dead lizard that had found its way into my jacket lining in Nigeria. The bone-dry lizard was odourless and didn't put me off, but the jacket didn't feel right for a film premiere and so I wore a leather one with an open-neck shirt. I didn't feel out of place, for the only bloke wearing a black bow tie and dinner jacket was a man from United Artists who shook everyone's hand – film crew, actors, guests – as we walked into the cinema.

Sitting in the dark that night, Jackie by my side, I feared Ken, who didn't know the first thing about hawks, would have made errors in editing the falconry scenes which would lead experts to deride the film's falconer. Waiting for the first flying sequence, where Billy Casper calls Kes across the field on the creance, was agony, but the scene worked well and contained a surprise. I'd assumed only Freeman and Hardy would appear but to my amusement and delight, there on the big screen, racked with indecision, was nervous wreck Willis, walking along a fence. She'd made it into the film after all.

In the lure-flying sequence, Hardy's first stoop sent her curving upwards and out of view at the top of the screen before she reappeared in another vertical stoop. David was flying her beautifully, keeping the lure just out of her reach as she plummeted downwards and then arced back into the sky to begin another stoop. I was thrilled, for this was what I'd worked and hoped for. I felt a sense of satisfaction that, despite all the setbacks throughout that cold, rainy summer, I'd succeeded. I'd done the job I'd been paid to do as the film's falconer, training the kestrels and working with David to make Billy a convincing falconer.

I was surprised how stirred my emotions were on seeing our village of Hoyland Common and its surroundings on the cinema screen. There was the slag heap of our local colliery where my dad had nearly broken his back and where my grandad had been killed. When Billy stooped his hawk to the lure beyond the fields I could see Tinker Lane, where Dad had led the way as we'd carried furniture from the terraced cottage we had rented to our new stone house further up the road. The familiar locations up on the screen acted as a vivid backdrop against which the significant events in my life had been played out: the Barnsley Library where, after being refused permission to borrow *A Manual of Falconry*, I'd copied parts of it out by hand; Bell Ground Wood where John and I carried the ladder in the moonlight; Tankersley Old Hall and the nest hole where my first kestrel, Kes, had come from; David as Billy raising his glove and calling 'Come on, Kes', using the very words I'd called to my first kestrel in the very fields in which I'd trained her, flown her to the lure and hacked her back to the wild five years earlier.

# PART THREE

# TWENTY-THREE

> . . . Faulconrie or Hauking. For the onely delight and pleasure
> of all Noblemen and Gentlemen. . .
>
> – George Turbervile, *The Booke of Faulconrie or Hauking*, 1575

In 1970, the year of the film premiere, I was in my third and final year at Leicester Teachers' Training College. I was now working hard to finish my Environmental Studies dissertation about how hawks had fallen from grace over the centuries. Before coming to college I'd read J. A. Baker's *The Peregrine*, his dramatic account of how peregrines might not survive as they died, 'withered and burnt away by the filthy insidious pollen of farm chemicals'. On my college course, a key book was Rachel Carson's *Silent Spring*, published in 1962, which told the same story, but more scientifically. By now it was well known that organo-chlorine pesticides, such as DDT, passed through the food chain and accumulated in hawks, causing death or reproduction problems, such as thin egg shells which broke when parents sat on the eggs. I'd done lots of research on this aspect of my dissertation, as well as gathering evidence and photographs of the poisoning, trapping and shooting of hawks by gamekeepers. I already knew a lot about falconry history but I'd read about the recently opened Falconry Centre in Gloucestershire, which had a falconry museum, and in the autumn term of 1969 I decided to visit.

Hawks were on the verge of extinction in Britain, but the Falconry Centre had a collection of imported hawks. When I saw a falcon on a block perch my heart raced. A peregrine! Eventually I stopped gazing and went into the small museum of falconry. I was reading information displayed on the wall and making notes when someone walked in. Having seen a photograph of him, I recognised Phillip Glasier, the falconer who had set up the Falconry Centre. Although I had no chance of flying a peregrine I wanted to impress him with my knowledge of game hawking, and so I asked him if he agreed with Jack Mavrogordato's view that stooping a falcon to the lure does *not* lower the falcon's 'pitch' – the highest point at which a falcon circles above the falconer before stooping on its prey.

Even before he opened his mouth I could tell from Glasier's face that he disagreed.

'If you are going to fly at grouse or partridge, you should never stoop your falcon to the lure,' he told me. He went on to explain that if you do, when out hunting, instead of climbing to a good high 'pitch' the falcon will most likely go up only a short distance, before circling around, as it waits for the falconer to take out the lure. What he said made perfect sense, and today his view is that of all falconers, but the way he said it, in his posh, loud voice, intimidated me so much I could hardly take in what he was saying.

Looking back over more than forty years, it seems incredible that the way someone spoke could have had such a profound effect on me.

My mother had recently told me how, before they were married, Dad had cycled over to visit her when she worked in service. She said he hadn't known that servants' visitors weren't allowed to go to the front door, and was curtly sent to the back door. Later, she'd overheard her employers mocking his accent. My only contact with the upper classes to date had been through my falconry books. Their posh-ness made me smile – 'When hawking in India one needs a horse' – and I enjoyed descriptions of their eccentric antics, such as the aristocratic falconer who flew his goshawk along a corridor past Ming vases and priceless paintings. Yet, to me, all that stuff about social division belonged in the past. So when Mother told me that story, I'd reminded her it was the 1960s, and that working-class blokes were now stars in films such as *Saturday Night and Sunday Morning*, and that Beatles songs and northern voices were on the airwaves. Accents and social class didn't matter any more.

I'm not criticising Phillip Glasier, for he can no more help the background that he was born into than I can, but back then upper-class accents were much more strikingly posh. This is apparent to anyone who goes online to watch documentary films made for the British Council in the 1930s and 1940s, the era in which Glasier was raised. Although it was now the 1960s, Glasier spoke in the manner of those times and his accent was far posher than that of today's royal family.

As I stood that day in his falconry museum, listening to him explain why he thought stooping a falcon to the lure *does* lower its pitch, and makes it a less effective hunter, I was astonished by the gulf between our classes. It wasn't just his accent that intimidated me, but his confidence, that sense of effortless superiority instilled by a public school educa-tion, and his lack of inhibition and booming voice as if he assumed what he was saying would be of interest to every-one within fifty yards. I didn't say a word, except to thank him, when he said that later he'd be flying a hawk if I wanted to watch, and then marched out.

Not long afterwards, when I was home from college for the weekend, a lad who'd kept a kestrel told me of the experience of a Yorkshire miner he knew. The miner had let it be known to a group of middle-class falconers that he was interested in joining their ranks, only to be mocked and snubbed by them. Later I read of an upper-class army officer falconer, who in the late 1880s abandoned flying his peregrine on Salisbury Plain to join his regiment to break a strike of half-starved Yorkshire miners like my great-grandad. It was only then that it dawned on me that the Royalist Sir Richard Fanshawe would most likely have seen me as an ill-bred plebeian. Rather than indulge my boyhood passion for hawks, he'd probably have set his dogs on me had I gone anywhere near Tankersley Old Hall to take a young kestrel.

It took meeting Phillip Glasier for me to realise how I'd been obsessed with an upper-class history and a world in which I wouldn't be welcome. It was a revelation which made me see things differently. For the first time I began to value my own heritage. In our village, as in many other working-class communities, the history of the community was passed down through stories from one generation to the next. I liked it when my mother told me about my grandad Westerman, who'd worn a pink dog rose in his lapel, and who'd later been killed in the mine. His hobby was racing pigeons over a distance of a mile. He had two champion 'milers', one called Semolina, the other Something Hot, and as a girl, mother told me, she liked to watch him rattling a tin of pigeon peas as he encouraged them back into the loft at the end of a race. Dad used to make me laugh with his stories of life in Hoyland Common in the 1920s and 1930s. I particularly enjoyed his tales of rent avoidance by men who'd blown their wages on drink, or were out of work through injury, or needed the money to pay a doctor's bill, or just didn't earn enough money to pay the household bills. On rent collection day one man would put the rent book and rent money on the windowsill, then hide upstairs. The rent collector could see the rent book and rent money through the window. But after knocking on the door and getting no reply he'd move on to the next house muttering: 'The man's willing to pay – but he's never in.' I also liked to hear tales of our village's past from other miners. One night in the pub a miner told me how, at the age of five or six, during the 1926 miners' strike his mother would send him to sing outside a strike breaker's house. Then, to the tune of 'Let Me Call You Sweetheart', in a surprisingly beautiful voice, he sang the song his mother had taught him as a child over forty years ago: 'Let me call you blackleg, I've no love for you. You have been working, this whole strike through.'

Both my mother and dad and other miners had told their tales of past pit village life with amused affection, but all of them seemed glad things had moved on from those harsh, poverty-stricken times. Although I enjoyed these tales, I saw them as the experiences of earlier generations, which had nothing to do with my life.

Yet after meeting Glasier, and realising things hadn't changed as much as I'd imagined, I developed a passionate interest in the history of my own social class; its humour, and the inequalities and hardships faced by people from my background. More crucially for my future teaching career, I became much more aware of how this legacy of disadvantage could still affect children's life chances. Back at college, alongside writing up my dissertation, I studied the influence of social class on children's educational achievement, as part of my other main subject, Education.

In the summer of 1970, both the Environmental Studies lecturer and the external examiner admired my dissertation about the decline of hawks, and I was awarded top marks. I'd also done well in the other subjects I'd taken. All I needed now was to pass my exam in Education. Everything was going perfectly. I was proud of the job I'd done as falconer on *Kes*, and I was looking forward to becoming a qualified teacher. Then I did something stupid.

It was the night before my exam. I'd been revising all evening in my room in the hall of residence, and, satisfied I'd done enough work, I decided to nip downstairs to see if the student bar was still open. It was in darkness; the shutters were closed but light was leaking out around the edges and I could hear voices. I tried the bar door. It was locked and the voices fell silent. I knocked.

'Who is it?'

'Richard.'

The door opened and I was invited in. Inside, seven or eight students were crushed behind the bar holding glasses of beer or whisky. One of the lads had sneaked into the room of the student who ran the bar and taken the key to the bar out of his pocket. Now they were all helping themselves to drinks to celebrate the end of their exams. I decided I'd only have one drink, but I was enjoying myself so much that I stayed for another pint, and then another, and another . . . By the time I staggered up to my room sunlight was streaming through windows on the stairs. It was dawn. Somehow I managed to set the alarm and clambered into bed.

When the alarm went off I was badly hungover and too ill to go to the exam, and, between vomiting, I lay in bed hardly able to believe my own stupidity. By the afternoon, feeling a bit better, I dressed and was sipping a coffee when there was a knock on the door. When I opened it, the lecturer who had taught me Education burst past me into the room.

'You stupid . . .' he said, just stopping himself. Face white with anger, he told me that after three years of work, and being awarded an A in my recent teaching practice, I'd blown it and was now going to be thrown out of college without my teaching qualification.

'You made your point in that article,' he went on. 'Couldn't you just have left it at that?'

'What?'

Then it dawned on me what he meant.

Earlier in the term, I'd written an article in the student magazine arguing that exams should be scrapped and replaced by ongoing assessment of course work throughout the year. He thought I'd missed the exam on principle.

'I was ill,' I insisted.

I don't know if he cottoned on that my illness had been self-inflicted, but to my huge relief he said, 'Send in a sick note, and I'll arrange for you to sit a different exam paper', then abruptly left my room.

I sat the exam a few days later with two or three other students who'd missed the original exam through genuine illness and passed with a good mark.

In that summer of 1970 I returned to the pit village, where I spent my summer working as a labourer on a building site, and walking the countryside with Jackie in the evenings and at weekends. I also applied for two teaching jobs. Had the head teachers who interviewed sober, respectful, enthusiastic me known about that irresponsible drunken night I'd spent crowded behind the shuttered bar, things might have been different. But they didn't know, and to my amazement I was offered both the jobs I'd applied for. In the end I chose to work in a junior school on the outskirts of Barnsley in an Educational Priority Area, the purpose of which was to try and improve the life chances of educationally disadvantaged kids.

# TWENTY-FOUR

Managing is to handle any thing with cunning according to the true nature therof . . .

– Symon Latham, *Latham's Faulconry, or The Faulcon's Lure and Cure*, 1615

The autumn of 1970 was an eventful time. In September, aged twenty-five, I became a school teacher. Jackie was working as a designer in a quilt factory in Barnsley, and we bought a detached 1930s house on the edge of the village. We enjoyed doing it up: sanding the floorboards, painting the walls white, Jackie making the curtains. We moved in after marrying in the October school holidays. The wedding was a funny affair. Neither of us had wanted to be the focus of attention, so we only invited two guests to act as witnesses, my brother, Barry, and his wife, Margaret. The four of us travelled together on the bus to Barnsley registry office. The others had boarded at earlier stops, and when I got on the bus I had to smile when I saw my bride, Jackie, sitting there dressed in a black crocheted beret, a dark green belted coat and black knee-length boots. Jackie's dad had found a wedding ring while renovating an old pawnbroker's shop and during the ceremony I slipped it on Jackie's finger. She also wore the bangle I'd bought her in Kano, and just as the bangle carried its fascinating history of Nigerian village life with it, so the ring from the pawnbroker's shop intrigued us and felt like a direct connection to our pit village's past. Even today we occasionally look at it and wonder what circumstances forced the poor woman, its previous owner, to pawn her wedding ring. Had her husband blown his wages on booze? Was he unable to work because of injury? Or did she need the money to pay a doctor's bill?

After the cinema release of *Kes*, newspapers reported how the film had sparked a craze for taking young kestrels from the nest to train, and one evening I came across what I suspected to be a victim of that craze. I was out walking through farmland at the edge of the village with our dog Gyp, a Labrador, when I met a man I knew who pointed across the fields and told me he'd seen a trapped kestrel. I followed his directions and soon I could hear the kestrel calling out in fear, 'kikiki . . . kikiki'. It was hanging upside down at the top of a wooden electricity pole. Whoever had tried to train that kestrel had committed the worst crime in falconry by letting it escape with its leash attached, and it was caught on the crosspiece that supported the electric cables. The circle of barbed wire wrapped around the top of the wooden pole meant I couldn't climb up that way, but to either side, like the guy ropes on a tent, were two steel ropes that helped secure the pole. So, hand over hand, my legs wrapped around the steel rope, I climbed up. Gripping the kestrel's leash between my teeth, I climbed down with the kestrel flapping around at the end of the leash calling, 'kikiki . . . kikiki'. Gyp went crazy, leaping up, trying to bite it. I couldn't open my mouth to shout 'No!' or the leash would have slipped from my teeth, but I managed to keep her away with my foot. Within an hour or two of her rescue the kestrel was flying free the length of our long sitting room to my glove, and after I'd fed her up on beef, she calmly stood on a block perch while Jackie drew her in her sketchbook.

Our house was surrounded by a garden in which I could have flown the rescued kestrel on a creance, and a few minutes' walk away were the fields in which I'd flown my two Keses and Freeman, Hardy and Willis for the film. I still loved hawks. Yet meeting Phillip Glasier and realising that I had been obsessed with a world which wouldn't have welcomed me had put me off falconry. In addition to that, after training so many kestrels I didn't want to stoop another to the lure; it would have felt repetitive. So, even though the rescued kestrel was beautiful, I passed her on to the son of a member of staff where I worked, who was interested in flying her.

One day my old friend Towser and his sculptor wife, who were visiting his parents in the village, called in to see Jackie and me in our new home. Handsome and as charismatic as ever, Towser sat on our green Chesterfield, talking to Jackie and his wife in his beautiful accentless actor's voice, and to me in Yorkshire dialect. To my surprise he'd decided not to take up acting, instead going on to become a successful writer for BBC Radio. Towser's wife was seriously posh and at one point in the conversation he told us that if we thought she sounded posh, we should hear her dad. He then made us laugh, his wife included, by impersonating his father-in-law's astonished words upon hearing they were going to the theatre before eating: 'But one has supper.' It was an enjoyable afternoon, all of us talking together, with Jackie and Towser's wife discussing art, and laughing as they listened to their husbands recalling their schoolboy antics. As they left Towser then commented on the large garden, and how it would be a good place to keep a kestrel. I told him I'd packed in hawking because of the lack of opportunity to fly other species of hawk, which were under threat of being poisoned into extinction by pesticides, rather than embarrass his lovely, friendly wife by explaining that it was an encounter with a man with a voice just like her father's that had prompted my decision.

Not long after Jackie and I had married we'd bought Gyp, our black Labrador, who I took to work. We travelled to the school by bus, or on fine sunny mornings walked the four miles to school through farmland. In autumn and winter, with her head down sniffing the trails of scent, and her tail wagging, she'd quarter the stubble fields and frost-covered meadows; in spring and summer, when the crops were growing, she'd walk at heel behind me along the field paths. The nine- and ten-year-old boys and girls I taught loved having a dog in the classroom, and the headmaster didn't mind, although he wasn't best pleased when one day I asked him if he could order me a new chair. Gyp spent a lot of her time lying under my desk and had chewed through the leg of my current one.

When I'd applied to college I'd intended to teach environmental science in secondary schools and my first stint of practical teaching, 'teaching practice', was in a secondary school. Then, while doing my next teaching practice and teaching a class in a junior school, I changed my mind. I enjoyed the variety involved in teaching all aspects of the curriculum to one class of children, rather than having different class after different class parading in for their science lesson.

I didn't regret my choice of age group and really enjoyed teaching the class of nine- and ten-year-olds. Each day the boys and girls would enter the classroom bustling with life and energy, some of them laughing and chatting with their friends, others greeting me cheerfully, while others would come up to my desk to tell me what they had been up to. Then it would be down to work. Whatever the subject – be it maths, English, history, art, drama, dance, or an environmental science field trip – I'd do my best to engage the pupils' interest, then keep them on task, encouraging them to do their best work, whatever their capabilities. At lunchtime and after school I'd mount children's work and put up classroom displays, always making sure each child had a turn to have work displayed on the wall. I was always on the lookout for opportunities to help boost the self-worth of less confident children. For example, one lad who had difficulty with his reading and spelling found that a technique I'd shown him – tracing the letters of a difficult word in the air with his finger – helped him remember the word and how to spell it. One morning I secretly asked him to learn to spell 'psychology', then later that day contrived to bring the word into a class discussion. When I asked if anyone could spell the word this boy was the only one to raise his hand. He spelt it correctly, to the astonishment of the rest of the class. When the other kids were working, we grinned at each other as we shared our secret.

Of course there were pupils in the class who didn't need me to contrive secret plans to raise their confidence. One day a pupil told me he didn't understand the difference between vertical and horizontal. I asked the class to stop work for a minute so they could all listen, but one lad continued to talk to a friend as I explained. Irritated, I asked him to give me an example of something that was horizontal. 'A ruler,' he said.

Seeing my chance to put him in his place, I picked up a metre-long ruler, held it up vertically with my fingers about a third of the way down from the top, and then asked: 'Is that horizontal?'

I should have known better. This lad was such a bright spark he pointed to the top edge of the ruler, which was one or two centimetres wide, and said: 'The top is.'

His answer brought laughter from all the children in the class, as well as me, as I conceded I hadn't thought of that myself.

Of course I had no control over my pupils' home lives. One morning I was sitting at my desk having just listened to a pupil read from a book, when a friendly girl, who was usually cheerful, approached me close to tears.

'I've got bellyache, Mr Hines,' she told me.

'Oh dear,' I said, before asking, 'Did you have some breakfast?'

'Yes.'

'What did you have?'

'A pork pie,' she replied.

Another morning one girl spotted something through the classroom window and laughed. Moments later, all the class, boys and girls, were on their feet, pointing out of the window in amusement, while some of them called out warnings, such as 'You're in trouble now, Mr Hines', or 'You've had it now, sir'. Hurrying to the window I saw for myself what was causing such merriment. I don't recall the circumstances – maybe he'd fallen out with another pupil, or perhaps I'd told him off – but whatever the reason, earlier a lad from my class had bolted out of the door and run home. And now, on the school field, there he was being half marched, half dragged back to school by his mother, a big woman with her sleeves rolled up to her elbows and with a grim, determined look on her face. The kids thought it funny, but my stomach churned when the classroom door opened, and, wearing a striped pinafore, the mother dragged her son into the classroom. Whatever the reason for it, to my relief she didn't hold me responsible for her son's flight from the classroom. It was him she was angry with for running home, and she apologised to me for her boy's behaviour.

I took my job very seriously, and by studying in the evenings, at weekends, and in the holidays, I added to my teaching qualifications by gaining a BA (Education) from the Open University. In 1974 I moved to another junior school in an Educational Priority Area in Doncaster, where I taught for a further two years. I then took a year's sabbatical in

1976 to study for a Master of Education degree at Sheffield University, and complete a thesis on how family background can influence educational achievement. That year was special, for one day in October our son John was born at 6.15 a.m. in Barnsley hospital. Perhaps it was frowned on in those days, but I wasn't encouraged to hold him. Still, that didn't dampen my joy. Later, after leaving the hospital, I caught a bus to the edge of town, and still smiling with delight I walked the rest of the way home through fields and woods as the cobwebs on the hedgerows glistened with dew.

I wasn't the only school teacher in our house. Soon after we'd been married, Jackie had left her job as a designer in the Barnsley quilt factory to study art as her main subject at a teacher training college in Doncaster. On gaining her teaching qualifications, just as I had she'd decided to teach primary school children, but in her case she taught five- to seven-year-olds in an infant school in a nearby village. She loved the job, so what happened one hot sunny day in 1976, before John was born, came out of the blue. While on holiday in East Anglia in the June school break, we visited an art gallery. I don't recall what kind of work was displayed but I remember Jackie looking at it with interest, and at one point leaning in so close to examine the brushwork on one painting that an attendant had walked up close to us, as if fearing she was about to damage it. When we walked out of the gallery into the sunlight Jackie began to cry, and cry, and cry.

I was in despair, begging her to tell me what was wrong. When she did eventually stop crying, she tried to put her feelings into words. She explained how she'd been overwhelmed by a sense of being unfulfilled, and how that awful sense of emptiness had been followed by an almost unbearable yearning to take up art again. On that lovely sunny holiday, as we walked hand in hand along the sea front, Jackie decided that, after our baby was born in October, she would leave her teaching job to look after the child while also developing her own artwork and teaching part-time art classes. These were plans that I wholeheartedly supported.

Twenty months after John's birth, in May 1978, our daughter Katie was born in Barnsley hospital at 4.15 a.m. Just as I had when John had been born, unable to contain my delight I walked all the way home smiling. On this beautiful morning there wasn't a cloud in the sky and the woods were full of bluebells. By the time of Katie's birth I had become deputy head of a junior school in another part of Doncaster. I enjoyed my job and planned to eventually apply for headships. Then, just as my youthful obsession with hawks had led to me working as a volunteer overseas, and later to my decision to become a teacher, my hawking experiences influenced another decision that dramatically changed my life.

# TWENTY-FIVE

RAKE AWAY. To abandon the flight and career away down wind.

– J. G. Mavrogordato, *A Falcon in the Field*, 1966

In 1980 I'd been deputy head for nearly three years at the junior school in Doncaster, and had already begun to look in the *Times Educational Supplement* for suitable vacant headships I could apply for, when, one Sunday night, I stayed up late to watch a 1940s black and white Hollywood film called *The Best Years of Our Lives*. Next morning at school a consignment of stationery arrived and, as I stacked the shelves with exercise books, paper, boxes of pencils, I couldn't get the film out of my mind. It haunted me. The stories of the men returning from the Second World War changed by their experiences, and having to adjust to civilian life; the women having to adjust to the return of their menfolk, and the loss of their war work and the independence that went with it; the title of the film, *The Best Years of Our Lives*, all combined to create a sense of yearning. By the time I arrived home that evening I'd realised what I was yearning to do.

'A film director?' Jackie asked, after I'd told her. Then, laughing, she added: 'You've only just learnt how to take a photo.'

This was true. I loved cinema: British social-realist films; American films such as *The Last Picture Show* and *Five Easy Pieces*; French and Italian sub-titled films. Yet I'd never given any thought to how they were made or to the cinematography. When I'd worked as falconer on the film *Kes* I'd never owned a camera, or taken a photograph or thought about framing a shot. Each time Chris Menges – who went on to win two Oscars for cinematography – invited me to look down the camera, to me the shot didn't look any different from the view I'd seen before. Once when I'd heard Chris talking to his assistant about emulsion I'd thought one of them had been doing a bit of home decorating; I'd never heard of film emulsion. Even so, working on *Kes* had sown the seeds for what I'd decided to do next.

When I told Jackie that I wanted to use film to tell the stories of working-class people like ourselves, she realised I was serious. And, just as I'd supported her decision to give up teaching to concentrate on her art, so she supported my decision. In the summer of 1980, aged thirty-five, I left my job as a deputy head teacher and gave up my good salary to begin a one-year film-making course at Sheffield Polytechnic.

I enjoyed the course but my elation at having taken a new direction didn't last, for after I'd completed it I found myself unemployed. A year earlier, my decision to give up my job had seemed exciting. Now, each morning as I awoke and remembered that, for the first time in my working life, I had no job to go to, I began to fear that my decision had not only been naive, but stupidly reckless. Although I wasn't entitled to unemployment benefit because Jackie worked part-time, I could have my National Insurance stamps paid by the state, and keep up my entitlement to health treatment and a pension, as long as I signed on at the Social Security Office, or the 'Dole Office', as we claimants called it. In the early 1980s the

Conservative government were closing mines and steelworks throughout South Yorkshire, and once every two weeks I'd join one of the queues of men – it was almost exclusively men – that snaked around the Dole Office as they waited to sign on. When I signed on – I think it was on Thursday mornings – it always seemed to be raining and I can remember how the breath and the damp clothes of the hundreds of queuing men steamed up the rain-spattered windows.

Even though I'd brought it on myself, the awful sense of shame I felt was even harder to bear than the lack of money. My feelings came as a shock. I hadn't anticipated the humiliation and embarrassment I felt at being without a job, and the way it led me to behave. For instance, I kept quiet about being unemployed and tried to avoid people I knew, fearing they would ask me about work. Once, when I was travelling home on the train after an unsuccessful interview for a director's job on a factual film, I ducked into the toilet when I saw an acquaintance walking down the aisle towards me. On another occasion when I went to sign on, I carried on walking past the Dole Office when I saw someone I knew; terrified they'd see me go in and then spread the word I was unemployed, I only returned once they were out of sight. I began to think I'd become paranoid. Yet I noticed other men in the queues that snaked around the Dole Office, their eyes staring straight ahead of them, as if they feared catching someone's eye, and I began to wonder if they felt like I did: emasculated without a job to define me and give me purpose. Ironically, it was the awful experience of being unemployed, and the unexpected effects this had on my state of mind, that gave me the idea that would turn my life around.

Back then, in the early 1980s, Yorkshire Arts, which was funded by the Arts Council of Great Britain, gave grants to artists and film-makers. I submitted a script for a thirty-minute drama film based on my experiences of being unemployed, called *After the Ball*, and was awarded a budget big enough to buy and process the 16mm film stock, hire a film camera, a tape recorder, lights and so on, and pay all the actors and film crew – except for myself. The story was about a redundant worker, who not only feels ashamed and emasculated after losing his job, but also fears local children will taunt and bully his son if they discover his dad is out of work. I wasn't happy with all aspects of the film, particularly the beginning, which felt too slow. Yet when I showed it to a commissioning editor for independent film at Channel 4 television he thought it worked well, and to my delight he bought *After the Ball* for broadcast.

Around this time, Channel 4 was looking for documentary programme ideas. Interested in how working-class history was passed down the generations through stories, I wrote a proposal for a series of programmes called *A Tale to Tell*. Fortunately my idea was commissioned by Channel 4, and with the help of a friend who was more technically minded than I am, I set up a film company called Banner Film and Television to make the four programmes and found myself once more in paid work.

I travelled around the pit villages of South Yorkshire, and sometimes into areas of Sheffield where the steelworks were by now empty, derelict buildings, in my search for men and women to participate in *A Tale to Tell*. It was my fascination with the stories of the mining community that had given me the idea for the series, so I also persuaded a miner called Harry, who was a brilliant tale-teller and a friend of my parents, to take part and tell stories from our pit village's past. For example, in one of Harry's stories, on smelling cooking drifting up from the kitchen a man who was dying in bed called to his wife: 'That ham smells nice.' To which she replied: 'It's not for thee. It's for the coffin bearers.' Another story that Harry told in *A Tale to Tell* was of a miner who was confused by the formal, unfamiliar vocabulary that was sometimes used in union meetings at our local colliery. After it had been reported that some miners hadn't paid their union subscriptions, a union official had said to the chairman: 'Mr Chairman, I propose you divulge their names.' This prompted one miner to angrily call out: '*Don't* divulge their names, Mr Chairman! Read the buggers out!'

And yet, in my experience, working-class people, if they are made to feel at ease, and trust you, are articulate, vivid speakers, even when being filmed. Particularly when they are fired up and feel strongly about a cause, as I discovered when I made two documentary films for Channel 4 during the 1984–5 miners' strike. In these films, miners and their wives eloquently and movingly put the social and economic case for keeping Britain's coal mines open. Britain's miners weren't striking for a pay rise, but to stop pit closures, protect their jobs and save pit villages. Yet the press and most of Britain were against them. Being a miner's son myself, who'd been raised in a pit village, this subject was close to my heart. I'm still proud that I made the first documentary shown on British television which supported the striking miners.

Later in that year-long strike I made a second television film in their support. In both of our documentaries we filmed the striking miners at home with their families, at their meetings, in their cars as we travelled with them to the picket lines. Unlike the television news footage of the picket lines, which was shot from behind the police and facing the miners, we were always with the miners, shooting from their viewpoint. I still feel angry when I recall those awful times. I remember laughing policemen waving fists full of the money they'd earned in overtime at miners now so hard up they had to rely on handouts from supporters to feed their families. I have memories of baton-wielding policemen on horseback charging into the ranks of legally picketing miners, many of who had wounds to the backs of their heads and on their backs from police batons, as they had tried to run away. Recently, while watching a BBC Yorkshire news programme, called *Inside Out*, I was stunned to discover that at the time we were filming the strike, high-ranking officers in the South Yorkshire Police Force had dictated identical statements to all police constables which said it was the miners who had attacked the police, rather than the other way round. As a result of those false police statements, decent hardworking miners were charged with the offence of rioting and faced life imprisonment.

Events from filming that strike still stay with me. One day tears rolled down my face as we filmed the miners, their wives and their children as they walked beside the colliery union banners, a brass band playing. My tears weren't sentimental, rooted in some romantic idea of a 'salt of the earth' community. What I found so moving was the overwhelming sense of admiration I felt for the people whose background I shared. To me the union banners and brass band spoke of the long struggle of our parents, grandparents and great-grandparents, for safer conditions and decent wages, in the dangerous industry around which our mining communities had been built. Now the miners and their families had been forced into a fight to save their livelihoods and the livelihoods of their children. I vividly recall a woman being arrested on a picket line and thrown into the back of a police van. I was interviewing her through an open window when a policeman banged the window shut. As the police van sped away the woman opened the window again and shouted: 'Tell my husband I've been locked up.' There were other moments when I was inspired and moved, such as when we filmed a group of miners' wives singing:

> We are women, we are strong, we are fighting for our lives
> Side by side with our men, who work the nation's mines.
> United by the struggle, united by the past

> And it's 'here we go', 'here we go',
> for the women of the working class.

I'll never forget those women. They valued the sense of community that existed in their mining villages, where people greeted each other in the streets and the shopkeepers knew your name. They also understood the pride and the camaraderie instilled in their menfolk from working in dangerous conditions deep underground. Yet I suspect, along with many of the miners themselves, that most of the women would have preferred their sons not to follow their dads down the mine. But as the Conservative government closed one colliery after another unemployment had risen to an all-time high, and alternative jobs were extremely difficult to find. Keenly aware of this, the women stood beside their menfolk as they fought for their livelihoods. They supported the strike, and tried to help save the jobs of their husbands, brothers and sons, and preserve their historic century-old communities.

# TWENTY-SIX

She was the dear companion of my travels and sorrows . . .

*— Memoirs of Lady Fanshawe, 1676*

In 1993, a quarter of a century after I'd given up falconry, and with me aged forty-eight, we were living in Sheffield, just a few minutes' drive from the moors. In early summer, patches of the moorland are turned white by cotton grass, and in August, when the heather blooms, the whole of the moorland is turned purple. I love the haunting sounds up there, the sad burbling song of the curlew, the forlorn call of the golden plover. Yet as much as I love those moors, I often found myself gazing into the distance, at the faint outline of Hoober Stand, a monument not far from Tankersley Old Hall. My fascination with that place had stayed with me.

On each visit to the ruined Hall, I'd gaze up at the nest hole where my two Keses and Freeman had hatched, walk my old haunts, and then visit my mother who still lived in Hoyland Common. After she'd made me a cup of coffee and cut me a piece of her home-made cake, I'd enjoy listening to the village news.

In the summer of 1993, my mother was diagnosed with stomach cancer and I visited her daily in Sheffield's Northern General Hospital. One evening my heart ached as she asked me to hold up her compact mirror, after weeks of being too ill to bother. 'I don't look too bad, do I?' she'd said, and she didn't. She even talked of her plans for the future that evening, of what she was going to do when she got out of hospital. Although she knew it, earlier she'd asked me to write my telephone number on a piece of torn napkin which she'd put in her glasses case. As I left the ward I saw her fear returning. She was clutching her glasses case with my telephone number in it to give her comfort.

The next evening, Mother had been moved from a shared hospital ward into a room of her own. Once installed, she asked me to help her move into a position that would let the air get to a deep bedsore on her leg. She said she needed to get it better, but I knew it would never heal. The doctor had told me Mother was in the last hours of her life. She became increasingly confused, and when Jackie smeared cream on her dry lips she asked her if she'd taken up nursing, which made us both smile. Moments before Mother became unconscious she'd been hallucinating. I'd hoped the imaginary person she'd been speaking to was Dad, but her tone suggested she was speaking to a friend she hadn't seen for a while. 'I'll miss Richard . . . I'll miss Barry,' she said, and then fell silent. I glanced at my watch, then, recalling something, I looked through the window. Mother had lost consciousness at the same time and on the same day and month as Dad had died thirty years earlier, and, once again, it was a beautiful late summer's night, with a large full moon in the sky.

Later Barry arrived and Jackie went home in a taxi to check our kids were all right. After he'd rung to check on Mother and I'd told him how seriously ill she'd become, Barry had flown home from holiday in Italy and come straight to the hospital from the airport. He was tired from travelling and suffering from a hornet sting he'd got in Italy. Barry lived in Sheffield now, too, so after we'd sat with our mother for an hour or two, I suggested that he go home for a sleep while

I stayed with her through the night. As I sat alone with my unconscious mother I noticed her small suitcase on top of a wardrobe. The thought of her suitcase being repacked with her clothes and personal possessions and carried back home without her brought tears to my eyes.

Next morning the nurses told me they wanted to give Mother a wash and change her bedding and suggested I go home for breakfast. I'd only been home a few minutes when the telephone rang. Mother had died while the nurses were changing her, and when Barry and I entered her hospital room she lay in her clean nightgown on a dazzling white bedsheet.

Mother's home was still in Hoyland Common, and within an hour or two of her death I drove over there to walk in the surrounding countryside. The following day I awoke at dawn. For the last seventy-six years the sun had risen on a world in which Mother was alive; this morning I watched it rise on a world in which she was no longer alive and once again felt compelled to visit my old haunts. Day after day I was drawn to walk through woods whose leaves had unfurled from buds when Mother was alive, to walk beside fields of golden wheat planted when she was alive. One morning I found a chaffinch's nest lying on a path, and as I examined the moss, roots and horsehair woven into it I thought I heard Mother calling my name, her voice carried on the warm September wind. At home one evening I turned and saw her sitting on the sofa with a blanket wrapped around her shoulders, momentarily rescued from death by my imagination.

After my dad's death, nothing had been left unsaid; no questions had been left unanswered. And on that sunny September day, when the grass had glistened with dew as my dad's coffin was lowered into the ground, the robin's song had caught perfectly the sad, sweet yearning that I'd felt at the loss of my beloved dad. I felt no sad, sweet yearning after Mother's burial. Instead I felt hurt and angry.

On the morning of her funeral I stood looking up the road. Recently I'd seen her tentatively cross this road wearing a head-scarf, but this morning she'd glided down it in a coffin lying in a black hearse. A neighbour from our childhood, our mother's friend of over fifty years, was too old and infirm to attend the funeral, so later that day Barry and I had called to see her. Two hours earlier I'd seen my mother lowered into her grave. Yet our old neighbour chose that time to make a heartbreaking revelation. Mother, she said, had once told her that Barry was everything to her, the most important thing in her life.

Later, when the family visited the grave to admire the flowers and read the tributes of love and respect, I stood in sullen silence. On the previous day in the Chapel of Rest I'd been unable to bring myself to leave Mother. I'd take a last look at her, close the door, then, unable to bear the thought that I'd never see her again, I'd go back in for one last look. Once, twice, maybe a dozen times. But now I felt betrayed. Only hours after her burial, as she lay in the silent blackness, I felt no tenderness or pity, only a selfish, impotent rage at not being able to confront her about what her friend had said. Too late now. Her chance to reflect, to explain, to reassure, had gone forever.

After Mother's death, on one of my compulsive early morning walks around the pit village, I stopped to sit on a wooden bench beside Tankersley church. With our new spaniel, Floss, lying beside my boots, I remembered an occasion from my childhood when Barry had accused Dad of favouring me. Dad had replied that he only made a fuss of me because I was the youngest, before adding, 'Anyway, your mother makes enough fuss of you'. At the time it had seemed a strange thing to say, because I hadn't been aware of Mother treating Barry and me differently. Yet, by making more of a fuss of me than Barry when I was little, perhaps Dad was trying to provide the affection he sensed I was missing from

Mother. It all suddenly seemed to make sense. The neighbour's comment about Mother's feelings about Barry must have unearthed some long forgotten, unconscious childhood hurt. Memories flooded into my mind. I recalled the overheard argument, before he'd apologised, in which Dad had accused Mother of only wanting me to pass the exam to go to grammar school because it would have been a feather in her cap. I searched for better memories. An incident came to mind which I probably hadn't thought about since it happened. When I was a child, as she'd tried to help me with my maths, Mother had put a full stop after a number. I'd told her that wasn't right and that it looked like a decimal point. She stared at the book a moment then opened her mouth as if to speak. The words she wanted to say wouldn't come, and, frustrated, she snatched up a duster. As I sat on the bench beside the church I wondered if it was Mother's embarrassment at her lack of education, her anger at her blighted life chances, which had set her off dusting so furiously. For centuries her ancestors had worked the fields and coal mines and served in the big houses of the rich, as had she. I conjured up an image of Mother as a young woman, anxiously looking up the lane for the postman, waiting to discover if Barry would break this legacy of hard labour and deference by gaining a place at grammar school. His success would confirm the restless intelligence she suspected she had. I convinced myself that she'd made those hurtful comments when she was wretched with concern about Barry's future. But I was kidding myself.

When I told Barry how upset I was he was understanding and kind. He then reminded me that he wasn't the only first-born child Mother had been obsessed with. She had been obsessed with his first-born child. She had been obsessed with our first-born child, John. So much so that our daughter, Katie, had almost rebelled and confronted her about her obvious favouritism. Yet when Katie had visited her grandmother in hospital, and had seen her with oxygen tubes up her nose, with hardly the strength to moisten her parched lips, and Mother had told her she couldn't die because she wanted to see what she did with her life, and that she loved her, Katie was glad she had never known her seething rage.

I had never shown affection towards my mother. At her seventieth birthday party, for instance, softened by the occasion she had sought out family members to kiss. When I saw her heading towards me I'd glanced around in panic, desperate to escape. Sometimes, when I'd called in to see her, she'd sought compliments by saying, 'You'll miss me when I'm gone'. I don't know why, but her saying that infuriated me and I never gave her the answer she was looking for. But she was right, I did miss her. And the intensity of my grief, and the tender way I touched her medical card as I handed it to the registrar when registering her death surprised me.

'It's not unlike a throstle,' Mother had said when I'd carried Kes into the house in 1965. Twenty-eight years later, on my compulsive walks, I'd stop and gaze at the now-exposed nest ledge in the ruins of Tankersley Old Hall, and remember those words and the fond way Mother had looked at my first hawk. In the midst of the ruins is an impressive fireplace, built of narrow bricks in a herringbone pattern. One day, as I stood on the cart track gazing at the Old Hall, I thought about Sir Richard and Lady Fanshawe sitting around this very fireplace with their daughter Ann. In her memoirs Lady Fanshawe wrote of how she and her husband had lived here 'with great content' until something happened which made them 'both desirous to quit that fatal place'. In July 1654 Ann had died of smallpox and Lady Fanshawe wrote, 'She was between nine and ten years old, very tall, and the dear companion of my travels and sorrows'. When Ann was buried in Tankersley church, Lady Fanshawe and Sir

Richard had 'both wished to have gone into the same grave with her'. Almost three and a half centuries later, as I grieved for my mother and gazed at the brick fireplace, I recognised the sense of loss the Fanshawes would have felt. And I felt we had a strange connection across the centuries.

# TWENTY-SEVEN

Sir Terence Falkiner . . . Lord Feversham . . . Lt-Col R. S.
Ryan . . . T. H. White . . .
Members as at November 2nd, 1937

   – *The Falconer*, the Journal of the British Falconers' Club, 1937

As the weeks after Mother's death ran into months, I
stopped being so compulsively drawn to the countryside around the pit village. Even so, over the following years
I continued to walk my old haunts, and although I'd abandoned falconry my eyes always scanned the skies hoping
to see a hawk. There seemed these days to be more kestrels
around, hovering over the fields and verges. Once I saw a
kestrel hunting from a tree branch, but each time it swooped
off its perch into the stubble it missed its prey and flew up
grasping a few strands of straw. At Tankersley Old Hall the
stones had fallen away around the nest hole from which my
two Keses and Freeman had been taken. But to my delight
the kestrels had adapted, using a new nest in an inside wall
of the ruins.

It wasn't only the kestrels whose numbers were improving.
Something amazing began to happen. Goshawks had become
extinct in Britain in the 1880s. Now they were back. One
day, a mile or so across the fields from Tankersley Old Hall,

I saw a pair of wild goshawks rising and tumbling through the sky. On another occasion I stopped dead on a field path behind the Hall, hardly believing my eyes. A dead wood pigeon lay on its back surrounded by a scattering of feathers, its white breast bone pecked clean of meat. It had definitely been killed by a hawk – a sparrowhawk, I presumed. After that, not far from the eighteenth-century dovecote where as a youth I'd gazed up at the spikes designed to impale marauding hawks, I saw the first sparrowhawk I'd seen in this country. The feeding pigeons were undisturbed by the lads riding past on mountain bikes, but a few moments later they exploded into flight and I instinctively looked up. One, two, three, glide – a sparrowhawk was flying overhead with its distinctive flying style. From then onwards I saw sparrow-hawks on many occasions, one flying low along the middle of the road chased by a crow, and another crashing into a bush to flush out sparrows. One day I had to duck when a sparrowhawk shot through a gap in a hedge, then with a flick of its wings whipped back over the hedge and flew low over a field of wheat. Another time I watched in amaze-ment as a male sparrowhawk, a musket, ran down the steep slope of the church roof and launched himself into flight to pursue prey I couldn't see.

In 1998, when I was fifty-three, I was a lecturer in Film and Television Writing at Sheffield Hallam University. After making films for Channel 4 for a few years in the 1980s I'd moved to the BBC. I'd written, produced and directed fifteen documentary films for national television on Channel 4 and BBC2 on a range of topics. By now it had become more diffi-cult to get commissioned to make the type of documentaries I wanted to make, in which characters told their own stories without a voiceover narrator. So when I'd been approached and offered a lecturer's job at the university, I accepted it. To my surprise, my teaching qualifications and strong interest in education, along with my experiences and interest in film-making, and my love of films, combined to make teaching at university my new passion.

Jackie had become an art lecturer in the mid-1980s, teaching adult education classes in Sheffield. Just as meeting Phillip Glasier had made me realise falconry had been dominated by the upper classes, adding to her teaching qualifications by gaining a BA in Fine Art had brought home to Jackie how men had dominated art. In the library at Sheffield Polytechnic, where she'd studied, it had struck her that there was room after room packed with books about artists who were men, but that there was only a single shelf devoted to women artists. Intimidated by the maleness of it all, she'd looked into women's art, both historical and contemporary, and this had provided her with the encouragement and inspiration for her own work, in which she tried to represent women differently from the way they had been historically portrayed by men. As well as doing commissions, Jackie had won both the South Yorkshire Open and the Derby Open art exhibitions. She'd had solo exhibitions of her work, and had work in group exhibitions. One of these, called Reclaiming the Madonna: Artists as Mothers, toured the country and we saw it in the Usher Gallery in Lincoln.

When the Sheffield Adult Education department was cut back, Jackie found a teaching job in an inner-city school in Sheffield. One evening in 1998 I drove past second-hand furniture shops, Asian grocers, a Chinese gift shop, and turned into the car park to pick her up from work. As I locked the car I sensed the presence of a hawk; its reflection in the car window probably registered on the edge of my vision. I turned quickly and there, flying towards me several feet above the tarmac, wild yellow eyes fixed firmly on my face, was a sparrowhawk. To my amazement I found myself remembering a line from a book I hadn't read for over thirty years: 'the horrible aerial toad, the silent feathered owl, the humped back aviating Richard the third, made toward me . . .' That's how T. H. White described his hawk flying towards him in *The Goshawk*. In the book T. H. White ducks. I didn't. I stood in awe as the sparrowhawk flew a couple of inches over my head and away across the car park. I was twenty-three when I'd last trained a hawk. Now, aged fifty-three, I'd assumed I'd got hawks out of my system. It seemed not. There was something in that moment, the sudden closeness of a hawk in a dull urban setting, the sound of its wingbeats and rush of air on my face, the instant recalling of a line from a book that had stoked my love for hawks all those years ago. Whatever it was, thirty years after I'd abandoned falconry I suddenly felt a desperate need to have a hawk in my life.

Although I always scanned the skies looking for hawks, I'd completely lost contact with falconry. I didn't know of any goshawk or sparrowhawk nests, or if it was even still possible to get a licence to take an eyas. I realised I needed help, and that the way to meet experienced practising falconers who could give me advice was to apply to join the British Falconers' Club, which I'd read about in the 1960s. My last encounter with a falconer had intimidated me so much that it had led to me losing interest in hawking for three decades, but I was older now and I'd had experiences which made me feel less awkward in the company of upper-class people.

Barnsley and Sheffield United were the football teams I supported, and when I'd worked for the BBC I'd snapped up the opportunity to produce and direct two films in a BBC2 series which followed Sheffield United's fight to win promotion back into the Premier League – they succeeded. The series received excellent reviews, and soon afterwards I'd found myself producing and directing two films for another BBC2 prime-time sports documentary series. This time the subject was horseracing. I'd read in the falconry books how King James I, while out hawking in 1605, had come across the small village of Newmarket in Suffolk and had established horseracing there. It was still an elite affair, and making these documentaries took me into a social world different from anything I'd experienced.

One day, as the cameraman set up an exterior shot of a stately home, its owner, who owned and bred racehorses, told me he knew this view would look impressive on the screen because he had an original J. M. W. Turner land-scape of the very same view hanging on a wall in his house. Later we filmed this same lord in the Jockey Club Rooms in Newmarket next to a portrait of his father, who, like him, had also been a member of this exclusive private members' club, with its eighteenth-century furniture and George Stubbs equestrian paintings.

I was struck by the fact that, although the racehorse owners I met had upper-class accents, they were less notice-able, less pronounced, and their way of speaking a great deal less intimidating and overbearing than Phillip Glasier's had been thirty years earlier. Only once, when a usually courte-ous aristocrat let his manners slip, was I suddenly reminded of my class. On that occasion I had rung to tell him about changes to our filming schedule. Who knows, but he may never before have been phoned on his private line by some-one with a working-class accent. Whatever, when I told him the reason for my call he said: 'I know that. Why else would I be speaking to you?'

I was momentarily stunned by his staggering rudeness but I managed – just – to restrain myself and let it pass. I badly needed him to participate in my film.

Yet most people were friendly. At one stately home, I arrived on the butler's day off and was made a cup of instant coffee by an apologetic Marchioness as I sat in a stately room with a high ceiling and paintings on the walls, waiting for her husband to return. Others I met were a little eccentric. I was interviewing Lord Carnarvon, the Queen's racing manager, in the office of his stud farm when he suddenly shot to his feet bellowing 'You'll want lunch' and marched out. Not sure if I'd been invited, I was following his car in my car when he pointed to a pub that served lunch and carried on driving towards Highclere Castle, his stately home.

On another day I did manage a pub lunch with one of the aristocrats. Lord Zetland, who we'd been filming that morning, talked about his schooling at Eton, and honestly told us how easy it had been for him with his privileged background to get a place at Cambridge. Interested, I asked what subject he had studied for his degree and to my amazement he said that he couldn't remember.

In her book *The Sport of Kings*, anthropologist Dr Rebecca Cassidy tells us how some upper-class people in the horseracing world believe in the importance of pedigree, even for human beings, because this belief protects their elite position in society. I don't know if Lord Zetland believed that, but in her research Cassidy had met upper-class people who felt contempt for intellectual and academic study. For them, lived knowledge is inherited through the right breeding. Perhaps it's the belief they are well bred that makes some upper-class people seem so confident, when, despite their privileged education, they seem no cleverer than the rest of us.

Of course, I had neither the pedigree, nor good breeding, nor private school education, but, after working on those two horseracing programmes, I no longer felt overawed in the presence of the well-to-do. I decided to apply to become a member of the British Falconers' Club. Although I was confident I wouldn't feel intimidated, I feared the interview board might have seen *Kes* and would ask if I was related to the chap who'd written it. Perhaps they would complain that the film had begun a craze for stealing eyas kestrels from the nest and given falconry a bad name. I found myself preparing and rehearsing answers to imagined questions: Barry could have had no idea his book would become so popular and be filmed. Besides, lads like me would have needed to be in a falconry club to be granted a government licence to take a hawk legally, but the British Falconers' Club wouldn't have us as members. The only reason I'd been granted the three licences I'd needed to train the hawks for *Kes* was because the film company had swung it for me. But my application went in, and, as I waited to hear from the British Falconers' Club, I took down and reread falconry books I hadn't read for more than thirty years. To my surprise, when I went on the internet I discovered the first editions of the books by Jack Mavrogordato that I owned, *A Hawk for the Bush* and *A Falcon in the Field*, bought for 50 shillings (£2.50) and £3, were each now selling for hundreds of pounds.

A few days after I'd submitted my application a letter arrived. Sensing I'd been invited for an interview, as I opened the letter I imagined sitting on a leather sofa being sternly questioned by a committee of aristocrats and ex-army officers. To my surprise, though, there was no mention of an interview in the letter. Welcoming me to the club, it gave a contact number and address for the secretary of our local branch, a man called Paul, who lived a five-minute drive away from our house.

As I drove along the street of semi-detached houses I spotted the Range Rover Paul had told me to look out for parked in a drive. I pulled up in front of the house, and was about to knock on the door when a brown and white German Pointer ran around the corner of the house followed by a friendly man in his forties. As we walked into the garden, I told Paul that I'd been surprised by the ease with which I'd been accepted into what I'd thought was an elite falconry club. He told me that the previously exclusive British Falconers' Club, while retaining its name and history, had merged with a far less exclusive hawking club in the 1970s. Now any falconer was welcome to join.

Suddenly I stopped in my tracks. I hadn't seen a trained hawk since 1968 and there on the lawn in front of me, standing on block perches, were two large falcons. I had no idea what species they were. They had the look of peregrines, but were far too light in their colouring. And I was in part right, Paul told me, for they were hybrid offspring of a peregrine and a saker, the Arab falconers' favourite falcon. I was amazed: I didn't know hybrid falcons existed. For me, though, who had found falconry's history as interesting as actually flying a hawk, I wanted to fly a pure-bred hawk, as falconers had done for centuries. After I'd explained I'd been away from falconry for thirty years, Paul told me that licences were no longer granted to take hawks from the wild. Hawks with the same nature as their wild cousins were now bred in aviaries by falconers, and if I wanted to get back into falconry I could now buy and fly any hawk I wanted.

Realising how out of date I was, I updated my falconry book collection and bought and read every back copy of the British Falconers' Club magazine, *The Falconer*. My heart missed a beat when, among the lords, lieutenant colonels, captains and sirs who were listed as members in the 1937 edition, I spotted the writer who had sparked my boyhood obsession for hawks: T. H. White, Stowe Ridings, Buckinghamshire. Thirty-five years on from reading *The Goshawk*, that location still lived on in my memory: its gamekeeper's cottage, where White lived; its barn, where he kept his goshawk, with its wooden slats nailed criss-cross on the windows and its brick floor.

A short drive from our house in Sheffield is a granite mill-stone which stands on its edge on a plinth of stones and has a plaque inscribed PEAK NATIONAL PARK. Beyond that, on either side of the road, are Burbidge Moor and Hallam Moor. These are the high heather moors I often walk, sometimes with Jackie, frequently alone. This wild, open landscape is the natural haunt of the peregrine and the merlin, the two falcons that have been flown by falconers for centuries. One day I watched as a wild peregrine soared high in the sky, maybe waiting for grazing sheep to flush a covey of grouse from the heather before closing its wings and stooping. Early one morning when out walking, for the first time in my life I saw a merlin. Slightly smaller than a kestrel, this was a male in adult plumage, its buff-coloured breast feathers dashed with black, its blue back shining in the sun as it perched on a rock, ready to pursue any small moor-land bird unwise enough to take flight. One day, up there on the moor, I gazed into the distance at Hoober Stand near Tankersley Old Hall. Then I turned my mind back thirty-five years, to recall how, as an eighteen-year-old, I'd copied out sections of *A Manual of Falconry* in Barnsley Library, and discovered that the countryside around Tankersley and Hoyland Common was 'shortwing' country. This landscape was suitable for flying goshawks and sparrowhawks, which pursued their prey across the fields in a sprint, desperately trying to catch them before they escaped into the bordering hedgerows. Back then, I couldn't have imagined that I'd live close to 'longwing' country, the open landscape needed to fly a soaring, stooping peregrine, or a merlin, that had evolved to outfly fast-flying prey over long distances.

Now I was a member of the British Falconers' Club I met falconers who flew peregrines at game. I watched their hawks fly so high they became black specks in the sky, before stooping to strike a wild grouse whirring across the heather. This was truly spectacular hawking, and it appealed to me, but I did have a problem. I'd been a vegetarian for more than a decade.

I became a vegetarian in 1984, after I'd met a vegetarian miner while making the miners' strike films. I loved meat and told him I disagreed with his views. Later, I began to think about his reasons for giving up meat and read a book by Peter Singer, the moral philosopher, in which he talks about the evolution of human concern and empathy. Initially, Singer writes, our species was concerned for family and tribe. Over the ages those boundaries of concern were enlarged to include other nations and races, and in societies where we don't need to eat meat to survive our boundaries of concern should now be extended to include other sentient creatures. To my dismay I found myself agreeing.

Had I not been a vegetarian I'd have flown a peregrine and eaten the game it caught. But I was and still am, so instead I chose to fly a merlin, which I would train to catch its natural prey of small moorland birds for its own supper. Although smaller than kestrels, merlins are feistier, faster flying. They have to be, otherwise they wouldn't survive. Unlike kestrels, which hover and drop on to easily caught voles and insects, merlins have to pursue fast-flying, difficult-to-catch prey across open moorland.

# TWENTY-EIGHT

... hawking ... is ... an extreme stirrer up of passions ...

– King James I, *Basilikon Doran*, 1599

Thirty-one years ago, aged twenty-three, I'd carried the eyas kestrel Freeman home from Tankersley Old Hall in a cardboard box. Today, in 1999, at the age of fifty-four, I brought my eyas merlin home to Sheffield in a pet carrier, the type usually used for cats. When I reached inside feeling for his jesses he backed away, striking at my hand with his talons, pecking at my fingers. I eased him out and he hopped on to my gloveless fist. We were in our living room and for a moment he seemed mesmerised by the array of colours, the books on the bookshelves, the paintings on the walls and then he lunged into mid-air.

Imagine his life until then. After hatching, for the previous month or so this captive-bred young merlin had lived with his siblings in an aviary in an isolated garden surrounded by wheatfields in Norfolk. Then, earlier this evening, in an explosion of flapping wings, he'd flown in a panic around the aviary trying to escape being caught in a large butterfly net. Finally, beak open and panting with fear, he was untangled from the net and held by the falconer who had bred him while I fitted the jesses. He was then subjected to my intense gaze as I checked his eyes were bright, that he had no sign of 'bumblefoot', an inflammatory foot infection, under his lovely yellow feet, and that he was feather-perfect. Heart racing, he'd then been bundled into a pet carrier, and trapped in this claustrophobic tomb he'd been driven from Norfolk up to Sheffield unable to escape the terrifying noises all around him. After the car engine, and the roar of overtaking motorbikes, and the whoosh of air from lorries speeding by, here he was in our living room hanging upside down at the end of his jesses calling 'kikiki . . . kikiki', in fear.

Jackie closed the curtains and I gently lifted the young merlin back on to my fist. In the half-light he was calmer and didn't bate. Holding a tea towel, Jackie tiptoed up behind him like someone on stage in a pantomime. She threw the towel over him and pinned his wings by his side, then, while she held him, I slipped a hood on to him. Jackie then put the merlin on to my now gloved hand and removed the towel. I touched the scales with the back of his legs and he stepped backwards. He weighed just under six ounces.

Screen perches were no longer used, as over the years there had been rare instances of falcons getting in a tangle with their jesses, and hanging upside down in the mews. So, in the mews I had made of a converted brick building in our back garden, I'd fixed a wide shelf perch covered with Astroturf to cushion his feet and prevent bumblefoot. That night my young falcon wasn't in danger of having problems with his feet, for he lay down on the shelf perch, and the next day when I tried him on his block perch in the garden, instead of standing on it he lay on the grass beside it. Yet he quickly got the hang of things. On the first day he stepped on to the glove to feed, and when I manned him by standing in the front window to let him watch people, dogs and cars passing by in the street, he didn't bate from the glove. Soon he was flying a leash length to the glove in the mews, then a leash length from a fence post in the garden. A little more than a week later I stood amid the purple heather on Burbage Moor, a few minutes' drive from our house, and with my glove raised I blasted on my whistle. The juvenile merlin powered off Jackie's fist and he flew with the creance trailing behind him along a sheep track through the heather, towards me and on to the glove to take his reward of meat. After that flight I flew him free.

My only problem was getting him used to a hood. I hadn't hooded my kestrels, but traditionally proper hunting falcons, such as merlins, were hooded to keep them calm while being transported or carried before flying. At first I made our spaniel sit in front of us, and while the hawk was looking at the dog I practised hooding him without too many problems. Later, however, when he'd become used to the dog, each time I tried to hood him his head ducked and writhed like a snake's, making it difficult for me to slip on the hood and tighten the hood braces with my teeth. One of my books suggested that the way to deal with a hawk that resisted hooding was to carry it under your arm and repeatedly hood it until it accepted the procedure. Suspecting it was my incompetence that was the problem, not my merlin, and realising he was so well manned that he didn't really need a hood, I decided against this drastic advice, accepted defeat and abandoned my efforts to get him used to the hood.

I'd intended calling my merlin Lilburne, after John Lilburne, a Parliamentarian hero of mine who'd helped to defeat Sir Richard Fanshawe and his Royalist mates in the English Civil War. However, I changed my mind while reflecting on Lady Fanshawe's memoirs. Although Sir Richard was the secretary of the Council of War for Charles I's Royalists, who I disagreed with, he was a fascinating character. He was a poet and a brave man. Once when he and Lady Fanshawe were walking by the sea in Portsmouth they were fired at from two Dutch ships. Hearing the musket balls whiz by, Lady Fanshawe began to run, but Sir Richard carried on walking and said, 'If we must be killed, it were as good to be killed walking as running'. According to Lady Fanshawe even Oliver Cromwell, his enemy and the leader of the Parliamentarians, had respect for him and 'would have bought him off to his service on any terms'. After the Battle of Worcester Sir Richard was captured and imprisoned in Whitehall where, penned up in a cold, small room, scurvy had 'brought him almost to death's door'. Finally, released on four thousand pounds' bail, he visited his friend William Wentworth, Earl of Strafford, who offered him the tenancy of Tankersley Hall a couple of miles away from Wentworth's own country house.

Although our ties to the Old Hall were very different, I felt a connection, and so I called my merlin Fanshawe.

Had Mother been alive to see Fanshawe, she'd have said he was not much bigger than a 'throstle'. At a flying weight of only five and a half ounces, he was a little beauty, with big brown eyes and buff and brown feathers in perfect condition, and his instinct to survive showed in spirited and endearing ways. Standing on his perch on the lawn, for instance, his eyes to the sky, he'd 'chup, chup, chup' at sparrowhawks soaring high overhead. He once 'chupped' at something in the cloudless sky – probably a soaring peregrine – which was so high I couldn't see it, not even through the binoculars that I hurriedly fetched from the house. Once he delicately pecked at a tiny spot of red among the swirl of colours on an empty coffee mug, as if it was a piece of meat he was about to feed to a newly hatched chick. On another occasion, when I'd brought him into the house to keep me company, he cocked his head to one side and looked under tables and chairs for the bird singing on the birdsong recording I was playing.

Fanshawe had a small wooden travelling box with an Astroturf-covered perch. One evening, to get my young falcon used to this and to man him, I drove over to my old haunts. After walking with him on my glove for a while I sat on a bench beside Tankersley church. Flat in the grass by my feet was a gravestone, and although the letters and numbers were green with moss, I could make out the words:

LVKE BVRDET
BU ͬ d 1680

As I gazed at his gravestone I wondered what Luke would have thought had he seen me with a merlin. The 1486 *Boke of St Albans* had been through many reprints, the last one in 1614, and coming from the landowning classes who'd been able to afford a gravestone I guessed that Luke would most likely have been able to read. Yet even if Luke hadn't read the book and come across 'Ther is a Merlyon. And that hawke is for a lady', he would have known that merlins were flown by women of high social standing. Until the death of her beloved daughter Ann had made her 'desirous to quit' Tankersley, Lady Fanshawe said she had 'found all the neighbourhood very civil'. So maybe Luke had even greeted her as she rode out of Tankersley Hall with a merlin on her glove for an afternoon's hawking on Tankersley Moor. He'd have been puzzled to see me, a man, with a merlin on my glove.

Sitting there on the bench beside Luke's gravestone, I began to wonder if Sir Richard Fanshawe, whose beloved daughter Ann was buried in the church behind me, had after a Sunday service ever stood in this ancient churchyard with Luke Burdet discussing country sports. Fluent in several languages, and later Charles II's Ambassador to Portugal, perhaps Sir Richard would have read the 1643 book *D'Arcussia's Falconry* in French. If so, maybe he'd put Luke straight, for the Abbess Juliana Berners hadn't got it quite right in the *Boke of St Albans*, as men, King Louis XIII of France among them, did occasionally fly merlins. In Britain, however, it wasn't until the nineteenth century that men began to fly merlins regularly. The most famous of these falconers was E. B. Michell, an Oxford scholar and champion boxer, who was said to have knocked two soldiers unconscious for throwing stones at his merlin.

It was a lovely early September morning with a clear blue sky. One knee of my jeans was wet with dew when I stood up from putting my young merlin on his block perch. During the summer, head cocked on one side, Fanshawe had watched the squealing swifts fly over the garden. Now that the swifts were on their way back to Africa for the winter, Fanshawe made do with watching me carry stones across the garden to an old rockery that I was rebuilding. I needed a couple of extra large stones and as I worked I remembered a demolished cottage where I could get them from. Later that morning, carrying a large stone under each arm, I was walking up a path opposite Tankersley church when a stern voice called: 'Hey! Where tha going with them?'

Heart racing, I turned. It was Budgie. Dog at heel, he was walking up the path behind me grinning at the fright he'd given me.

After loading the stones into the car boot I called in at Budgie's house and was sitting in a garden chair while he fetched his pet rabbit out of the shed to show me. It was a sweet little thing and sat on its haunches on the lawn while Budgie, sleeves rolled up as usual on his tattooed arms, fed it from his fingers.

'I never thought I'd see thee hand-feeding a rabbit,' I said, before reminding him of his wild young days when he used to poach rabbits.

'I couldn't bear to do that now,' he told me.

Budgie loved birds and had listened intently when I told him about my merlin. So when he came to the car to see me off I suggested he could come out hawking with Fanshawe, once he'd started catching his supper on the moors. But, rather than looking pleased by my invitation, Budgie suddenly looked uncomfortable and brusquely said: 'It's too far – travelling over there.'

'It's not. It wouldn't take thi long,' I said naively.

'I'm not bothered about going,' he said more forcefully.

'Keep thi timber up,' Budgie called to me as I drove off. It was an old mining farewell, meaning take care of yourself by setting your pit props properly. Despite our friendly good-byes, Budgie had made clear his disapproval of my plans to fly Fanshawe after his natural prey. Since I'd recruited Budgie for the part in *Kes*, we'd rekindled our childhood friendship. Our shared histories and the history of the village were important to us. Budgie had got his job back at the local pit and, when it was open to the public on its centenary, he had pulled aside sacking which signalled an out-of-bounds area, and taken me on an unofficial tour of the dark tunnels where my dad and grandads had worked. Then, when I left the village for Sheffield, we fell into the habit of meeting up for a drink every couple of months or so. He was a dear friend. His disapproval upset me, and as I drove home, and later worked on the rockery while Fanshawe watched, I couldn't stop my mind going over arguments I thought I'd already put to rest.

With his dogs and ferrets and rabbit nets, Budgie had been a hunter as a young man. Once when we'd walked together in the countryside, mid-conversation he'd suddenly dived into a patch of long grass, stood up holding a flapping pheasant, wrung its neck and had it for his dinner next day. When working on *Kes*, Ken Loach had told me how he didn't look for actors to play a part so much as seek actors who *were* the part. Budgie was certainly that when he took on the role of a poacher in Ken's television film of Barry's book *The Gamekeeper*. Now Budgie had turned against all that, and regarded hawking for live prey as cruel.

As a youth I'd taken my guidance from M. H. Woodford, a vet who had spent his life caring for animals. In *A Manual of Falconry* he wrote: 'There has never been a slur cast on falconry on the grounds of cruelty' because 'all quarry have sanctuary and frequently outfly their pursuer'. To me, as a vegetarian, it seemed fairer to let a hawk catch animals that have had an independent life in the wild, and which have evolved to escape, than to feed it on farmed animals. Yet even before Budgie had disapproved, I'd felt uneasy.

When I'd discovered it was possible to buy any captive-bred hawk you wanted, I'd at first considered stooping a lanner or peregrine to the lure, without letting it fly at quarry. I'd flown my kestrels like this but now it seemed wrong. It seemed to me that if I did get a hawk I needed to give it a life as near as possible to the life it had evolved to live. Had I bumped into Budgie months earlier, maybe I would have overcome the yearning to bring a hawk back into my life, but it was too late now. As I worked on the rockery, there was Fanshawe on his perch on the lawn and I'd no choice but to do what I was convinced was best for him.

# TWENTY-NINE

ENTER, to fly a hawk at quarry for the first time.

– J. E. Harting, *Bibliotheca Accipitraria*, 1891

It was early evening, time to fly my merlin. Keen to get on my glove, Fanshawe raised his wings when I approached him on his perch on the lawn. In the mews he hopped from my glove on to the scales. He weighed five and a half ounces. Spot on. He hopped back on to the glove and the moment I opened the door of his small wooden travelling box he eagerly stepped on to its little Astroturf-covered perch. I fastened the door, checked my pocket for the licence allowing Fanshawe to catch his natural prey – chiefly meadow pipits, which were common at that time – then carried the travelling box out of the mews and headed for the car.

Within a couple of minutes I was driving past Burbage Moor, where I'd trained Fanshawe. On this moor, the meadow pipits would have simply disappeared into the heather the moment he left the glove. So, to give my young falcon a chance to learn to hunt for himself, and the chance to survive in the wild if he ever got lost, I was taking him further afield. I passed the DERBYSHIRE sign and left South Yorkshire. Slowing down for sheep wandering on to the road, driving across cattle grids, and with views of peaks stretching into the distance before me, I drove across the moors. Leaving the heather moors behind, I drove down into the valley and through a softer landscape, with wooded hills and green fields. Then, after driving up a steep, narrow street of stone cottages, and up a lane no wider than a cart track, I reached Bradwell Moor. Burbage Moor had been purple with heather. Here, on his new flying ground, the grass was heavy with seed and the moor the colour of ripe corn. Crucially, from the viewpoint of Fanshawe, on this moor the meadow pipits would need to outfly him rather than just drop into the heather to escape.

At the top of the moor I parked beside a cart track, took out Fanshawe from his travelling box in the boot, then slipped on to my shoulder the strap of what looked like a canvas fishing-rod case; this was my telemetry. I hadn't walked far when Fanshawe hurtled off my glove, his jesses slipping through my fingers. I desperately looked down the moor, trying to spot what he'd seen. Wings flapping furiously, my young falcon was powering up into the sky towards a raven, as if about to drive it off and establish this moor as his terri-tory. If that was his intention it was about to be thwarted, because flying towards him was another raven, and moments later I watched in horror, as, jet black against the sky, the two ravens, which were twice as big as Fanshawe, chased him across the moor and out of sight.

I jogged across the moor to where Fanshawe had disap-peared. Out of breath, I stopped at the edge of a disused quarry, took the telemetry receiver from its case and unfolded what looked like a small television aerial. BEEP-BEEP-BEEP. To my relief the tiny transmitter attached to Fanshawe's leg was sending a signal. He wasn't far away. I aimed the receiver at the steep rock face on the other side of the quarry and slowly swept it in front of me. At first the signal wasn't strong, but when the receiver was pointing directly ahead the signal became much louder: BEEP-BEEP-BEEP. Raising my binoculars I scanned the rock face opposite. There was no sign of him standing in the grass on top of the rock face, or perched on any of the ledges. I was about to put the receiver on the ground and take the lure from my pocket when I saw Fanshawe standing between my boots. I don't know if he'd flown in low and landed there, or if I'd almost trodden on him.

I was soon walking through the grass with my young merlin back on my glove. Although merlins, as falcons, are called 'longwings', their wings are broader than peregrines, and almost hawk-shaped to aid acceleration. Again he hurtled off my fist, and again I didn't see what he was pursuing. After the experience with the ravens, I held on tight to his jesses. By the time I saw the pipit that had flown out of the grass, Fanshawe was already hanging upside down by his jesses screaming with rage. Lifting him back on to the glove, I walked on. Again he launched into flight at something I hadn't seen, but this time I didn't hold him back. It turned out that this instinctive response had been triggered by nothing more than a moth fluttering out of the grass, and turning in the air he flew back to the glove. I was concentrating hard, trying to make sure I saw what had caught his eye, so I could decide whether to hold on to his jesses, or let him fly, when once again he shot off my glove. His jesses slipped through my fingers, and this time the young hawk was chasing prey which was so far away that he wouldn't have been able to catch it even if he'd been able to fly ten miles an hour faster. Fuming, I blasted on my whistle and swung the lure. Giving up the chase he turned and flew low over the moor towards me, and rather than throwing the lure into the grass I pulled it on to my raised glove for him to land on.

Poor Fanshawe. It was hard enough for him trying to catch prey that had evolved over thousands of years to escape his

258

clutches without me making it even more difficult. I'd read that at least six out of ten young wild hawks and falcons die in their first year, mostly because they can't catch enough food. I hadn't thought much about the reality of those young hawks' lives until this evening, watching my juvenile merlin's heart-rending attempts to catch his quarry. One chase ended with him crashing into a bed of nettles near a derelict stone barn. When I got to him he was hanging upside down, his wings spread out among the nettles, panting with anger and frustration. On the final flight of the evening my young falcon followed a pipit into long grass. When he didn't fly up I thought at last he must have nailed his supper, but the small brown moorland bird he thought he was killing turned out to be a dried-out sheep's dropping.

The next evening, my dread that Fanshawe would get lost and die of starvation before he could fend for himself subsided a little. He still hadn't caught anything, but I began to think it wouldn't be too long. I began to recognise when I needed to hang on to the jesses and when I needed to let them go. Fanshawe was more settled and seemed to be honing his evolved survival instinct. Each time he pursued a pipit, after about twenty or thirty yards he seemed to spot something about its flight which told him whether it was worth carrying on. If he sensed he had little chance of catching his quarry he circled around and flew back to the glove. If he felt there was a chance, however, he pursued his fleeing prey in deadly earnest. One such chase led him into a field beside the moor. When I arrived at the stone wall I saw him chasing a pipit through a herd of cows, flying over their backs and under their bellies, brushing past their legs as the cows deftly tried to back-heel him with kicks that would have killed had they connected.

Outflown by this particular pipit, Fanshawe had returned to the swinging lure and I was once again walking the moor with him on my glove. I must have almost trodden on the pipit before it sprung up from grass near a boulder. Fanshawe shot off my glove and was after it. I'd read how, instinctively fearing a night with an empty stomach and possible starvation, falcons pursued their quarry with more determination as the sun sank lower in the sky. Perhaps it was this fear, or the anger and frustration of continually being outflown by his quarry, but Fanshawe refused to give up. On and on they flew, prey and predator, across a moor now turned the colour of copper in the rays of the setting sun, and on over the green fields beyond until, with dismay, I watched through my binoculars as they disappeared beyond a distant hill.

After stopping to raise the telemetry receiver to check I could still hear the faint BEEP-BEEP-BEEP, I ran on, recklessly clambering over walls and dislodging stones, climbing fences, running across fields, until I came to one in which a bull with massive shoulders and a ring in his nose was throwing back his head and bellowing. Skirting the large field took ages, and the telemetry receiver had gone silent by the time I reached the other side. No longer running, I wandered on, holding the receiver above my head at arm's length, standing on the third bar of a five-bar gate to get more height as I swept the transmitter in every direction. Still there was no signal. Back at the car, my heart ached when, through the open door of his travelling box, I saw his little Astroturf-covered perch. It was awful driving home without him, the car headlights lighting up the narrow lanes and the road across the moor where I'd trained him to fly free.

I hardly slept that night, worried that I'd never see my young falcon again. Fanshawe wouldn't be able to fend for himself, and he might starve to death. I was up before dawn, driving back over the moors to a narrow lane near where I'd searched for him the previous evening. Again, there was no signal from the transmitter. Stopping in another lane near a cement factory with a tall chimney, I got out and clambered up to the top of a pile of rocks and rubble and held up the telemetry receiver. Still no signal. Thinking that the transmitter battery might have gone flat, I took the whistle from my pocket and blew it. Fanshawe didn't appear, but a couple of night watchmen did and stood in a doorway in the cement factory, obviously wondering what kind of idiot would repeatedly blast a whistle at sunrise. I then drove to the moor, where I should have gone first, and the moment that I turned on the receiver it beeped. Loudly. I could see a bird perched on the large boulder near where Fanshawe had begun his desperate chase last evening. It was him. When I blew the whistle, he launched himself off the boulder and flew low over the straw-coloured grass and swooped up to land on my raised glove.

That evening, with Fanshawe in his travelling box, we were once more driving past Burbage Moor on our way to his flying ground on Bradwell Moor. Once again Fanshawe hurtled off my fist each time a pipit flew up out of the grass, either turning back if he sensed he'd no chance of catching it, or pursuing it relentlessly until, closing its wings, the pipit would escape by dropping into long grass beside a wall, or into a patch of thistles, or a bed of nettles, and out of Fanshawe's reach. On each occasion, raging with frustration after yet another failed flight, the young hawk flew back over the moor and on to my raised glove.

Since coming up here, I'd been surprised how tramping Bradwell Moor with my merlin had affected my emotions. Earlier in the day, Jackie and I had driven for half an hour or so from our house to visit the Yorkshire Sculpture Park. While there, to my surprise I'd smoothed my hands over the stone sculptures, eager to touch the earth's raw materials they'd been hewn from. I'd held up Jackie's wrist to examine the bangle I'd brought her from Nigeria, touching the bands of tiny metal studs which had been mined from the African earth, rubbing my finger on the smooth golden brown bone which had once been part of a living animal. That evening, as I walked on, with Fanshawe gripping my glove – alert, ready to power off my fist at the slightest movement in the grass – I was reminded of those prehistoric hunters who made handprints on cave walls. This process, some archae-ologists speculate, could have given these ancient people the sensation of reaching through the cave wall into an animal world beyond. Each evening, when we'd arrived on Bradwell Moor and I'd pulled on my falconry glove, I'd had a simi-larly strange sensation of reaching into the wild. Walking this moor with Fanshawe on my glove made me keenly aware of being *in* nature. Never before had I felt so vividly aware that all of us, all species, share an evolutionary origin and live fragile transient lives, in which chance and the tiniest inher-ited advantage or the wrong decision can mean the difference between life and death.

It was a fatal decision made by his prey that finally led to Fanshawe catching his own supper. After he had chased it across the moor, the pipit found sanctuary in the long grass surrounding a derelict barn, but instead of staying in the safety of the grass, the pipit inexplicably flew out. With a tilt of his wings Fanshawe was on it in an instant. When he delivered a swift peck to the back of the pipit's neck, the notch on Fanshawe's beak, evolved for this purpose, killed the pipit instantly.

Fanshawe was already plucking and flicking away the pipit's breast feathers when I knelt down beside him. I held his jesses between gloved finger and thumb, wrapped my other three fingers around the pipit and stood up. After he'd plucked its breast feathers, Fanshawe delicately ate the warm dark red meat of the pipit's breast, occasionally stopping to wipe his bloodied beak on the fingers of my glove. Some falconers raise their hip flasks and take a sip of sloe gin in a respectful toast to the quarry their hawk has caught, but the practice of the Kalahari hunter-gatherers, of tenderly stroking the dead quarry, while singing a prayer for it, seemed to catch how I felt towards the beautiful pipit Fanshawe was eating on my glove.

I flew Fanshawe each evening for the following few weeks of autumn until the nights drew in and the pipits had left the moors to winter on lower ground. Fanshawe became a skilful hunter, knowing when to circle around and fly back to the glove, knowing when to pursue his prey. Sometimes he stopped flapping his wings and glided, as if he'd given up the chase, only suddenly to begin his pursuit again and nail his prey. Very occasionally he 'flew cunning', which is considered a vice in trained merlins and annoys the falconer. On one occasion, for instance, instead of flying back to my raised glove he landed on a boulder, where, fluffed up and appearing harmless, he looked across the moor. Moments later a pipit, seemingly taken in by his posture, took flight nearby. His feathers immediately sleeking to his body, Fanshawe was off the boulder like a shot and caught the poor pipit before it had flown ten yards. On another occasion he hid a pipit he had caught under a rock. I discreetly removed it and fed it to him later for his supper, but the next evening on his first flight he flew across the moor and peeped under the rock, looking for the pipit he'd cached there the previous evening.

I was pleased Fanshawe had become a successful hunter. To a limited degree, he was living the life that he'd evolved to live, and it was a relief to know that if I lost him he would most likely be able to fend for himself. Letting him hunt and eat his natural quarry was the right thing to do, I was convinced, and I hoped my heart would harden to the sight of him catching his supper. It never did.

The following summer he moulted and the brown feathers on his head, back and wings were replaced by slate-blue feathers, and once again I flew him to the lure on the heather moor to get him fit for an autumn of flying quarry on the grass moor. But after an unexpected phone call I changed my plans. A falconer-conservationist contacted me to ask if I'd be interested in Fanshawe becoming part of his merlin-breeding programme. In Britain in the 1950s wild merlin numbers had declined to as few as 550 pairs. Now that number had risen to around 1,300 pairs, but the loss of their nesting sites, as moorland was overgrazed by sheep and planted with conifers, could prevent any further rise in their numbers. If there was another fall in the wild merlin population, I liked the thought of Fanshawe's descendants helping to repopulate the wild, as falconers' peregrines had already done in North America. So, in the autumn of 2000, I took Fanshawe to Lincolnshire and released him into a large aviary, to join a fine-looking female merlin.

I knew I wouldn't fly another hawk.

# EPILOGUE

It was late April 2012, a warm and sunny morning after days of heavy rain. Now aged sixty-six, I walked along a muddy farm track and sat on a bench opposite Tankersley Old Hall. Almost twelve years had passed since I'd flown Fanshawe, but I still loved hawks. I knew kestrels roosted in the ruined Hall, but today I was curious to see if they were nesting. Earlier, as I'd driven along the boundary of the Old Hall's medieval deer hunting park, I'd seen a kestrel hovering, but I had yet to see a kestrel flying into the Old Hall.

I had recently attended an event in Oxford at which writers, artists and scientists who love the natural world gave presentations of their work. There I met a writer named Conor Jameson who shared my love of T. H. White's book *The Goshawk*. I told him the address of the cottage where White had trained Gos – Stowe Ridings, Buckinghamshire – and of my excitement when I'd discovered it alongside his name in the 1937 edition of *The Falconer*. Then writing a book on goshawks, Conor had managed to find White's remote cottage and he kindly offered to take me.

So, two months later, on a cold winter day with a clear blue sky, I drove down to Buckinghamshire. There, I met up with Conor in a car park near what had been a stately home called Stowe House, until it had become Stowe School in 1922. This was the public school in which T. H. White had taught

English, before abandoning teaching to rent the cottage on the Stowe estate, where he'd written *The Goshawk*. We'd walked through the parkland of Stowe estate, through a wood, and were now walking down a narrow road, when I felt my heart quicken. Across a field, beyond two grazing horses, I'd seen the gamekeeper's cottage and barn where, over seventy years ago, T. H. White had lived and trained Gos.

The image from the book of the barn, Gos's mews, with its wooden slats nailed criss-cross on the windows, had been etched on my mind for almost half a century, but as we approached I saw it had been rebuilt and given a new roof. Conor walked past the cottage, but this place had been in my imagination for decades, and I stopped at the garden gate to gaze at the stone cottage with its red-tiled roof. And there in front of me was the garden in which Gos would have arrived in the basket covered in sacking, 'bumping against it from underneath: bump, bump, bump, incessantly, with more than a hint of lunacy', before T. H. White picked it up 'in a gingerly way and carried it to the barn'. There in front of me was the door that T. H. White was about to paint when disaster struck. Carrying a tin of blue paint he discovered Gos had gone, the twine securing him to his outdoor perch snapped. As I walked back through the fields and ridings which White had walked with Gos on his fist, I guessed that this was the stream in which Gos took a bath, and these the very woods where poor Gos had come to his end, his jesses entangled in a tree. There I'd experienced a sense of reverence, a strange palpable connection with T. H. White, the lonely, obsessive, brilliant writer, whose book had fired my passion for hawks.

Back at Tankersley, along the cart track, a few yards from where I was sitting on the bench, was where, forty-seven years ago, on one sunny evening in June 1965, I'd come across my friend John, who'd eventually agreed that we could go together to take a kestrel each from the nest in the ruined wall of Tankersley Old Hall. Three summers later, on the very spot of the cart track where I'd come across John, I'd sat at a trestle table eating lunch with a film crew, and for the first time reflected on the unexpected turn of events my hawk obsession had brought about. It had led me to become a volunteer overseas, a falconer on a film of my brother's book, and to study Environmental Studies. I still found it extraordinary how my love of hawks had made me see the world differently. It was the posh, booming voice of a falconer that had led me to realise I was obsessed with a history that was not my own. This had ignited a passion for the history of my own class. That in turn had prompted me to study for a Master's degree, and become a deputy head teacher, then a television producer and director, and finally a university lecturer. Jobs I would have thought were beyond me when I was a secondary modern school write-off.

A childhood friend, after he'd passed his eleven plus exam and won a place at grammar school, had taken every opportunity to tell me that he was in the top percentage of the most intelligent people in the country. At college, I remember one student who'd attended grammar school proudly claiming he was part of the 'intelligentsia', and thinking to myself, 'God help the rest of us'. Yet both those grammar school boys became successful in their chosen fields, so perhaps they were right to be so confident. Having been branded a failure at the age of eleven, and sent to a secondary modern school where I was no cleverer than the other lads there, I see things differently. My own experiences, along with working as a teacher and a lecturer, and making television programmes with working-class people, have convinced me that all of us have something of worth; a hidden potential, a talent or aptitude, which, if, through our home circumstances, our education, or by chance, we are fortunate enough to unearth it, this talent can inspire us to do things in life we might have thought impossible.

At Tankersley Old Hall there was still no sign of a kestrel. Looking around I noticed the gap through which, almost fifty years ago, I'd emerged from Bell Ground Wood into the moonlight, heart racing with excitement. Getting up from the bench, I crossed the muddy cart track, clambered over the stone wall and walked across the field towards the ruins. Suddenly, out of the blue, a kestrel flew directly towards me at head height. Fleetingly, I relived what it feels like to train and fly a hawk: being close to a creature that never loses its wildness, but which through gentleness can be trained. Then, when the kestrel was only a few wingbeats away, its lovely brown eyes focused on my face, it suddenly curved upwards over my head, flew up and over Tankersley Old Hall, and was soon out of sight.

# Acknowledgements

I would like to thank my wife Jackie for her encouragement in the early stages of writing. Also, thank you to Alan Payne, Frances Byrnes, Conor Jameson, Miriam Darlington, David Llewelyn and Will Atkins, who all read various edits of the manuscript and made insightful suggestions. I am grateful to Andrew McNeillie for publishing an early piece I wrote about training hawks in Archipelago. I would like to say a special thank you to Michael Fishwick at Bloomsbury for his belief in my book, and also to my agent Patrick Walsh, who took a chance on me and encouraged and helped me throughout the writing of this memoir. Thank you too to everyone at Bloomsbury: the design team, Anna Simpson, Rachel Nicholson and Marigold Atkey for their help and support; to Richard Collins for a meticulous copyedit and Catherine Best for reading the proofs.

The author and publisher would like to thank Mal Finch for permission to reproduce lyrics from 'We are women. We are strong.'

## A NOTE ON THE TYPE

The text of this book is set in Linotype Sabon, a typeface named after the type founder, Jacques Sabon. It was designed by Jan Tschichold and jointly developed by Linotype, Monotype and Stempel in response to a need for a typeface to be available in identical form for mechanical hot metal composition and hand composition using foundry type.

Tschichold based his design for Sabon roman on a font engraved by Garamond, and Sabon italic on a font by Granjon. It was first used in 1966 and has proved an enduring modern classic.